The Empire Has No Clothes
U.S. Foreign Policy Exposed

More Praise for *The Empire Has No Clothes*

"Focusing on the post–Cold War period, Eland brings together the American actions in Kosovo and Gulf War I & II in a discussion of the ways in which our 'nation-building' has become a new form of empire. And what was disastrous for other ambitious world powers going back to Rome, he suggests, will fall upon us—sooner than we think. The heart of the book, moreover, are the chapters showing how both liberals and conservatives need to rethink their positions, and join in an effort to challenge the empire on grounds of self-interest. It is a great book!"

—LLOYD C. GARDNER
Charles and Mary Beard Professor of History, Rutgers University

"The Empire Has No Clothes offers a powerful and persuasive critique of recent U. S. foreign policy. It deserves the thoughtful attention of conservatives and liberals alike—indeed, of all Americans disturbed by the imperial pretensions evident in Washington since the end of the Cold War."

—ANDREW J. BACEVICH
Professor of International Relations, Boston University

"An eloquent and well-researched argument that very much needs to be heard, contending that Americans have become ensnared in an imperialism of which they are largely unaware, and of which they should disapprove. The book will play an important role in structuring a major debate about American foreign policy."

—GEORGE H. QUESTER
Professor of Government and Politics, University of Maryland

"Ivan Eland's provocative and well-researched critique of America's interventionist foreign policy makes a powerful case for returning to the practical principles of the Founding Fathers. With convincing examples that range across history, he clearly demonstrates that our current democratic empire is a dangerous oxymoron."

—MELVIN SMALL
Distinguished Professor of History, Wayne State University

"Think a U.S. empire is desirable and viable? Read Ivan Eland's highly insightful, essential book, and you will change your mind."

—EDWARD A. OLSEN
Professor of National Security Affairs, Naval Postgraduate School

The Empire Has No Clothes

U.S. Foreign Policy Exposed

Ivan Eland

The INDEPENDENT INSTITUTE

Oakland, California

The Independent Institute
100 Swan Way, Oakland, CA 94621-1428
Telephone: 510-632-1366 | Fax: 510-568-6040
Email: info@independent.org
Website: http://www.independent.org

Library of Congress Cataloging-in-Publication Data

Eland, Ivan.
The Empire Has No Clothes : U.S. Foreign Policy Exposed / Ivan Eland.
p. cm.
Includes bibliographical references.
ISBN 0-945999-98-4 (alk. paper)
1. United States—Foreign relations—20th century. 2. United States—Foreign relations—2001- 3. United States—Territorial expansion. 4. Imperialism. 5. Intervention (International law) 6. United States—Foreign relations—Philosophy. I. Title.

E744.E437 2004
327.73'009'04--dc22

2004015409

10 9 8 7 6 5 4 3 2 1

The INDEPENDENT INSTITUTE

THE INDEPENDENT INSTITUTE is a non-profit, non-partisan, scholarly research and educational organization that sponsors comprehensive studies of the political economy of critical social and economic issues.

The politicization of decision-making in society has too often confined public debate to the narrow reconsideration of existing policies. Given the prevailing influence of partisan interests, little social innovation has occurred. In order to understand both the nature of and possible solutions to major public issues, The Independent Institute's program adheres to the highest standards of independent inquiry and is pursued regardless of political or social biases and conventions. The resulting studies are widely distributed as books and other publications, and are publicly debated through numerous conference and media programs. Through this uncommon independence, depth, and clarity, The Independent Institute expands the frontiers of our knowledge, redefines the debate over public issues, and fosters new and effective directions for government reform.

THE INDEPENDENT INSTITUTE
100 Swan Way, Oakland, California 94621-1428, U.S.A.
Telephone: 510-632-1366 Facsimile: 510-568-6040
Email: info@independent.org Website: www.independent.org

Contents

1

Introduction: History of the U.S. Empire

Americans don't think of their country as having an empire. U.S. presidents have often disclaimed imperial intent while engaging in what suspiciously appear to be imperial adventures. After going to war in 1898 to grab Caribbean and Pacific possessions from a weakened Spain—America's first imperial foray—President William McKinley disclaimed any imperial intent: "No imperial designs lurk in the American mind. They are alien to American sentiment, thought, and purpose. Our priceless principles undergo no change under a tropical sun. They go with the flag."[1]

Such rhetoric is strikingly similar to that of President George W. Bush. During his campaign for president, Bush asserted flatly, "America has never been an empire."[2] Similarly, when speaking about the U.S. invasion and occupation of the sovereign nation of Iraq, Bush stated, "Our country does not seek the expansion of territory" but rather "to enlarge the realm of liberty."[3] In his 2004 State of the Union speech, the president declared, "We have no desire to dominate, no ambitions of empire."[4]

Even at the neoconservative American Enterprise Institute, which advocates an expansive U.S. foreign policy, the audience—in a poll taken after a debate on the proposition "The United States is and should be an empire"—rejected the notion.[5]

Yet an American overseas empire has existed since the turn of the last century and a global U.S. empire since the advent of the cold war under both Democratic and Republican administrations. After George W. Bush became president and the neoconservatives gained ascendancy within his administration's national security apparatus, their jubilant brethren on the outside began to use openly, and even extol, the "E"-word when describing U.S. foreign policy. Writers such as Eliot Cohen, Max Boot, Ernest Lefever, Robert Kaplan, Lawrence Kaplan, Charles Krauthammer, and William Kristol have made discussion and debate about the American empire trendy in the foreign policy salons of Washington and New York. The "outsider" faction of the neoconservatives has done a great service to the post–cold war and post–September 11 foreign-policy debate by imprudently broaching that taboo subject.

Even current and future high-level administration officials have openly used the terms *empire* and *imperial* to apply to the United States. In a 2003 vice-presidential Christmas card, Dick Cheney quoted Ben Franklin to imply that God was watching over and aiding the U.S. empire: "And if a sparrow cannot fall to the ground without His notice, is it probable that an empire can rise without His aid?" Similarly, after the 2000 election, Richard Haass, future policy-planning director of the Bush II administration's State Department, urged Americans to "reconceive their global role from one of a traditional nation-state to an imperial power." Although Haass distinguished between an "imperial foreign policy" and "imperialism," the imperial foreign policy he championed would recognize the "informal" U.S. empire.[6]

Neoconservatives and others from the right are not the only advocates of empire. For example, Ivo Daalder of the Brookings Institution and Sebastian Mallaby, a columnist for the *Washington Post*, are more liberal advocates of empire. Of course, while currently fashionable, all of those advocates of empire—both on the left and on the right—are more than a hundred years too late in discovering that the United States has had an overseas empire. Furthermore, a global empire, which, since the Korean War, has lasted through both Democratic and Republican administrations, will likely continue after President George W. Bush leaves office.

America's own Colonial subjugation at the hands of the British has bequeathed an anti-imperialist self-image—even as the United States engaged in blatant imperial behavior. How did this empire come about? Until recently, the anti-imperialist self-image held so much sway that anyone labeling U.S. foreign policy as "imperialist" was immediately thought to be a leftist or a communist. People from that camp were the only ones who regularly asserted that the United States had an empire. How times have changed! Niall Ferguson, a British historian and proponent of U.S. empire, noted that, "The greatest empire of modern times has come into existence without the American people even noticing."[7] Exiled German economist Moritz Bonn perceptively noted a paradox of World War II: "The United States have [sic] been the cradle of modern Anti-Imperialism, and at the same time the founding of a mighty Empire."[8]

THE SEEDS OF EMPIRE

Most historians would agree that the first American imperial conflict was the Spanish-American War, which began in 1898. But some analysts would say that U.S. imperial behavior began as America expanded westward, pushing out other powers and Native American populations, and that U.S. overseas imperialism started when that continental expansion was complete. Although the latter argument is probably true and was reflected in the rhetoric at the turn of the last century, the former argument is not true.

The westward expansion should be labeled as nation-building, not empire-building. That classification is in no way designed to develop a euphemism for the grabbing of what is now the southwestern United States by provoking a war against Mexico or for the ethnic cleansing and brutal treatment of Native Americans in the westward push by white settlers. In fact, nation-building can be more brutal than the quest for empire. In an empire, conquered populations are left intact and dominated, at least partially, using local elites. They often keep their own language and laws. In nation-building, foreign populations are either "integrated" with conquering peoples through forced assimilation, or annihilated or driven from their land and forcibly resettled to make room for colonies of conquerors. Often, they are forced to speak the conquerors' languages and obey their laws.

As the United States moved west, it bought and annexed territories of other powers, eliminated peripheral Spanish and Native American elites, extended U.S. legal, military and administrative systems, and populated the new territories with nonnative settlers.[9] The western territories of the United States were never meant to be ruled as colonies but to enter the union as states.[10] (In a more benign example of an empire turning into a state, the Roman empire technically came to an end in 212 C.E.—long before it physically expired—when the Emperor Caracalla extended Roman citizenship to all the empire's free peoples. Such full integration of subjects should really be called a multinational state.)

In 1897, the inauguration of William McKinley ended the era of congressional domination. It was the culmination of a redistribution of power from the Congress to the executive branch in the late 1800s. A strengthening executive branch and the expansion of federal bureaucracy had allowed a naval buildup that permitted America's first imperial adventure—the Spanish-American War. When the ship U.S.S. *Maine*, on a show-of-force mission to Cuba, blew up in Havana Bay, hawks in the United States used the event—now believed by most historians to have been an accident—as a pretext to grab a declining Spanish empire's possessions.[11]

In the aftermath of the Spanish-American War, the United States—now a world power—tried for the first time to rule a foreign people using brutal force without annexing their territory and integrating their citizens into the American nation. Although the seeds of war began in the Caribbean, the outcome helped the United States compete with other imperial powers that were carving up China. Already in 1900, as part of the multilateral mercantilist effort to force China to trade with the west, President McKinley, without getting congressional approval, sent five thousand troops to help the other imperialist powers repress a rebellion by the Chinese "Boxers." Ironically, the American overseas empire began around the beginning of the last century and spanned the globe after the Korean War because American policymakers essentially bought into now-discredited theories by Vladimir Lenin and others. Lenin's theory of imperialism was that capitalist nations were intrinsically prone to industrial overproduction, and thus underconsumption (as well as oversaving and underinvestment), and needed to develop overseas markets for their products to avoid domestic unemployment and accompanying social unrest.[12] After the American frontier was closed in the 1890s, some observers bought into this fallacy. But many countries did not have open (free) trade policies, so the neomercantilist policy of opening markets at gunpoint was adopted by the United States. Yet, in reality, any American overproduction was caused by excessive domestic prices maintained by America's failure to observe the principles of free trade through the enactment of high tariffs.

After drubbing a weak Spanish empire in the Spanish-American War, the United States obtained Guam and the Philippines and also annexed Hawaii, all of which would be used as naval bases in the competition for China. With the addition of Wake Island and a strategic deepwater port in Samoa in 1899, the United States had obtained a chain of naval coaling stations across the Pacific, including California, Hawaii, Midway, Samoa, Wake Island, Guam, and the Philippines. Hawaii and the Philippines were America's first true colonies.[13]

The naval build-up and war also allowed America to dominate the Western Hemisphere and bring Cuba under U.S. military rule. That "strategic" island guarded the Caribbean approaches of the planned canal through the Central American isthmus—the building of which would allow U.S. naval vessels to pass into the Pacific without making the long southern trip around the tip of South America. Thus, the canal would also facilitate American participation in the great power competition for China. In 1903, President Teddy Roosevelt began the quest for the trans-isthmus waterway by assisting Panamanian guerrillas in a revolt and separation from the uncooperative parent Colombian government. The United States subsequently signed a one-sided treaty to dig the canal with the much more cooperative Panamanians.

Roosevelt, as Assistant Secretary of the Navy before he became president, was also one of the chief architects of the naval buildup, the Spanish-American War, and U.S. overseas imperialism—the last of which he euphemistically had to dub "Americanism" because of American aversion to the concept. During and after the conflict, an anti-imperialist backlash served up harsh criticism of the American empire for, among other reasons, violating constitutional principles and draining the Treasury.[14]

Because of such popular sentiment, American imperialism was sporadic during the first half of the twentieth century. Up until the beginning of World War II, the platforms of both the Democratic and Republican parties opposed U.S. involvement in wars overseas.[15] The post-Spanish-American War presidencies of Teddy Roosevelt, William Howard Taft, and Woodrow Wilson restricted the new imperial policy to small interventions in Latin America. Teddy Roosevelt, for example, formulated a corollary to the Monroe Doctrine (the United States would stay out of Europe's wars and European powers were to stay out of the Western Hemisphere) that promised U.S. intervention in the Western Hemisphere to ensure internal stability. Woodrow Wilson sent forces to Latin America in an ineffectual attempt to teach them to "elect good men." And during the interwar period, despite the horrors of World War I, the U.S. Marines upheld the new tradition of meddling in Latin American affairs by periodically occupying Caribbean and Central American nations. In all, during the first decades of the twentieth century, the United States intervened militarily in Cuba, Mexico, Nicaragua, Haiti, the Dominican Republic, Honduras, Guatemala, Panama, and Colombia.[16]

Despite interventions in the traditional U.S. sphere of influence in the Americas, however, the U.S. military demobilized after each of the world wars to its traditional small size and was not used to build a more expansive empire. In short, despite the fact that the United States had become a world-class economy by 1830, a potential great power by 1850, the largest economy on the planet by the 1880s,[17] and a great naval power by 1907, the American popular aversion to imperialism constrained U.S. imperialists from creating a large peacetime army and a global empire until the advent of the cold war. Prior to the Pax Americana of the cold war period, even U.S. military interventions in the Philippines, Latin America, and World Wars I and II were done either unilaterally or with an ad hoc coalition of allies in the founding tradition of avoiding the obligation of permanent, entangling alliances.[18]

A GLOBAL U.S. EMPIRE RISES

After the massive destruction inflicted on all of the other great powers by World War II, the United States, geographically removed from the conflict, came to dominate the world because all of its competitors had been crippled. During the early cold war years, the United States had 50 percent of the world's remaining Gross Domestic Product (GDP) and began to remake the world essentially because it could, not because it needed to for reasons of security.

The perceived lessons of World War II, the power vacuum created by the debilitation of other powers, the slow rise out of the war's ashes of a second-class Soviet competitor, and the desire to use American power to open the world to trade and investment from dominant U.S. companies (that goal had existed since the Spanish-American War at the turn of the last century) led to the creation of a truly global American empire. Although the Bush II administration has blatantly emphasized preemptive actions (really preventative actions to keep future threats from coalescing) and neoconservatives outside and inside the administration have openly talked about a global American empire, the United States has pursued both policies since the beginning of the cold war. For example, the United States ousted Mohammed Mossadegh in Iran in 1953 and Jacob Arbenz Guzman in Guatemala in 1954 because of fears that they were taking those countries down the wrong road for U.S. interests. The United States also intervened militarily or covertly in many countries during the cold war and created an empire by forming alliances, establishing bases around the world, and dumping large amounts of military and economic aid into many countries to pay for access to those bases.

Learn Lessons from World War I, Not World War II

The perceived lessons from British appeasement of Adolph Hitler during a summit in Munich in 1938 have influenced U.S. postwar foreign policy for decades. Almost sixty years later, Madeleine Albright, President Clinton's Secretary of State, was still invoking this event to warn against appeasing the Serbs in the Balkans. The general premise in U.S. foreign-policy circles is that appeasing a foe—and hawks can easily label any negotiations as appeasement—might appear as weakness and cause the opponent and other observing nations to commit aggression. Also, any sign of aggression, direct or indirect, or instability must be nipped in the bud early and in remote locations overseas before it snowballs or spreads closer to home.

There are logical and historical problems with putting too much weight on this historical example to drive policy, but the U.S. government nevertheless has given excessive emphasis to the event during the cold war and thereafter. First, every potential opponent is not a jingoistic, rich, and well-armed Germany that has the potential to overrun a region of high economic and technological output—that is, Europe. Second, in World War II, Central Europe was much more strategically important to Britain and France than most of the world is to the United States today. Third, today's high-technology weapons take at least twenty years to research, develop, produce, and field—making the rapid rise of a peer competitor, such as Hitler's Germany from 1933 to 1939, much less likely. Fourth, negotiations can and should be undertaken with a potential foe before military action is taken. Fifth, Neville Chamberlain may have had little choice but to negotiate with Hitler. The British and their French allies were so overstretched policing global empires that they could not deal with a potentially much bigger threat closer to home—a lesson that the U.S. empire should learn in the wake of the September 11 attacks and with the potential for China or India to rise as a great power. In addition, in response to the German threat, Chamberlain had ordered military improvements, but in 1938 his armed forces were not yet up to the task of taking on a Germany that was ahead on the rearming curve. He had to stall for time. The world's first integrated air defense system—including new radar technology that Winston Churchill scorned while in opposition to the British government but later, as Prime Minister, used in the decisive Battle of Britain—was made possible by the governments of Chamberlain and his predecessor.[19]

Sixth, and most important, today's proponents of an interventionist U.S. foreign policy read history selectively. They blame Nazi aggression on the absence of a continuing U.S. military presence in Europe after World War I. There is no proof that even this commitment would have prevented a German nationalist regime from trying to win back lands lost from a peace that was perceived as unfair. Instead, if the interventionists looked farther back in history, they might realize that U.S. intervention in World War I tipped the scales on a stalemated battlefield toward the allies and contributed greatly to the rise of Hitler. John Mearsheimer, an academic who has studied wars of the great powers, notes: "Germany almost won the subsequent war of attrition between 1915 and 1918. The Kaiser's armies knocked Russia out of the war in the fall of 1917, and they had the British and especially the French armies on the ropes in the spring of 1918. Had it not been for American intervention at the last moment, Germany might have won World War I."[20]

After 1776, the United States, in keeping with the founders' policy of military restraint overseas that the country had followed for most of its history, stayed out of numerous European wars. The idealistic Woodrow Wilson, however, decided to get involved in World

War I to fight the "war to end all wars." Curiously, in that European conflict, unlike numerous past wars, many of the opposing belligerents had participative governments—for example, Britain, France, and Germany. In fact, Germany, the country later blamed (probably unfairly) for starting the war, had the broadest voting franchise among them.

With the U.S. entry into the war, the allies won and imposed a draconian peace on Germany. In a bid to purify the German constitutional monarchy, Wilson insisted that the Kaiser be removed from his throne. Now that the major barrier to the rise of a dictator was removed, Hitler used weaknesses in German society caused by the war and the heavy reparations imposed by the allies—that is, the torn social fabric and the squalid economy—to catapult himself to power. He rekindled the nationalistic fire in the German people by bashing the less-than-gracious treatment of the allies toward a vanquished foe. Instead of leading to Hitler and World War II, following traditional U.S. foreign policy, staying out of World War I and at worst allowing the Germans to win the Great War would merely have caused the borders of Europe to be readjusted and balance of power to be reestablished. Although Germany had the largest economy in Europe before World War I, the combined GDP of the Triple Entente of France, Russia, and Great Britain had been slightly larger than the combined GDP of Germany and the Austro-Hungarian Empire. Thus, Germany, even as the winner of World War I, would have been far from becoming a hegemonic European power, especially after a devastating large-scale war.[21] So a closer examination of history yields the opposite conclusion from that of the interventionists: less American intervention, rather than more U.S. meddling, would have led to a better outcome.

Fight Against Communism Used as Cloak for U.S. Empire

When combined with the perceived lessons of Munich and the nascent cold war, the power vacuum arising from the debilitation of all other great powers during World War II was too good a chance for the United States to pass up. In addition, after World War II, the "isolationist" consensus dominant in both political parties morphed into an interventionist one, with the "American century" proclaimed as the buzzwords for the ascendant American empire. If the new policy was to mount an aggressive "forward defense" against future threats, a global power vacuum provided the opportunity to station forces overseas, create alliances to justify such deployments, provide arms sales and military assistance to those allies, and win influence where exhausted powers could no longer tread.

In addition to courting countries liberated from German and Japanese hegemony, the United States sought to make inroads in the spheres of influence of France and the United Kingdom, colonial powers that had been drained by two world wars and could no longer maintain their empires. For example, the United States eventually replaced France as the dominant power in Indochina and the United Kingdom as the dominant power in the Middle East. Also, the British could no longer dominate Greece and Turkey. So President Truman announced the Truman Doctrine and provided $400 million to those nations, marking the first time in U.S. history that America had intervened in peacetime in areas outside North and South America.[22] A global empire was about to be born.

Of course, if the post–World War II rising of the Soviet Union is added to the mix, the U.S. urge to fill the power vacuum in key regions, before the Soviets did, became even more intense. But historians and policy analysts have probably made too much of the cold war rivalry with the Soviet Union as a genuine driver of U.S. foreign policy in the postwar period. The rivalry was certainly there, and the communist threat was used by policymakers to justify the U.S. turn away from its traditional foreign policy toward a policy of global intervention. The cold war was also used to justify a large peacetime military. After World War II, the nation once again demobilized, as it had after all prior wars. But the Korean War and the ensuing cold war were used to justify a military remobilization on a permanent peacetime basis—again, a first in U.S. history.

U.S.-Soviet competition, however, was far from the whole story. Both the United States and the Soviet Union used the exaggerated threat from the other side as an excuse for their forward-deployed empires. For example, a memo in 1965 by John McNaughton, Assistant Secretary of Defense, which laid out the rationale for the massive U.S. military intervention in Vietnam, stated that 70 percent was to escape tarnishing the U.S. reputation as a security guarantor and only 20 percent was to keep Indochina from being controlled by the communists.[23] If the main goal of post–World War II U.S. foreign policy had been to fight communism, the Pax Americana that spanned the globe would have been dismantled after the Soviet empire fell. Yet more than a decade after the cold war ended, about two hundred and fifty thousand troops are deployed overseas in thirty-eight countries and at sea. The United States has legally binding commitments to provide security to at least thirty-six countries.[24] In 2003, the U.S. Military's Special Operations Command was deployed in at least sixty-five countries.[25]

In addition, after the cold war, the U.S. government changed justifications for its forces and weapons from containing the Soviets to defending other interests. For example, despite years of rhetoric to the contrary, the Bush I administration declared in 1990 that the United States maintained forces for intervention in the Middle East to defend its interests against threats other than the Soviet Union. And despite the demise of that rival superpower, U.S. military spending never dropped below cold war levels. Similarly, the F-22 fighter aircraft and Comanche helicopter, originally designed to fight the Soviets, subsequently have been justified on other grounds.

In fact, the United States is by now busily extending its influence into the new power vacuum left by the demise of its only remaining great power rival. It has expanded the North Atlantic Treaty Organization (NATO) into the former-Soviet sphere of influence in Europe and intervened militarily in the Balkans, a region not deemed to be strategic for the United States during the cold war. In East Asia, the United States has augmented its military presence[26] and enhanced its formal and informal alliances with Japan, South Korea, Taiwan, Australia, Thailand, and the Philippines. Only since the cold war ended has the United States created a permanent land-based military presence in the Persian Gulf. Although Iraqi forces were severely crippled after the first Persian Gulf War, the United States continued to vilify Saddam Hussein (there were other dictators equally as brutal) to keep forces permanently stationed in the oil-rich region in order to dominate that resource.[27]

In the wake of the September 11 attacks, in the name of fighting the "war on terror," the U.S. military invaded and occupied Iraq, took advantage of the war in Afghanistan to establish "temporary" bases in Central Asian countries formerly in the Soviet Union, built bases in Bulgaria and Romania, and sent forces to help suppress insurrections in the backwaters of Georgia, Yemen, and the Philippines. Fighting such insurgencies had little to do with fighting terror and more to do with gaining U.S. influence in "strategic" areas. Similarly, in Azerbaijan, under the banner of the "war on terror," the U.S. Department of Defense (DoD) provided funding for the training of the Azeri military and financing to buy U.S. arms, but later acknowledged that the assistance was designed to ensure U.S. access to Caspian Sea oil. In short, the war against Serbia in 1999, two wars against Iraq, and the war in Afghanistan allowed the United States to enlarge its empire into the southern Eurasian region from the Balkans to the border of China, a region that is both oil-rich and formerly in the Soviet Union or its sphere of influence.[28] To battle "narcoterrorism," the United States has dramatically increased anti-drug aid to the government of Colombia, which is fighting an insurgency.

Similarly, with the collapse of the Soviet Union and thus the lifting of the main constraint on U.S. meddling overseas, U.S. military interventions increased dramatically in the decade after the end of the cold war. From 1989 to 1999, the U.S. intervened nearly four dozen times, as opposed to only sixteen interventions during the entire cold war.[29]

The rationale for an ever more expansive U.S. foreign policy and larger and larger defense budgets has changed from containing the Soviet Union to spreading democracy, free markets, and respect for human rights around the globe. And even though threats to the United States requiring a response by large military forces have declined dramatically, U.S. spending on defense is now 10 percent higher than the cold war average and more than the average spent during the Korean and Vietnam Wars.[30] The Pentagon justifies that increase because of the war on terror and the potential rise of China as a competitor, neither of which will soon be as great a threat as the Soviet Union. The failure of the U.S. defense perimeter to contract after the demise of the Soviet Union, and its actual expansion, are the best indicators that the expansive post–World War II U.S. foreign policy would probably have arisen even if the Soviet Union had never posed a threat.

Although the Soviet Union was a military threat to Western Europe and to a lesser extent East Asia, two regions of high economic and technological output, its economic system was pathetic, greatly diminishing its worldwide threat to the United States. The "Soviet threat" was magnified by the U.S. foreign-policy apparatus to gain support for profligate military and political intervention in the affairs of other nations worldwide and for the excessively high defense budgets to carry out that policy. In 1947, President Harry Truman appeared before Congress in an attempt to replace a faltering British empire by aiding the governments of Greece and Turkey against communist insurgencies. To get the money from the frugal legislators, Truman was advised by Senator Arthur Vandenberg (p. 63) to "scare the hell out of the American people." He did so in what became the Truman Doctrine, the keystone of the U.S. containment policy for decades during the cold war. He implied that dominoes would fall and thus turned a regional problem into a global crusade against communism. His words, "It must be the policy of the United States to support free peoples who are resisting attempted subjugation by armed minorities or by outside pressures," were used by later presidents to justify profligate overseas interventions.[31] In short, the cold war permitted those wanting to build an American global empire with the justification to do it.

After World War II, the Soviet empire was confined to Eastern Europe. The informal empire of the United States stretched around the world. All of the other great powers were decimated and exhausted by the world conflagration. Only the United States, in the secure bastion of placid North America and separated from the locus of conflict by two vast oceans, escaped massive destruction on its own territory. At the end of the greatest war in history, the United States was really the only great power left standing. In 1947, Harold Laski, a British scholar and politician, wrote, "America bestrides the world like a colossus; neither Rome at the height of its powers nor Great Britain in the period of its economic supremacy enjoyed an influence so direct, so profound, so pervasive."[32]

The idea that protectionism had caused the Great Depression and World War II led to a continuing belief in the "underconsumption" of advanced capitalist nations (such countries allegedly produced more than they consumed), which in turn caused the push to create an open world commercial order in which the overflowing U.S. products and investment would dominate. Thus the rival regional trading blocs of the 1930s would be avoided. The United States wanted unrestricted access to Asian and European resources and markets. The thinking was that U.S. military power would provide the stability on which an unfettered global commercial order depended. Thus, despite its anti-imperialist self-image, the United States—like many nations in history that have sought empire—could not resist the temptation of world domination.

THE POST–COLD WAR EMPIRE

Today, after the fall of the Soviet superpower rival, the desire for U.S. global dominance—present even during the bipolar environment of the cold war years—has been reenergized. And if any doubt existed about the imperial ambitions of the U.S. government, they were exposed in a 1992 Department of Defense planning document. The document was drafted by Paul Wolfowitz, then-Undersecretary of Defense for Bush I's administration and now Deputy Secretary of Defense for Bush II's administration. The text laid out in blunt language the goal of American global dominance and the need for unparalleled U.S. military power to intimidate potential rivals from even competing and to give allies confidence that the American security umbrella would continue to obviate the need for them to conduct military buildups.[33] At the time, the leaked document caused an uproar and was disavowed by the first Bush administration. How times have changed! The second Bush administration is much more hawkish and blunt than the first. Most of those formerly forbidden thoughts have since been enshrined in the official U.S. National Security Strategy. The Bush II administration initially dropped much of the veneer of Wilsonian idealistic doublespeak from U.S. foreign policy discourse, exposing the U.S. quest for world dominance.

Downplaying the idealistic rhetoric that cloaks the American empire got the Bush II administration into trouble with certain quarters of the generally idealistic American public and also U.S. allies. Although the Bush II administration is more overtly hawkish than any U.S. administration since Ronald Reagan, all post–World War II administrations—including Clinton's—have tried to maintain U.S. dominance in the world. But they did so either with the Wilsonian rhetoric of intervening militarily for humanitarian purposes or to preserve, or actually enlarge, the community of free-market, democratic nations. Such was the rhetoric of Anthony Lake, President Clinton's National Security Advisor, when he said that "enlarging the world's community of free nations" would make the world "more humane and peaceful" and would make the United States "more secure, prosperous and influential." Andrew Bacevich, a prominent scholar of the American empire, alluded that preserving U.S. preeminence was only implied in Lake's statements, thus avoiding impolitic sentiments, such as those from Wolfowitz.[34]

Unlike large grass-roots protests before and during the Bush II administration's invasion of Iraq, no large movement arose to criticize Clinton's attack on the sovereign nation of Serbia over the Kosovo issue. The less hostile public reaction to military action occurred because Clinton billed the bombing of Serbia as a humanitarian mission to stop Serbian ethnic cleansing of Kosovars in Kosovo, though it inadvertently fueled the ethnic cleansing.

In contrast, although the Bush II administration did mention that removing the despotic regime of Saddam Hussein from Iraq would have humanitarian benefits, the major rationale for the invasion was that Saddam was reconstituting his weapons of mass destruction and that they were an imminent threat to U.S. security. Paul Wolfowitz even admitted that Hussein's human rights violations alone would not constitute a justifiable reason to remove him from power. The administration changed its tune and began touting that Iraqis were better off without Saddam only when no weapons of mass destruction were found in Iraq after the war, and accusations were made that the administration had hyped the threat. So rhetoric does matter greatly in the solemn decision to take the nation to war.

DEBATE ON U.S. WORLD ROLE HAS FINALLY BEGUN

Curiously, the Bush II administration's unfortunate "in-your-face" policy of world domination may have a silver lining. That more blatant policy has emboldened neoconservatives inside and outside of the administration openly to acknowledge and praise the quest for such domination by using the term *American empire.* By bringing out of the closet the American desire to dominate the world—a policy hidden since its inception during the early years of the cold war—the Bush II administration has spurred a much-needed debate on the proper role of the United States in the world.

When the cold war ended, that debate should have commenced. But after the collapse of the Soviet Union, those who wanted to maintain U.S. global dominance—that is, most of the American foreign policy elite—had to search for new fig leafs to hide the empire from an unsuspecting public. The elder President Bush removed the drug-running thug who was president of Panama and rolled back the aggression of another despotic dictator in Iraq. In reality, the first intervention was probably undertaken to intimidate the leftist Sandinistas before an election in Nicaragua and to restore U.S. prestige after Manuel Noriega, a tin-pot dictator of a banana republic, had tweaked a superpower's nose in its own hemisphere. In other words, the intervention was undertaken to uphold the revised Monroe Doctrine, not solely to remove a Latin American dictator participating in the drug trade. The leaders of other Latin American nations were also involved in the trade and were not ousted. Most analysts believed that the first Gulf War was fought to eliminate the threat that the Iraqi army in occupied Kuwait posed to Saudi Arabia, the world's largest oil producer.

Bill Clinton was equally haphazard. In the most interventionist presidency in the last twenty years, he flailed about with "humanitarian" interventions in Somalia, Bosnia, Haiti and Kosovo. In reality, the interventions in Bosnia and Kosovo were most likely undertaken to give the NATO alliance a new mission. The United States wanted to keep its "influence" (what the American taxpayer gets from that amorphous buzzword is unclear) in Europe. To do so, a rationale had to be developed to keep U.S forces on the continent after the cold war. To retain the forward–deployed forces, NATO, an alliance created originally to counter the now-defunct Soviet Union, had to be expanded in territory and mission. The perception was that NATO must "expand or die." Contrary to the NATO charter, which envisioned it as a defensive alliance, NATO's new mission was offensive. The alliance would now send forces outside the treaty area (Western Europe) to pacify "failed states." The NATO military interventions in Bosnia and Kosovo fulfilled the objective of giving it something to do in the post–cold war world. (In the Bush II administration, NATO is now involved in peacekeeping in Afghanistan, a nation nowhere even close to Western Europe.) In Haiti, although the Clinton administration claimed that the intervention was undertaken to help stabilize that poor, corruptly governed nation and restore an elected leader, the reality was that the United States wanted to stanch the flow of Haitian refugees to U.S. shores.

The lack of interventions where human suffering is at its worst also belies the humanitarian rationale. More than three million people have been killed in each of the civil wars in Sudan and the Congo. About five to eight hundred thousand people were killed by civil strife in Rwanda. The suffering in those nations made the suffering in Kuwait, Panama, Somalia, Haiti, Bosnia, and Kosovo look mild. Yet the United States did not intervene directly in any of those African conflicts.

The Bush II administration did not like softheaded humanitarian rationales for war. So, in the wake of the September 11 attacks, that administration invented an "axis of evil" (despite the uncomfortable fact that its members—Iraq, Iran, and North Korea—were not only not allies but, in some cases, enemies of each other) and developed the "preemptive strike" doctrine to counter it. Although the Bush II administration is removing some of the Wilsonian idealism from U.S. foreign policy rhetoric, it is being forced to use other deceptive means to cloak the American empire. Clearly, the administration deceived the American public and exaggerated the threat from the relatively poor nation of Iraq, which had already had its military destroyed by a superpower and had endured more than a decade of grinding economic sanctions. The Bush II administration probably fought this war as a demonstration-effect for other members of the "axis of evil" and additional rogue states (such as Syria and Cuba); to help its ally Israel; for bases to guard Persian Gulf oil that were less vulnerable to instability than those in Saudi Arabia; and to restore U.S. prestige in the region that had been tarnished by years of Saddam's continued defiance of U.S. military muscle-flexing and economic coercion.

Although the Bush II administration's strategy to maintain and expand the empire is more blatant and aggressive than the last two post–cold war administrations—for example, Bush II prefers ousting leaders using ground invasions rather than Clinton's method of bombing countries from the air—the policy is not new and remains as operationally fuzzy as ever. The Bush II administration has intervened overseas as haphazardly as the Bush I and Clinton administrations. Some interventions were necessary to fight the war on al Qaeda—for example, military action in Afghanistan—but others have had no significant relationship to that war. For example, the invasion of Iraq and the small-scale military interventions in the backwater nations of Georgia and the Philippines were unnecessary to battle effectively the terrorists of al Qaeda. Also, much has been made of Bush's seemingly decisive inclination toward preemptive and preventative war. But Bill Clinton alleged that he was preempting imminent follow-on attacks on U.S. targets by al Qaeda (after the group's bombings of U.S. embassies in Africa) when he launched cruise missiles against the group's training camps in Afghanistan and a pharmaceutical plant in Sudan. This claim was shaky because of the nature of the targets and the concurrent Monica Lewinsky affair, but the preemption doctrine was used as a justification. Moreover, in 1994, Clinton threatened a preventative war if North Korea continued a nuclear program designed to make it a nuclear power. When North Korea admitted that it had continued the program in secret, the Bush II administration actually preferred the milder approach of negotiation.

The fuzzy criteria that the U.S. government uses to determine whether and where American forces should intervene indicate that American foreign policy is askew. Unlike the empires of old, which limited their military interventions to certain parts of the world, the United States is trying to police the entire globe. This book offers an alternative vision of a more restrained U.S. foreign policy that is more focused, more achievable, less costly, and a lot less dangerous.

2

Does the United States Really Have an Empire?

Although to the popular Bush II–era pundit Robert Kaplan, "It is a cliché these days to observe that the United States now possesses a global empire—different from Britain's and Rome's but an empire nonetheless" and "It is time to move beyond statements of the obvious,"[1] academics might still debate whether the United States qualifies as an empire.

Academic treatises usually begin their discussion of empire with lengthy and dry discussions about the definition of the concept. There are many varying definitions about what constitutes an empire. The traditional meaning was territorial—that is, an empire acquired and held colonies and dependencies. Of course, the United States still holds Guam, Puerto Rico, the U.S. Virgin Islands, and other dependencies not considered as states. From 1945 to 1972, the U.S. military directly ruled Okinawa. Even the nation's capital, Washington, D.C., is considered a dependency by some. It is not a state, and the people living within its borders are not represented by voting members of Congress (although they do get to vote in presidential elections). In addition, the U.S. military is occupying Afghanistan and Iraq. So, technically, the United States is an empire, even under the narrowest territorial definitions of that concept.

EMPIRE IS MORE THAN SIMPLY TERRITORIAL CONQUEST AND RULE

Territorial definitions of empire, however, are too restricted, particularly in an age in which nationalism and nuclear weapons impose constraints on blatant territorial conquest and annexation by great powers. Such narrow territorial definitions take Roman territorial conquest and subjugation as a model for empire, but there are many other models.

In the premodern era—for example, during the Roman and Assyrian periods—empire was financed through plundering precious metals in peripheral areas or heavy taxes on trade from those regions. Even during the transition from the premodern to the modern world, during the mercantilist era in the 1600s and 1700s, empires were based on coercive tribute gathering and plundering. The Spanish and Portuguese empires and the initial British and French acquisitions in India used such methods. But then more modern empires came along. They financed their realms with economic growth and regulated international trade to garner hard currency. The metropolis exported manufactured goods to the periphery, and the periphery exported food and raw materials back to the metropolis, with all trade transported by the metropolis's ships.[2]

At the turn of the last century, Alfred Thayer Mahan, an influential American naval strategist who convinced Teddy Roosevelt and others in the U.S. government to begin to build an American empire based on the worldwide use of naval power, defined imperialism as, "the extension of national authority over alien communities."[3] This definition emphasizes a political dimension to the central authority's control over the periphery and does not necessarily require the central authority to conquer and occupy a country to exercise imperial authority over it. Also espousing a broader, more political definition of empire rather than a narrower territorial one, David Lake notes that, "in empire, one partner cedes substantial rights of residual control directly to the other; in this way, the two polities are melded together in a political relationship in which one partner controls the other."[4] Similarly, apparently making no distinction between hegemony and empire, George Lichtheim defines empire as the "relationship of a hegemonial state to peoples or nations under its control."[5]

There are even broader definitions of empire, whereby the central authority dominates, rather than controls the peripheral entity.

Alexander Motyl suggests that in an empire, "a nonnative entity dominates a native entity"and that "because the empires with which we are concerned belong, above all, in the realm of politics, the nonnative entity must at a minimum exercise *political* [emphasis in original] dominance."[6] In one of the broadest definitions, Gier Lundestad even seems to toss out the need for one entity dominating another: "Empire simply means a hierarchical system of political relationships, with one power being much stronger than any other."[7] In only a few instances—in Bosnia, Kosovo, Afghanistan, and Iraq, for example—has the United States followed the Roman model of indefinite and involuntary territorial occupation, but the modern-day superpower would certainly have no trouble in qualifying under these broader definitions of empire.

The United States, however, which usually opts for coercive influence rather than annexation, also fits even narrower definitions of empire. According to Motyl, hegemony occurs when the dominant polity influences the external policies of the peripheral polity but has no voice in its internal matters. An informal empire exists when central authority determines the periphery's external policies but has only influence on its domestic matters. A formal empire determines both the external and internal policies of the peripheral polity.[8] Using Motyl's classification scheme, the United States would seem to fit easily into the informal empire category. As the leader of a worldwide system of alliances, the United States effectively controls the security policies of allies and also has influence on their domestic policies—especially in the traditional U.S. sphere of influence in Latin America, where it is involved in neighboring countries' drug, terrorism, immigration, and human rights policies.

Michael W. Doyle makes a different distinction between hegemony and empire and defines hegemony as one polity's control over another polity's foreign policy, but not its domestic policy. He defines empire more restrictively than Motyl, as the first polity's control over both of the second polity's policy sectors. He further subdivides empire into informal and formal categories. An informal empire is one where the central authority governs through local elites that are legally independent from the center but politically dependent on it. A formal empire comes about via annexation of the specific territory, which is then ruled by a colonial governor and collaborating local elites.[9] Although wider than defining empire merely as territorial conquest and annexation on the Roman model, Doyle's definition of empire is one of the narrower typologies.

Even under Doyle's more restrictive definition of empire, the U.S. superpower probably qualifies. Certainly, although U.S. allies such as Japan, South Korea, Taiwan, Israel, Australia, and the European NATO allies are independent countries, they follow the U.S. lead in security and foreign policy matters. In absolute terms, compared to the massive amounts spent by the United States on national defense, those rich allies spend very little on security (See Table 2.1 and Figure 2.1).[10] Also, most of those allies spend very little of their GDP on defense and rely on the United States to provide their security.[11] In return, they defer to the United States for leadership in external security matters. Even the sovereignties of Italy and the United Kingdom, and especially Japan, Germany, and South Korea, have been effectively limited by the presence of U.S. military forces on their soil.

Some academics would argue, in keeping with Doyle's definition, that the United States is better termed a "hegemonic power" rather than an empire. They would assert that the United States, while controlling the allies' external relations, does not have control over the domestic policies of those nations. Although their argument is true on a day-to-day operational basis, it is ultimately untrue in a larger systemic sense.

During the cold war, the United States would not have allowed any of those major allies to go in a "negative" direction domestically—that is, move toward communist rule—without direct or indirect intervention in their internal politics. For example, in the years following World War II, the United States imposed its own

TABLE 2.1: TOP 20 NATIONS BY DEFENSE SPENDING* 2002

		Defense Spending (D.S.)	Percentage of GDP	Country D.S./ World D.S.
1	**United States**	**$348.50**	3.4%	37.8%
2	China	$51.00	3.9%	5.5%
3	Russia	$50.80	4.8%	5.5%
4	France	$40.20	2.5%	4.4%
5	Japan	$39.50	1.0%	4.3%
6	United Kingdom	$37.30	2.3%	4.0%
7	Germany	$33.30	1.5%	3.6%
8	Italy	$25.60	2.0%	2.8%
9	Saudi Arabia	$22.20	12.0%	2.4%
10	India	$13.80	2.7%	1.5%
11	South Korea	$13.30	2.8%	1.4%
12	Brazil	$10.20	2.3%	1.1%
13	Israel	$9.90	9.6%	1.1%
Subtotal, Countries 2–13		**$347.10**		
14	Turkey	9.20	5.1%	1.0%
15	Spain	$8.70	1.2%	0.9%
16	Canada	$8.20	1.1%	0.9%
17	Australia	$8.00	2.0%	0.9%
18	Taiwan	$7.90	2.7%	0.9%
19	Netherlands	$7.70	1.6%	0.8%
20	Indonesia	$6.60	3.7%	0.7%
Subtotal, Countries 14–20		**$56.30**		
European Union Total		**$185.42**	2.1%	
World Total		**$914.84**	2.7%	

*Measured in billions of 2002 U.S. Dollars. Source: International Institute for Strategic Studies, Military Balance 2003–2004 (London: Oxford University Press, 2003).

political system on Japan, France, Italy, Germany, and other European countries in Western Europe. In addition, the Central Intelligence Agency (CIA) intervened in the elections of Italy and France when the United States believed that the communist parties in those nations had become too strong. In other words, the United States would not have tolerated any communist governments in important allied nations. The United States also intervened, directly or indirectly, in far less important nations—for example, Iran, Chile, Argentina, Cuba, El Salvador, Nicaragua, Guatemala, Granada, Laos, Cambodia, and South Vietnam—to try to prevent them from "going red" or to reverse communist takeovers.

FIGURE 2.1: TOP 13 DEFENSE SPENDERS IN THE WORLD

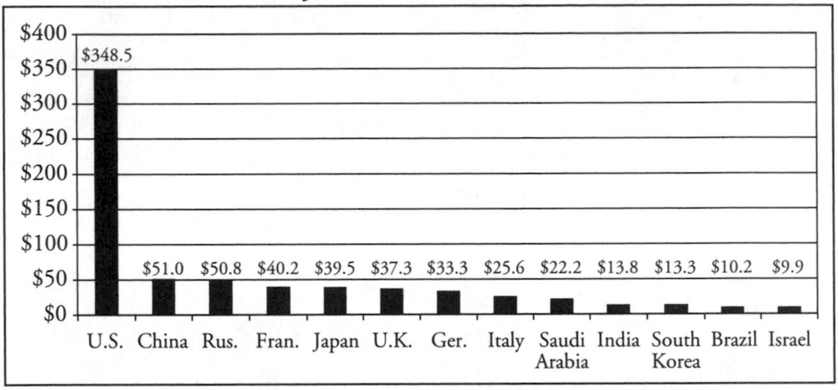

*Measured in billions of 2002 U.S. Dollars. Source: International Institute for Strategic Studies, Military Balance 2003–2004 (London: Oxford University Press, 2003).

Similarly, in the post–cold war world, does anyone think that the United States would allow major U.S. allies—for example, the economic powerhouses of Japan, Italy, France, Germany, and the United Kingdom—to move from democratic to authoritarian or totalitarian rule? Even in the less important nation of Haiti, the Clinton administration intervened to restore an elected leader who was the victim of a coup attempt.

Therefore, although relatively disengaged on a day-to-day basis from the domestic policies of most countries, the United States ultimately acts to guarantee "friendly" governments in important and not-so-important nations. Thus, even under Doyle's overly restrictive definition of empire, the United States appears to be an informal empire, albeit a loose one that normally allows states flexibility to determine domestic policy on a day-to-day basis (less so, of course, in Latin America). That type of imperial control most closely resembles that of ancient Sparta, rather than that of Rome or Britain, which form the common image of empire in the popular mind.

AMERICAN EMPIRE IS NEITHER ROME NOR BRITAIN

The American public's perception of imperialism has been colored by film and television depictions of the quintessential formal em-

FIGURE 2.2: COMPARISON OF U.S. AND "ENEMY STATE" DEFENSE SPENDING

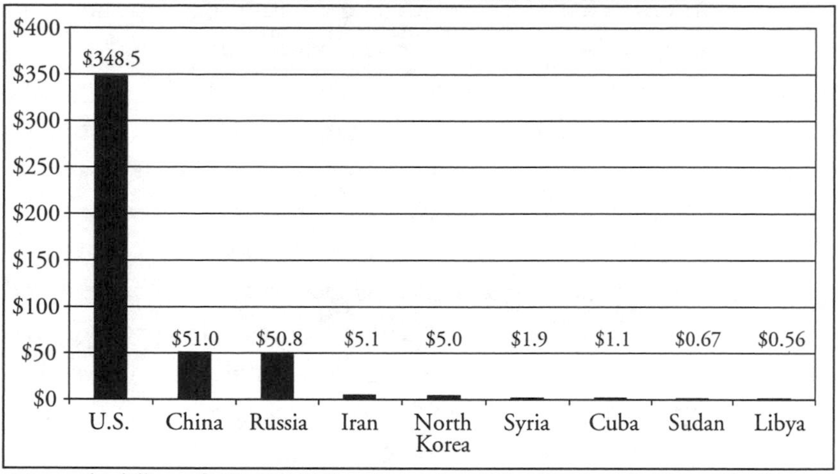

*Measured in billions of 2002 U.S. Dollars. Source: International Institute for Strategic Studies, Military Balance 2003–2004 (London: Oxford University Press, 2003).

pires—ancient Rome and nineteenth-century Britain. The American empire has some similarities with those empires of yesteryear. Rome (at times) and the United States (post–cold war) enjoyed the distinction of being the sole world powers of their respective times—a situation unrepeated in history, except by China during certain periods.[12] Rome and Britain dominated the globe militarily during their eras, but, in both relative and absolute terms, post–cold war American military dominance is the greatest in world history. The United States spends on national defense about what the next thirteen countries spend combined (see Table 2.1).[13] Its spending for future military dominance (expenditures for military research and development) is two-thirds of the world total and seven times that of the second-highest-spending nation (France).[14] The United States' defense budget is roughly seven times that of Russia or China and massive compared to the six "rogue" states—Iran, North Korea, Syria, Cuba, Sudan, and Libya (see Figure 2.2). The British empire at its height had no such military dominance over its competitors. Britain always had a smaller army than European continental powers and a navy that equaled the next two rival navies combined.

To justify their expansion, the Roman, British, American and other empires have had defining ideologies about the superiority of their system of governance. For example, Vergil, ancient Rome's greatest poet, maintained that the domination of Rome was willed by God to bring peace to the warring world.[15] That rationale sounds similar to Woodrow Wilson's "war to end all wars" justification for U.S. entry into World War I. The Romans also believed they brought benefits—for example, their system of government—to conquered peoples.[16] The British believed that they had replaced the Jews as the Elect Nation and had the mission to spread Christianity throughout the world. The urge to be civilizing missionaries was transplanted to the United States in the breasts of the first English colonists in the new world.[17] In the case of the United States, with the demise of a constraining Soviet adversary, the principal ideology changed somewhat from containing communism to the more ambitious goal of spreading democracy and free markets. Strangely, this new rationale harkened back to the originators of the American overseas empire—Teddy Roosevelt, Henry Cabot Lodge, and John Hay. They believed that America had a civilizing mission overseas,[18] which had been transmitted down the generations from the original English settlers. As hard as it may be for many contemporary Americans to accept, both late nineteenth-century and modern versions of "American exceptionalism" are similar and imply superiority over other peoples.

But the similarity between the empires ends there. Although both the Roman and British empires, as well as Alexander the Great's Macedonian empire and the Russian empire, relied to some extent on local administration (the exception was the direct British rule of India from the mid-nineteenth to the mid-twentieth century), they were created, for the most part, by removing the sovereignty of the peripheral polity. This was done through territorial annexation and the imposition from outside of a ruling regional governor. Both the Roman and British empires often ruled ruthlessly. Even Adolf Hitler noted that the means by which

Britain acquired colonial territories "were those of force and often brutality." The British empire was the largest formal empire in history, dominating one-quarter of the earth's surface, one-quarter of its population, and all of its oceans.[19] The informal U.S. empire spans the globe.

AMERICAN EMPIRE RESEMBLES ANCIENT SPARTA

The American empire—with its alliances and military bases spanning the entire globe—most closely resembles the informal empire of Sparta in the 400s BCE, before and during the Peloponnesian War. Sparta's superior military capacity allowed control of the foreign policy of the Peloponnesian League, an alliance of oligarchic city-states in ancient Greece that opposed the democratic Delian League, led by Athens. Sparta cared little about the day-to-day domestic policies of its smaller allied city-states but made sure that they all retained their oligarchic form of government.[20] There is a dispute in the academic world about whether or not Sparta was an empire or hegemonic state.[21] Although Michael Doyle concludes that Sparta was a hegemonic power,[22] ultimate Spartan control over the forms of government in its allies would seem to meet even Doyle's overly restrictive criteria for an informal empire. In short, Sparta was an informal empire that was loosely controlled. Just as the founders of the United States modeled their new republic after Sparta—which was controlled by an oligarchic and aristocratic Senate—rather than the more democratic Athens, the post–World War II American empire, perhaps out of necessity, resembles the more loosely controlled Spartan empire rather than the more tightly controlled Athenian realm.[23] Athens demanded mandatory contributions of funds from allies and forbade them to withdraw from the alliance. The looser Spartan alliance required a majority vote to go to war but effectively gave Sparta a veto over alliance policy.[24] Similarly, the modern-day NATO operates on a consensus of its members but gives the United States, which provides security for the other nations, a veto over alliance actions.

But recently, the United States, emboldened by the end of the cold war, has used military force to conquer and conduct long-term occupations and reconstructions of Bosnia, Kosovo, Afghanistan, and Iraq. Its governance of those new areas in an expanding empire is becoming tighter than the loose control exerted over traditional allies. Although less repressive, American governance of the new territories resembles that of the tight, informal Soviet rule in Eastern Europe during the cold war. Eastern European states were nominally sovereign, but their domestic and foreign policies were controlled by Moscow.

At least theoretically, however, the United States asserts that it will not rule those regions forever. In fact, throughout U.S. history, the American model has been to teach such people to, in the euphemism of Woodrow Wilson, "elect good men." Often that slogan has meant ensuring at gunpoint the election of leaders friendly to the United States and then withdrawing U.S. forces or retaining military bases but not engaging in the day-to-day running of the country. That informal mode of empire has allowed the United States to preserve its anti-imperialist self-concept at home.

Similarly, the British empire started out as an informal empire with coastal bases and informal spheres of influence. Threats and perceived threats to British commercial interests turned the informal realm into a formal one. The same transformation could happen to America. During the cold war, the superpowers did not usually rule formally in competitive regions of the world, because the countries could bolt to the other camp. That constraint on the method of U.S. rule is now gone. Also, in fragile societies, if the United States commits to rule at arm's length, it may eventually have to tighten its rule if a societal collapse becomes imminent.[25]

Today, the array of U.S. military bases around the world looks a lot like the panoply of British naval bases and garrisons around the world at the height of a declining Britain's imperial overstretch in the early 1900s.[26] The post–cold war conflicts in Bosnia, Kosovo, Iraq (two), and Afghanistan have greatly expanded the number of

American bases. Also, American foreign policy has become militarized: overseas regional military "proconsuls" or CINCs (commanders in chief) possess many more resources to conduct diplomacy than State Department officials and have become more assertive in doing so.[27]

Although most of the American empire generally resembles the Spartan empire's informal and relaxed reins of control, it resembles the democratic Athenian empire in its more offensive orientation, commercial nature, and pursuit of democratic revolutions on the periphery. Fifth-century BCE Sparta was a status-quo power that wanted to be left alone and thus created a defensive alliance.[28] In contrast, Athens was more offensively oriented and wanted to foster and protect democratic revolutions in Sparta's oligarchic allies. Such behavior resembles the Bush I administration's invasion of Panama, the Clinton administration's "engagement and enlargement" policy intended to enlarge the number of "democracies," sometimes by force (as in the U.S. interventions in Bosnia and Kosovo), and the Bush II administration's invasion to "liberate" Iraq and convert a dictatorship into a democracy.

When recalcitrant Athenian allies tried to leave the Delian League or exit the democratic fold, they were dissuaded by military action. Such actions are similar to the Eisenhower administration's CIA-sponsored coup against the more independent Mohammed Mossadegh to restore the more U.S.-friendly Pahlevi dynasty in Iran; the Kennedy and Johnson administrations' battle against the Viet Cong, who were trying to take South Vietnam into the communist camp and out of the U.S.-led Southeast Asian Treaty Organization (SEATO); the Nixon administration's CIA-sponsored coup against the newly elected socialist Allende government in Chile; the Reagan administration's invasion of Granada to rescue that nation from a new socialist government, and its attempt to reverse the socialist takeover of Nicaragua by supporting the Contras; and the Clinton administration's restoration of a democratically elected leader in Haiti after he had been ousted by a coup. Also, like Athens (and Rome), the American empire uses commercial ties with lesser states to reduce the need for coercion.[29]

Thus, the Athenian empire was feared, hated, and revered (at least by the democratic factions in the peripheral city-states).[30] The British and Roman empires were greeted with an equally expansive range of sentiments. Around the globe, the same variety of emotions greets the American empire.

WHY DOES THE UNITED STATES HAVE AN EMPIRE?

At its founding and for most of its history, America successfully avoided empire. There are many opinions about why the United States is now in charge of policing the globe.

One View: Empire Is Needed for Security

Many politicians, numerous pundits, and even some academics have adapted the convenient myth that the United States never intended to be an imperial power and that it acquired its empire by accident. In comparing the Roman and American empires, Peter Bender is a proponent of that typical view:

> Rome and America both expanded in order to achieve security. Like concentric circles, each circle in need of security demanded the occupation of the next larger circle. The Romans made their way around the Mediterranean, driven from one challenge to their security to the next. The struggles against Hitler, Stalin, Mao, and Japan brought the Americans to Europe and East Asia; the Americans soon wound up all over the globe, driven from one attempt at containment to the next. The boundaries between security and power politics gradually blurred. The Romans and Americans both eventually found themselves in a geographical and political position that they had not originally desired, but which they then gladly accepted and firmly maintained. Neither power, it would seem, corresponds to the distorted picture painted by their ene-

mies or to the ideal portrait depicted by their admirers. They were neither world conquerors nor unwilling world powers.[31]

Although Jack Snyder argues that a belief in "security through expansion" was the primary cause of every instance of excessive expansion by the industrial great powers, he also calls it the central myth of empire. In extreme cases, that belief remained in spite of evidence that aggressive policies were eroding a nation's safety. According to Snyder, statesmen overestimate the benefits of offensive expansion and underestimate the costs. They also underestimate the benefits of a defensive strategy.[32]

The case of imperial Japan, however, seems to debunk the notion that states expand only for security rather than for less legitimate reasons. As John Mearsheimer notes, attacks across water are difficult, but the imperial Japanese government, despite its secure position on an island, nevertheless chose a policy of excessive expansion. Supposedly, the Japanese were expanding to get resources to make their military-industrial complex autarkic. But a rational examination (which the realist proponents of the "security through expansion" view should like) would have reached the conclusion that Japan's intrinsic security was so good that it could have allowed the much more efficient system of free trade to provide resources from overseas. Thus, Japan's aggressive attempt to militarily acquire an East Asian empire was probably done more for glory rather than for security.

In another refutation of the "security through expansion" principle, Spain and Britain each acquired control of a significant portion of the known world but not for any immediate gains in security. Similarly, in the late 1800s, the scramble for colonies by European powers had little to do with security. The Germans and French acquired colonies merely for prestige. In fact, in the quest for colonies, the British and the French sacrificed the much more important European balance of power.[33] Those two countries later behaved the same way in the 1930s, maintaining their empires in the face of a rising Nazi Germany.

However, even some in the "security through expansion" school—the so-called offensive realists—believe that the United States, because of its remoteness from the centers of major conflict, will eventually pull back from its overseas empire now that the Soviet threat is gone. For example, John Mearsheimer believes that the security of "offshore balancers," such as Britain and the United States, does not depend on the micromanagement of affairs overseas but only on ensuring that a hegemonic great power does not grab the resources and technology in a key region(s) of the world. He predicts that if no such aggressive power arises in Asia or Europe, the United States will withdraw its forces from those two areas.[34]

Yet even during the cold war, a rational analysis would have probably concluded that it was questionable for the United States to station forces overseas to ensure the security of the U.S. homeland. The United States was geographically removed from possible conflicts and had a huge nuclear arsenal to deter any attacks on its homeland. Thus, the U.S. government had no need to create an empire for security reasons. Geography and a history of being invaded gave the Soviet Union an ostensibly better excuse than the United States for an imperial stationing of forces in foreign countries to ensure security at home. But even the Soviets did not need an empire for security, because they too had a robust nuclear means of deterring attacks on their homeland.

If only the U.S. government would be so rational as Mearsheimer predicts. The problem with Mearsheimer's hope is that the cold war has been over for fourteen years and a "more humble" U.S. foreign policy has not ensued. He admits that the continued U.S. presence in Europe and Northeast Asia in the 1990s does not fit well with the prognostications of offensive realists, but says that too little time has elapsed since the end of the cold war to know whether they are true.

But fourteen years is a long time, especially when the United States is moving in the opposite direction of Mearsheimer's prediction. Taking advantage of the absence of a hegemonic rival, America is expanding, not contracting, its defense perimeter. With no new hegemonic threats to Asia and Europe on the horizon, the United States has been strengthening its Asian alliances[35]—with Japan, South Korea, Taiwan, Australia, Thailand, and the Philippines—and taking on new allies and an expanded mission in Europe (for example, offensive operations outside of the NATO area in the heretofore unstrategic area of the Balkans). Also, to contain China and Russia, the United States now has bases and is seeking influence in the newly independent states of the former Soviet Union.

Similarly, Britain, another relatively secure offshore balancer, did not confine its army and navy solely to shoring up the balance of power on the European continent. The British acquired a far-flung empire around the globe, which had little to do with its security. In fact, British (as well as French) imperial overextension overseas inhibited its response to a potent Nazi threat closer to home.[36] U.S. security is also undermined—in the form of blowback terrorism—by empire-building and profligate military meddling in other nations' affairs all over the globe (see Chapter 5 for more details on this point).

So although Mearsheimer and the offensive realists have much to contribute in the foreign-policy debate, they are not being very realistic about why the United States has an empire. It seems a bit naïve to believe that states always behave rationally, make policy with one voice, respond only to external stimuli, and expand only for reasons of security. In fact, as Jack Snyder notes, there are contradictions in the thinking of the offensive realists: if states were always rational, they would realize that expanding to achieve security would probably not be successful because other nations would feel threatened, band together, and balance against the expanding country.[37] States should realize that such balancing, and the possibility of war, could ultimately lead to reduced—not enhanced—security for the expanding nation.

In contrast, defensive realists acknowledge that states do not always try to expand. They only expand when the benefits of expansion exceed the costs. Expansion often requires the diversion of material and human resources from other more important priorities. There are many cases in which states forgo the opportunity to expand. According to defensive realists, that conservative behavior explains why there have been long periods of stability in the international system.[38]

But if defensive realists are right and nations are more conservative about "expanding for security" than the offensive realists claim, then the American empire becomes even more mysterious. The United States possesses a secure geographical position and the costs of the American empire exceed its benefits. The realists prize the "rationality" of states, but the American empire appears irrational even by the realists' own standards. Even Thucydides, the original realist, notes that other factors besides security—profits and prestige—can drive the quest for empire.[39]

Domestic Causes of Empire May Be More Potent

Unlike many realists, who postulate countries with unitary decision-making processes responding to like nations in the international arena, Snyder and Charles Kupchan emphasize more realistic, fragmented domestic decision-making processes that lead to the building of empires. Kupchan and Snyder reject the dominance of international concerns over domestic interests in elite decision-making.[40] (Intuitively, their view makes sense because domestic issues, rather than foreign policy matters, usually decide U.S. elections; thus, politicians are more attuned to the domestic scene.) Also, both Kupchan and Snyder believe that empires are outmoded and harmful to the countries creating them, leading to overextension and perhaps exacerbating decline. Kupchan emphasizes that policy elites get caught in counterproductive policies of their own making and cannot reverse course because of their own mythmaking and rhetoric.[41]

Snyder, a defensive realist, on the other hand, says that such elite rhetoric is only window dressing that the proimperial interests use to justify expansion. For example, Snyder notes that proimperial interests frequently propound the domino theory, tout the advantages of the offense and preventative action, and claim that assertive behavior will create allies and not adversaries.

Snyder applies political science theory to imperial expansion to show that the concentrated benefits of empire accrue to narrow, powerful, and well-organized groups (groups who benefit from overseas expansion, from increased military spending or from the domestic political climate brought about by international military competition). The costs of empire are spread out over the less well-organized general population (the general citizenry of consumers and taxpayers). In this situation, not only do the motivated, narrow interests with close ties to the state prevail over the broader and more apathetic interests, but logrolling (horse trading) among the narrow interests also results in an even more expansive foreign policy than any one expansionist group would have wanted. For example, he notes that U.S. worldwide containment policy during the cold war resulted from domestic logrolling between the Europe-first internationalists and the Asia-first nationalists, who wanted to use atomic weapons to prevent the advance of communism. Snyder also perceptively identifies the state apparatus as an interest group that receives net benefits from imperial expansion. He notes that war strengthens the state vis-à-vis other groups by giving it more resources and authority over civil society. [42]

Snyder's analysis of domestic determinants of empire comports well with public choice economics, which notes that various interest groups, including members of the state bureaucracies (in this case, the military and the foreign-policy apparatus), try to hijack state policy for their own ends. An example will demonstrate the power of this analysis. In the face of Russian opposition, the Clinton administration was initially lukewarm about the first round of NATO expansion. But then the administration realized that a critical "swing" portion of the electorate in key Northeast and Midwest states was ethnic Eastern Europeans—especially Poles—who supported giving security guarantees to the nations of their ancestry. Needless to say, major progress was made on the path to admitting Poland, Hungary, and the Czech Republic during 1994, a year of congressional elections, and 1996, a presidential election year. The American military and foreign-policy elites supported the policy goal of those ethnic groups because after the cold war ended, they were afraid that NATO had to expand or die. Also, the death of NATO probably would have meant that U.S. military personnel and American diplomats assigned to NATO and NATO countries would have had to leave Europe and might even have been released from service.

There is some evidence to show that Snyder's theory has more validity than Kupchan's. In general, Bush II-administration officials have been quick to avoid any causal link between U.S. foreign policy and al Qaeda's attacks against U.S. targets. President Bush has argued that the United States was attacked on September 11 because the terrorists hated American freedoms (not because they hated U.S. foreign policy toward the Middle East). Yet Bush II's own Deputy Secretary of Defense, Paul Wolfowitz, dispensed readily with that strategic myth by arguing for an invasion of Iraq so that the United States could lower its target profile vis-à-vis al Qaeda by withdrawing U.S. forces from Saudi Arabia.[43] Wolfowitz's implied belief—also held by terrorism experts—was that one of the main reasons al Qaeda had attacked the United States was the U.S. military presence in the Islamic holy land. That example seems to indicate that U.S. policymakers know the terrible costs of their interventionist foreign policy and are not trapped by strategic myths. They seem to opportunistically adopt previously rejected lines of argument when they support the policy goal of the moment.

THE DEMOCRATIC PEACE THEORY

Snyder's approach has great merit, but one flaw. The implication is that the less cartelized—that is, the more democratic—the decision-making becomes, the less likely that war and empire-building will occur. Thus, Snyder's approach backs into the notion that democracies are more benevolent than most other regime types.[44] But in refuting the "democratic peace theory"—the view that democracies do not fight each other—the realists have also poked many holes in that broader thesis. According to Christopher Layne, if the open debate and checks and balances of democracies cause the costs of war to be brought to the fore and are used to counter military and imperialist interests, then democracies should go to war against both democracies and nondemocracies less frequently.

In fact, Layne notes that democracies are no less war-prone than nondemocracies.[45] (In a footnote, Snyder even admits that fact but does not seem to see the problem for his thesis.)[46] Furthermore, the three greatest imperial powers of the nineteenth and twentieth centuries—France, Great Britain, and the United States—were democracies. Maintaining those empires has required many military interventions around the globe. Alexander Motyl agrees with Layne and best sums up the point:

> The [democratic peace] thesis does not, and plausibly cannot, claim that democracies are intrinsically more humane, more peaceful, or less interventionist, because such dispositions should be displayed toward all countries regardless of regime type. Instead, the historical record clearly shows that democratic elites have been perfectly capable of genocide, war, and gross interference. By the same token, democratic publics have been happily supportive of the genocides, wars, and bullying pursued by their democratically elected leaders. The United States, arguably the most democratic state of the nineteenth and twentieth centuries, illustrates the point. Even if their reasons for doing so were beyond reproach, Americans did massacre Indians, drop two atomic bombs on the Japanese, assist in the fire bombing of Dresden, provoke war with Mexico and Spain, gratuitously incinerate retreating Iraqi soldiers, and intervene—militarily, diplomatically, and surreptitiously—in scores of states. French and British behav-

> ior in their Asian and African empires was no less egregious, amounting to what, by today's standards, would have to be termed crimes against humanity.[47]

Motyl might also have mentioned the barbarous conduct of U.S. forces in battling the Philippine insurgency after the Spanish-American War. U.S. forces burned villages, destroyed crops and livestock, tortured and executed prisoners, and slaughtered innocent civilians.[48] John Mearsheimer also agrees with Layne and Motyl: "It is not the case that there is at least one type of political system or culture—including democracy—that routinely eschews aggression and works instead to defend the status quo."[49]

Sometimes democracies behave more aggressively than oligarchies or dictatorships. For example, in ancient Greece, after the Athenian fleet failed to take Syracuse, an oligarchic coup occurred in Athens. When democracy was finally restored, Athenian policy again became more bellicose.[50] In fact, democratic Athens was more aggressive than oligarchic Sparta. An example of Athenian ruthlessness was the treatment of the residents of the island of Melos. As the Athenians assembled a powerful force to conquer Melos, the Melians attempted to make a moral case for peace. The Athenians slaughtered all the men, sold the women and children into slavery, and colonized the island.[51]

And despite the democratic peace theorists' argument that democracies expect other like-minded states to apply their peaceful internal means of resolving disputes to external relations with each other, wars among democratic nations do occur. Layne argues that throughout history, war and democracies have both been rare, so that not finding many wars among democratic nations does not necessarily prove very much. Thus, the importance of any wars among democracies—for example, the War of 1812, the U.S. Civil War, and World War I—should be magnified.[52] One could also add British atrocities during the Boer War in South Africa, the Israeli invasions of Lebanon in 1948 and 1981, and the ancient Athenian attack on Syracuse.[53] Also, after World War I, the United States and Great Britain had the largest navies in the world and began war-planning for an eventual clash.

In those examples and others, the democratic peace theorists frequently and unconvincingly try to tweak the definition of democracy to exclude those cases from the category of "wars within the democratic family."[54] For example, for obvious reasons, democratic peace theorists attempt to exclude Wilhelmine Germany from the category of democratic states. Yet just before World War I, during a time of rising liberalism in Europe, Germany had the broadest voting franchise on the continent. Germany also had constitutional checks on the executive, parliamentary government, and civil liberties. In the late nineteenth century, American policymakers viewed Germany as a progressive constitutional state. But as U.S.-German relations eroded prior to World War I, Americans began to perceive Germany as more militaristic and authoritarian than its continental competitors.[55] In addition, although Germany often gets too much blame for causing World War I[56] (history is written by the winners), the reckless German behavior prior to the war was caused by democratic pressures. The German government, threatened from gains by the Social Democratic Party, attempted to unify the country with overly competitive behavior overseas.[57]

As Layne convincingly argues, the U.S. Civil War may be a particularly important case. According to Layne, although the democratic peace theorists argue that the war was an internal conflict as opposed to an international one, the core of their hypothesis is that peaceful norms and culture within democracies are used in their relations with other democratic polities. Layne then notes that if the United States—as a democracy bound by tight political, economic, and cultural ties—could split into two warring states, then democracy will not prevent wars between great powers with looser ties in the competitive international arena.[58]

In 1917, the Bolsheviks in Russia had a naïve theory similar to the democratic peace theory. They believed that after communist revolutions spread across the world, communist countries would no longer use the balance-of-power concept and would live in peace and harmony (a "communist peace theory" of sorts). The China–Soviet Union border war in 1969, the Vietnam-China war in 1979, and the Vietnamese invasion of Cambodia in 1978—all wars between two communist countries—made this theory as ill-suited to the historical record as the democratic peace theory.

Even though the realists have shot the democratic peace theory full of holes, it is still advocated by pundits on the left and right and by both Democratic and Republican administrations. The dubious theory that democracies do not fight each other is important for this book, because U.S. imperial behavior is often justified on the implicit assumption that creating more democracies will make the world a safer place. Acceptance of this erroneous premise has helped bias U.S. policy toward military interventions to remake the world in the American image.

Yet even if democracies did go to war less frequently with other democracies, the doctrine of bringing peace to the world by forcibly installing democracies, which the Clinton and two Bush administrations have repeatedly practiced, is essentially fighting perpetual war in the quest for perpetual peace (to paraphrase the sarcastic comment by historian Charles Beard). This U.S. policy is equivalent to the much-lampooned quote from Woodrow Wilson: "the war to end all wars." Even Spencer Weart, an avid proponent of the democratic peace theory, notes that democracies have historically crusaded to create more democracies in order to attempt to enhance security. But he concludes that, more often than not, they have been too heavy-handed and have failed. For example, Woodrow Wilson's war to "make the world safe for democracy" created the seeds for totalitarian regimes in Europe because most nations still had authoritarian political cultures. Also, repeated U.S. military interventions in the Caribbean during the early 1900s brought neither democracy nor prosperity to the region. Weart notes, furthermore, that trying to impose democratic systems by using force can subvert any attempt to cultivate a peaceful climate among republics.[59] An example of this phenomenon is the excited and hostile reaction of other democracies, especially in Europe, to the U.S. attempt to bring democracy to Iraq by invasion.

Worse, many of the democracies created at the point of a gun are either only quasi democracies—for example, those in Bosnia, Kosovo, and Haiti—or are unstable. Nations "in transition" to democracy tend to go to war with other countries at higher than average rates.[60] Also, democratic transitions can be reversed. Furthermore classical economists such as Adam Smith, cast doubt on the cost-effectiveness of forcing open markets with military power instead of relying on uncoerced, mutually beneficial free commerce. Thus, much doubt can be cast on the U.S. foreign policy, endorsed by the dominant schools of left-wing and right-wing Wilsonianism, of exporting democracy and free markets to the world at gunpoint.

PEACE FROM SPREADING LIMITED GOVERNMENT, NOT DEMOCRACY

If Snyder's theory of the domestic roots of empire is valid, why are democracies as warlike as nations with other forms of government? When the general public of taxpayers and consumers is not paying much attention to what is happening in the capital city—which is the case with the majority of issues—the concentrated, motivated vested interests triumph by controlling the war-making state apparatus. Snyder believes that when the masses are energized on an issue, they have a better chance of realizing the costs of the policy and countering the clout of the vested interests. Yet that assumes that the public opposes the policy of the vested interests (including the state bureaucracies).

War, unlike other issues, brings an outpouring of nationalism and patriotic fervor. The only thing more important to the public than the costs of war is national pride. The state and the vested interests supporting it can use such pride to sway the populace to their side of the debate. Snyder himself notes that the proexpansionist interests can often get control of the state's propaganda apparatus.[61] That apparatus is a powerful tool that can be used to stoke war fervor among the public and demonize anti-imperial interests as appeasers of the enemy, the adversary's unwitting accomplices, or outright unpatriotic traitors. In fact, in democracies, the government may start a war to counteract a loss of public support at home, whereas authoritarian governments can substitute internal repression by the security forces for external war. Thus, democracies are not always peaceful and dictatorships are not always aggressive externally.[62] A current example of a nonaggressive authoritarian regime is the Burmese junta.

In democracies, with the expansionists manipulating nationalism and patriotism and attempting to use powerful propaganda tools to quell dissent, the open public debate may not be so open, and the checks and balances of democracy may not, in practice, reduce the chances of war very much. For example, U.S. public opinion was jingoistic about war against Spain in 1898, and French and British public opinion were equally enthusiastic about war with the Germans in 1914.[63] More recently, the U.S. public wholeheartedly supported the Bush II administration's invasion of the sovereign nation of Iraq. Although China is no longer a totalitarian communist nation and is now closer to the fascist-like nations of Taiwan, Chile, Spain, and South Korea before they became democracies, rising nationalism could still make even a future democratic China more assertive, at least regionally.

A more plausible theory is that of Ludwig Von Mises, a well-known free-market economist, who suggested that war can only be eliminated if governments become very limited in all nations.[64] Von Mises is on the right track, but not so much because like-minded governments would necessarily live in harmony. Instead, there would simply be little government apparatus that the vested interests in any country could control and mobilize the public for war. Of course, a crusade to induce other nations to shrink their governments would not be possible because that would expand the government in the crusading nation. So each society should work within its own boundaries to reduce government and thus the potential for war. This approach may be a Herculean task but it is still probably the best way to eventually eliminate war from the planet.

Unfortunately, the U.S. and other governments today are very large by nineteenth-century standards, and proimperial interests can easily mask the costs of empire to a public that will end up paying them. Thus, a quick rundown of the drawbacks of empire is warranted. Moreover, the American empire is even less cost-effective than the empires of old.

AMERICAN EMPIRE: NONE OF THE BENEFITS AND ALL OF THE DISADVANTAGES OF TRADITIONAL EMPIRES

The loosely regulated, informal American empire is subject to many of the costs that eventually broke the backs of past formal empires but has none of the benefits.

Benefits of U.S. Empire are Scarce

The Roman empire sent its legions to grab land, plunder, tax revenues, and slaves. The French expropriated native land in their colonies of Algeria, Vietnam, and New Caledonia. The Spanish, like the Romans, believed that the property of the conquered passed to the conquerors; they plundered gold, silver, and the best land from their American empire.[65] Gold, silver, and taxes from the new world were the lifeblood of the Spanish empire. The Spanish and British tried to restrict the trade of their colonies to only the motherland. Such regulation ensured a captive market in the periphery for the center's goods and guaranteed that vital raw materials were sent only to the motherland. The British also wanted new investment possibilities for their commercial class. The ancient Athenians got naval tribute from allies, imported raw materials from and exported agricultural products and crafts to their empire, and seized slaves, land, and mines in conquered territories.[66]

Some would argue that the two U.S. wars with Iraq were motivated, at least in part, by the desire to ensure the supply of resources (oil) for the American empire. But modern-day nationalism and the resulting decolonization of the nineteenth- and twentieth-century European empires probably inhibits the United States, or any other great power today, from reaping the traditional benefits of empire. Today's nationalism likely renders any blatant policy of invasion, annexation and plunder difficult and possibly even dangerous. Countries are often ungovernable when nationalism causes even a portion of the populace to resist the occupying power. The United States, although a loose, informal empire, occasionally has to be reminded about the forces of nationalism that can face an occupying presence—for example, in Vietnam and occupied Iraq. Such experiences of resistance to American force, combined with the comparable experiences of the Soviets in Afghanistan and the Russians in Chechnya, should demonstrate to the great powers that formal empires in the modern world are probably nonviable. The way scholars think about empire should be altered to reflect this new reality.

Costs of Empire Are High

So if the United States is constrained from invading, annexing, plundering, and enslaving foreign peoples and demanding preferential trade with them, what does it gain by providing—at great expense—security for the entire globe? The answer is, very little. Even the best U.S. allies—for example, Japan, South Korea, and the European Union (EU)—ignore U.S. pleas to open their markets to American goods. More important, the United States is spending billions of dollars to defend rich allies that could defend themselves. Those allies instead have the opportunity to use those saved resources to better compete with the United States economically. Table 2.1 indicates that the United States spends much more of its GDP on defense than most of its major economic competitors. Robert Gilpin contrasts the more benevolent British- and American-headed international systems—which provide security, economically beneficial trade relationships, and a shared liberal ideology—with empires based on dominance.[67] Of course, authors differ on whether the U.S. system is an empire.

Although he does not agree that the United States has an empire, conservative Victor Davis Hanson best sums up the cost-benefit problem with the globe-spanning interventionist U.S. foreign policy (no matter what it's called):

> ... [I]f we really are imperial, we rule over a very funny sort of empire.
>
> We do not send out proconsuls to preside over client states, which in turn impose taxes on coerced subjects to pay for the legions. Instead, American bases are predicated on contractual obligations—costly to us and profitable to their hosts. We do not see any lucre in Korea, but instead accept the risk of losing almost 40,000 of our youth to ensure that Kias can flood our shores and that shaggy students can protest outside our embassy in Seoul. ... In sum, our more abstract reasons for stationing troops overseas in the post–cold war—secure global trade, safe sea lanes, and consensual government—would leave the Roman Senate singularly unimpressed.
>
> Athenians, Romans, Ottomans, and the British wanted land, colonies, treasure, and grabbed all they could get when they could. The United States hasn't annexed anyone's soil since the Spanish-American War. ... Britain talked about a mercantile system, and so did Napoleon—more modern ways to emulate the slanted commerce that in antiquity used to drain colonies and subject states in order to enrich Athens or Rome. America instead runs vast trade deficits with everyone, from protectionist Japanese and Koreans (our "clients") and Europeans (our "allies") to communist China (our "competitor") and Russia (our "former enemy"). ...
>
> Imperial powers order and subjects obey. But in our case, we offer the Turks strategic guarantees, political support—and money—for their allegiance. Before we can invade Iraq—which

> we fear has both terrorist liaisons and weapons of mass destruction to facilitate deadly attacks against our homeland in the aftermath of September 11—we extend debt relief to Egypt, some $15 billion in aid to Turkey, and advanced munitions for the Gulf States. France and Russia ponder about going along with us in the UN—but only if we ensure them the traffic of oil and security for outstanding accounts. In fact, both Germany and France vent a virulent anti-Americanism even as they continue to expect the protection of the American military. . . .
>
> Our bases dot the globe to keep the sea lanes open, thugs and murderers under wraps, and terrorists away from European, Japanese, and American globalists who profit mightly by blanketing the world with everything from antibiotics and contact lenses to BMWs and Jennifer Lopez—in other words, to keep the world safe and prosperous.[68]

Hanson never questions whether the expensive activist U.S. foreign policy is necessary for the security of the United States—as opposed to that of the world—or whether it may even be counterproductive to both. Hanson is right that America's behavior is not as overt or directly coercive as the formal empires of old, but he is essentially arguing that because the United States is not raking in piles of booty from overseas, its worldwide military presence cannot be called an empire.

Ronald Steel, who does believe the United States has an empire, says much the same thing as Hanson but does appropriately question the wisdom of U.S. foreign policy: "Unlike Rome, we have not exploited our empire. On the contrary, our empire has exploited us, making enormous drains on our resources and energies."[69]

Similarly, G. John Ikenberry notes the benefits received by U.S. allies under the umbrella of the American empire: "As Geir Lundestad has observed, the expanding American political order in the half century after World War II has been in important respects an 'empire by invitation.' The remarkable global reach of American post-war hegemony has been at least in part driven by the efforts of European and Asian governments to harness American power, render that power more predictable, and use it to overcome their own regional insecurities." Ikenberry further observes: "The United States provided its partners with security guarantees and access to American markets, technology, and supplies within an open economy. In return, East Asian and European allies would become stable partners who would provide diplomatic, economic, and logistical support for the United States as it led the wider American-centered, non-communist post-war order."[70] One might conclude from Ikenberry's summary that the vague contributions from U.S. allies were exchanged for costly elements of "U.S. leadership"—that is, by an invitation to pay other nations' bills for security.

Economics of Empire Don't Pay

Adam Smith and other classical liberals (for example, Richard Cobden and John Bright) believed the British empire was a waste of money for the homeland. In the liberal view, distortions of the market from imperialism—the use of military power and tariffs to help the center's businesses, the shift to the periphery of investment that could have been more efficiently used domestically, the excessive taxes spent on the military and the private consumption forgone to pay those taxes that could have modernized industries at home—made the center poorer. In their view, voluntary economic integration with the world was better economically and financially for the home islands than coercive imperial interaction. Because of mutual benefits of commerce to the trading parties, trade would naturally occur even without empire.[71] (In Chapter 3, I discuss that line of reasoning in more detail.) Many of the costs of the British empire are also incurred by the more informal American empire.

Of course, some ardent proponents of American empire will say that, historically, empires have rarely met the cost-benefit test. Niall Ferguson, a proponent of both the British and American empires, admitted that British colonial possessions cost more to administer than they generated in revenue. Ferguson quotes Winston Churchill as saying that he had not become the King's First Minister "in order to preside over the liquidation of the British empire."[72] But by vociferously urging that Britain get involved in both world wars, Churchill set himself up to do exactly what he had attempted to avoid. Britain had been the world's chief creditor, but after World War II, it owed the world $40 billion. According to Ferguson, the foundation of the British empire had been economic, but that had been eaten away by the cost of war.[73] In the late 1800s, the British empire spent 2.6 percent of GDP on defense. Between 1947 and 1987, defense spending accounted for 5.8 percent of GDP. And if the formal empires of old were a financial drain—even with their invading, annexing, plundering, and enslaving ways—the loose, informal, and less exploitative American empire, also supported by economic wealth, is likely to be even more so.

Is Empire Needed for Security and Stability in an "Age of Collapsed Distances"?

Proponents argue that the American empire is needed for security of the U.S. homeland in an "age of collapsed distances" and for ensuring an orderly world by the global expansion of liberal, civil society to create societies with political and economic freedoms.[74] For some with special Wilsonian missionary zeal, using American power to spread "freedom" around the world is an end in itself.

Later in the text, the myth of "security through empire" will be debunked in detail. In fact, worldwide U.S. meddling in the affairs of other nations makes the American homeland more vulnerable to attack, as demonstrated by the anger that U.S. foreign policy generated among the September 11 hijackers. So even if the U.S. government could successfully make the world better by invading, coercing, or socially engineering nations to "encourage" them to convert from authoritarianism to democratic governance (dubious and ineffective ways to create lasting, non-sham republics), it may be endangering the American homeland by doing so.

The myth that democratic nations avoid war with each other has already been debunked. But even if the theory of "democratic peace" were true, the many U.S.-led wars needed to oust the plethora of dictators and tyrants left in the world would lead to a state of "perpetual war for perpetual peace." And as the American occupation of "liberated" Iraq shows, even if the wars are won, totally restructuring societies to ensure genuine, viable, and self-sustaining liberal democracies is a Herculean task, especially in the developing world.

Of course, with empire comes the "influence" and prestige of being the world's top dog. The U.S. president gets to stand in the center of summit photographs, and the world hangs on every word of the imperial bureaucrats, parliamentarians, and foreign policy elite in American universities and research institutes. This American "influence" (whatever that vague term means) over political happenings in faraway lands, most of which are unimportant to U.S. security, seems a scant reward for the all of the blood, treasure, and goodwill squandered in subduing, policing, and socially engineering the world. As with the empires of old, imperial prestige and glory for America's elite come at a steep price for the common citizenry.

The founders of the United States had those failed empires in mind when they gave the peoples' branch of government, not the president, the power to declare war. Unfortunately, during the cold war and its aftermath, an increasingly powerful presidency has ignored that constitutional provision.

Also ignored has been the traditional U.S. foreign policy that served the country well for about a hundred and seventy-five years. That policy was to take advantage of America's uniquely secure geography to exercise a policy of military restraint overseas, stay out of disputes among nations where possible, and thus reap the domestic benefits of low military spending and a small standing army. Despite the collapsed distances of the modern world, this volume will argue that the founders' vision is more relevant than ever for a sound U.S. foreign policy. The original statesmen of the great republic would be appalled to learn that America is now a militaristic global empire on the ostensible mission of converting the world to democracy and free markets, while at the same time destroying its own republic.

3 Why Conservatives Should Be Against Empire

Although some traditional conservatives (sometimes called paleo-conservatives) are against empire and believe that the quest for one undermines the republic, most conservatives agree with an expansive and militaristic U.S. foreign policy. Neoconservatives (that is, liberals who turned conservative), want to spread democracy and freer markets around the world at the point of a gun. A free society, both economically and politically, is a superior form of social organization; but using force to export economic and political freedoms means adopting harsh methods similar to those of the now exhausted international communist movement. Strangely, although neoconservatives often prefer unilateral U.S. military action overseas, and the old (Wilsonian and Clintonian) left opts for U.S. armed force cloaked in a multilateral veneer, they both end up with similar global, interventionist foreign policies.

At this point in history, the new, McGovernite left makes up a larger group among liberals than the traditional conservatives do on the right. But after World War II, both the new left and old right—the guardians of the torch for the more traditional and restrained foreign policy of the founders—both became minorities in their respective camps. A cold war consensus formed around a new policy of global intervention and expansion. The debacle in Vietnam made the anti-interventionist wing of the left stronger. As the memory of Vietnam faded, however, that group lost influence but still makes up a potent and vociferous element of the left coalition. As the Bush II administration prepared to invade Iraq, the new left again began to make noise through large street demonstrations in major U.S. cities.

Although a few conservatives spoke out against the invasion and occupation of Iraq, the new left unfortunately shouldered the bulk of the burden of the antiwar movement. To support a Republican president or avoid being labeled as "unpatriotic," most conservatives, some of whom had questions about the necessity for war, chose to ignore that President George W. Bush was doing what his campaign had accused the Clinton administration of doing—conducting open-ended deployments with unclear missions that strain U.S. forces. In his campaign, Bush II vowed to put an end to such operations, but instead he has strained U.S. forces more than Clinton by initiating huge open-ended nation-building commitments in Afghanistan and Iraq and additional peacekeeping duties in Macedonia. Bush also reneged on a pledge made during his campaign to disengage from other nation-building efforts in Bosnia and Kosovo and to adopt a more "humble" foreign policy. Instead, Bush rashly plunged into a hyperexpansionist foreign policy.

But conservatives have not always been so timid in their criticism of an interventionist U.S. foreign policy. Before, during, and after World War I, many conservatives opposed overseas military interventions and empire-building. Before World War I, most members of the Anti-Imperialist League, who opposed U.S. colonialism in the Philippines after the Spanish-American War, were Republicans. They astutely realized that republican (small "r") and imperial values were contradictory.[1] During and after World War I, many conservatives were pitted against Woodrow Wilson and the old left. During the interwar period, the Democrats were the party of overseas intervention. At that time, many conservatives advocated small government, fiscal austerity, and keeping alive the founders' tradition of restraint in foreign policy. They realized, as Bruce Porter cleverly sums up, that "war makes death and taxes not only inevitable, but inseparable as well."[2] And from 1945 to 1950, noninterventionists came mainly from the right side of the political spectrum.

Today's conservatives should revisit that fine tradition and avoid becoming mesmerized by chauvinistic arguments for "national greatness" through global military intervention or idealistic Wilsonian arguments about spreading democracy and free markets around the world through armed force. Conservatives should be against empire and the profligate foreign military interventions needed to police it. This chapter presents arguments showing that an expansionist U.S. foreign policy violates the principles of the nation's founders and the tenets of conservatism, both of which entail restraining the growth of government.

WARS AND BIG GOVERNMENT IN THE UNITED STATES: A HISTORICAL OVERVIEW

In the United States, a nation that had minimal government in the 1700s and 1800s, "big government" began with World War I. Prior to that time, throughout most of American history, the central government remained small because geographic detachment from potent enemies allowed the U.S. military to be kept small. The tradition of small government was inherited from Britain, which also has geographical separation from continental European foes.[3] The U.S. government was small in the nineteenth century because the United States was involved in few wars of any size (the Civil War being the only exception). In contrast, the twentieth century was the most violent in world history and unsurprisingly led to the rise of big government, including totalitarian regimes overseas and a greatly enlarged government in the United States.

World War I was the first to require the full mobilization of American society. Although the Civil War led to the income tax and increased government intervention in the economy, it did not result in the mobilization of the entire society, and the expanded government apparatus was largely dismantled after the war.[4] Instead of the traditional American policy of allowing the free market to operate, the large-scale conflict motivated the government in World War I to plan industrial production, commandeer private resources and property, conscript men for the armed forces, and, in general, penetrate the civilian economy and society to an unprecedented degree.

Federal spending increased 2,500 percent in less than three years during the war and remained at four times prewar levels in the years after the conflict. Federal employment more than doubled during the war and then fell back after the conflict to 30 percent above prewar levels, growing in both defense and nondefense agencies.[5]

The mobilization of society during World War I set the precedent for the federal government's response to a subsequent crisis in the 1930s—the Great Depression. Many of the agencies that managed civil society and the economy during the war were brought back under new names during the New Deal, and even some of the same people were brought back to manage them.

Robert Higgs describes the effect of the World War I mobilization on the postwar peacetime society:

> The dominant contemporary interpretation of the war mobilization, including the belief that federal economic controls had been instrumental in achieving the victory, persisted, especially among the elites who had played leading roles in the wartime economic management. Economic czar Bernard Baruch did much to foster the postwar dissemination of this interpretation by historians, journalists and other shapers of public opinion. But many interest groups, like the farmers, needed no prompting to arrive at a Baruchian conclusion. "By the time the Food Administration dropped its wartime controls, it had weakened farmer resistance to governmental direction of their affairs. Having observed how the government could shape wartime food prices, farmers would expect it also to act in peacetime to maintain the prosperity of America's farms." Big businessmen in many industries took a similar lesson away from the war.
>
> In the depths of the Great Depression, the federal government employed the wartime measures as models for dealing with what Franklin Roosevelt called "a crisis in our national life comparable to war." Hence the War Finance Corporation came back to life as the Reconstruction Finance Corporation, the War Industries Board as

> the National Recovery Administration, the Capital Issues Committee as the Securities and Exchange Commission, the Fuel Administration as the Connolly Act apparatus for cartelizing the oil industry and the Guffey Act apparatus for cartelizing the bituminous coal industry. The military mobilization of young men came back as the quasi-military Civilian Conservation Corps. The Muscle Shoals hydroelectric munitions facility became the germ of the Tennessee Valley Authority. The wartime U.S. Housing Corporation reappeared first as part of the Public Works Administration in 1933 and then as the U.S. Housing Authority in 1937. The New Deal's federal social security program harked back to the wartime servicemen's life insurance and payments made to soldiers' dependents. . . . Obviously the wartime precedents were crucial in guiding the New Dealers and helping them to justify and gain acceptance of their policies. . . . Most importantly, the scope of federal regulation had increased immensely to embrace agricultural production and marketing, labor-management relations, wages, hours, and working conditions, securities markets and investment institutions, petroleum and coal marketing, trucking, radio broadcasting, airline operation, provision for income during retirement or unemployment, and much, much more.[6]

American societal mobilization to fight World War II surpassed even the massive effort during World War I. The U.S. government's tentacles slithered ever deeper into the civil society. Similarly in Britain, although the first post–World War II prime minister, Clement Attlee of the Labour Party, usually gets credit for establishing the British socialist welfare state, British society already had been socialized during the war under the Conservative prime minister Winston Churchill.[7]

And there was no relief after the second great conflict was over. In the aftermath of World War II, the activist government left over from the conflict received public approval.[8] Federal involvement in daycare resulted from wartime daycare for mothers working in defense plants. The federalization of American medicine began with wartime extension of military healthcare benefits to dependents of army personnel.[9] Government wartime economic controls and management of the war effort caused the American public to accept the Keynesian notion that the government should foster full employment and prevent economic maladies, such as recessions. The war also put in place the tax revenue machine that funded the rise of the welfare state in the postwar era.

Thus, the crises of World War I, the Great Depression, and World War II had replaced the free market with government management.[10] World War I and especially World War II created a greater governmental bureaucracy than even the New Deal.[11] During World War II, even the nonsecurity parts of the U.S. government grew faster than during the New Deal. The huge bureaucracy sired in the war became a greater tool for promoting social and economic regulation than any created in World War I or the Great Depression. Postwar federal expenditures reached equilibrium at nearly three times their prewar levels.

A cold war with a former ally ensued, and the United States maintained heretofore the largest peacetime military in the nation's history. During the Korean and Vietnam Wars, large increases in federal employment occurred. The precedent had already been set for a level of government encroachment never envisioned by the nation's founders, and President Lyndon Johnson decided to take full advantage of it by pursuing a disastrous policy of "guns and butter"—Great Society social programs and increased defense spending to fight the Vietnam War. The Republican Nixon administration did not reverse such policies. George W. Bush, also a war president from a Republican party that has traditionally touted fiscal responsibility and the lowering of government spending, has increased federal discretionary spending faster than any president since Johnson.[12] He is pursuing a Republican version of Johnson's "guns and butter" policy.

In short, federal spending as a portion of the U.S. economy went from less than two percent in 1914[13] to a little less than 20 percent today. At the turn of the last century, total government spending (federal, state, and local) accounted for about 8 percent of the U.S. GDP; at the turn of this century, government spending had increased dramatically, to nearly a third of the GDP.[14]

Robert Higgs explains the rapid growth of the U.S. government in the twentieth century as being caused by the government's response to crises beginning with World War I and continuing through the Great Depression, World War II, and the cold war. But he says that his theory fails to explain why crises in the nineteenth century did not lead to governmental growth.[15] Perhaps Higgs's theory should be amended to more narrowly focus on wars—rather than the more general category of crises—as a cause of government expansion. The nineteenth century had many economic and other crises but few major wars. Only during the dire conditions of a large war (or cold war) can a significant government takeover of the economy and society be justified. Not even severe economic crises can be sufficient excuses for such intrusion by the state. As noted above, the expansion of government that came during the Great Depression was both overrated and rooted in the war mobilization of World War I, which came just before it. Severe economic crises in the 1800s did not result in such government enlargement. In short, war causes the precedents for big government, not economic crises. Data developed by Bruce Porter provide evidence for the amended thesis. Writing in 1994, he notes that war occurred in forty-eight years of American history (just over 20 percent) and that during those years all but five Cabinet departments and a majority of federal agencies were created.[16]

WAR AND EMPIRE CAUSE GOVERNMENT GROWTH

Free market economist Ludwig Von Mises perceptively noted that global peace would never happen until the central governments of all nations were limited in scope and power (this goes a step further than the democratic peace theory).[17] Yet bigger government in the form of the nation-state originally came about because the expenses for warfare became too great for feudal rulers to handle. Thus, war caused big government in the first place. As Randolph Bourne famously stated, "War is the health of the state."[18]

Taking their cue from the founders, conservatives have championed small government—at least theoretically. Yet many on the right who are skeptical of government action at home applaud armed adventures and military social engineering by the government abroad and the huge defense budgets and large peacetime military organizations needed to carry them out. As Bruce Porter notes, "American political dialogue . . . reveals the irony of pro-military conservatives railing against Big Government, while forgetting that coercive taxation and bureaucratic organization are the sine qua non of funding and equipping forces in the industrial age."[19]

If anything, the U.S. government is likely to be even less effective in social engineering abroad than at home, because the cultures and problems are foreign, the distance of governance is much greater, and Uncle Sam possesses far less legitimacy overseas than at home. Even Max Boot, a well-known neoconservative advocate of American empire, admits that "the American track record of imposing liberal, democratic regimes by force is mixed" and that the United States has been less than successful at doing so in the third world. Yet he advocates fighting wars to do just that.[20]

In the next chapter, I will demonstrate that wars for nation-building have been disingenuous and the results abysmal.

More important, war and empire cause the government to grow substantially at home. In the 1600s, as nation-states evolved in Europe, their main function was intended to be security. City-states and feudal lords could not afford to buy the new weapons of war—for example, artillery, sailing ships, and standing armies—and so larger nation-states had to be created to do so.[21] As Charles Tilly summarized it, "war made the state and the state made war."[22] Among others, Carl Von Clausewitz, one of history's most famous military commentators and a favorite of conservatives, saw war as a tool for expanding and rejuvenating the state.[23]

Even Exaggerated Threats Can Cause Expanding Government

In a reversal of Snyder's domestic causes of empire (see Chapter 2), Otto Hintze believes that external factors affect the internal political structure of states. This realist view argues that states that were secure because of geography—Britain and the United States—were allowed the luxury of having smaller governments. They did not need a powerful state to mobilize resources and personnel for war against potent external threats. In contrast, the greater the external threat facing a state, the bigger and more autocratic its government will become.[24] Christopher Layne argues that during both world wars, the governments of Britain and the United States, at least temporarily, became so strong that they became autocratic. He further notes that during the ensuing cold war, the U.S. government evolved into a "national security state"—still a democracy but one in which government powers expanded greatly and the executive branch dominated the legislative branch in foreign policy.[25]

Concurring with Layne, Martin van Creveld, a well-known military strategist, notes that in 1913, prior to World War I, the U.S. government still had only two hundred and thirty thousand employees. He points out that Franklin Roosevelt's New Deal led to only a limited expansion of government, and that World War II and the cold war really created the age of big government. (Similarly, Canada did not become a European-style welfare state until its national mobilization for World War II.[26]) In short, the U.S. government's mobilization on a grand scale for the Second World War and the creation of an informal global empire during the cold war led to big government at home.

Although they take opposite perspectives, Hintze's approach and Snyder's analysis are not mutually exclusive. External factors affect internal political systems, and internal politics affect nations' foreign policies. The main drawback to Hintze's "outside-in" approach is that it doesn't explain why, despite their very secure positions geopolitically, Britain and the United States ultimately ended up with empires and ballooning government. For example, remedying an external threat does not explain the U.S. government's launching of its first imperial foray, the Spanish-American War. In fact, internal U.S. developments caused the quest for empire. The election of William McKinley in 1896 was the culmination of a redistribution of power from Congress to the executive branch. That development led to a U.S. naval buildup, which permitted the United States to grab Spanish possessions in the war.[27] Ironically, the architects and proponents of this first imperial war—for example, Theodore Roosevelt and Albert J. Beveridge—were big government Republicans, who advocated activist government both at home and abroad during the "Progressive Era" that followed the war. They actually bear some resemblance to the hawkish, big government neoconservatives in the Bush II administration. (The correlation between wars abroad and increases in nonsecurity government spending will be explored later.)

Although in retrospect World War I and World War II seemed like times of dire peril for the United States, it was not quite so clear cut for most Americans in the periods before the wars. Prior to World War I, the United States had purposely stayed out of all of Europe's many wars. But the crusading and idealistic Woodrow Wilson, with the zeal of a missionary, decided to tip the balance of the Great War to the allies. In doing so, he inadvertently planted the seeds of World War II and the cold war (by unintentionally helping the Bolsheviks take power in the Soviet Union). World War I destroyed the social fabric of Germany, and the subsequent oppressive peace imposed, both financially and psychologically, by the allies on Germany led to the rise of the Nazis and World War II. U.S. plans to intervene in World War I also led to Russia's staying in the war longer, making Aleksandr Kerenski's provisional government (which took power after the czar was deposed) vulnerable to the Bolsheviks. The Bolsheviks championed pulling out of the horrendously costly war.

Ultimately, during the cold war, the fear of that same Soviet communism going global was real but overblown. The United

States enjoyed the same secure geographic position that it always had, and nuclear weapons were the ultimate deterrent against attack or invasion. Because of its grossly inefficient communist system, the Soviet Union never had a GDP—wherefrom all other indices of national power emanate—or derivative economic influence anywhere comparable to that of the United States. During the cold war, the U.S. economy was between two and five times greater than that of the Soviet Union.[28] In fact, some analysts derisively called the USSR an "Upper Volta with missiles."

Contravening the realists' concept of a state with a rational, unitary decision-making process, American leaders during the cold war knew the reality that the United States was a much stronger superpower than the Soviet Union on any combined index of military and economic power. But they exaggerated the communist threat to win popular and governmental support for a veiled empire and an interventionist foreign policy to maintain it. Republican Senator Arthur Vandenberg advised President Truman, a Democrat, that to get key provisions of the Truman Doctrine—that is, U.S. assistance to countries fighting communism—passed, he would need to "scare the hell out of the American people." The Truman administration obliged. Dean Acheson, President Truman's Secretary of State, one of the architects of the post–World War II imperial policy (admirers of the British empire), later admitted euphemistically, "If we made our points clearer than the truth, we did not differ from most other educators and could hardly do otherwise. . . . The purpose of NSC 68 [the famous 1950 national security directive, which first enshrined the containment of communism as national policy] was to so bludgeon the mass mind of 'top government' that not only could the President make a decision but that the decision could be carried out."[29] In a more specific case, American officials admitted years after the fact that they had overstated the strength of communist movements in Iran during the 1950s. Those overstatements led to a CIA-backed coup that destroyed Iranian democracy under Prime Minister Mohammed Mossadegh, whose government had nationalized the Anglo-Iranian oil company.[30] During the cold war, the Defense Department and the CIA had incentives to exaggerate the Soviet threat to get more money and personnel for their bureaucracies.

Even President George W. Bush, in his National Security Strategy of 2002, admitted that "[i]n the cold war, especially following the Cuban missile crisis, we faced a generally status quo, risk-averse adversary."[31] As one foreign policy writer noted, that admission never would have been made during the cold war.[32]

There is another indication that the Soviet threat might have been inflated to justify America's imperial concern with maintaining "stability" around the world: after the Berlin Wall came tumbling down, the American ambassador to the Soviet Union practically invited the Soviet military into Eastern Europe to ensure stability there.[33] In fact, even before World War II ended, President Franklin Roosevelt was resigned to the fact that the Red Army would make Soviet domination of Europe a reality.[34]

Similarly, before the North Korean invasion of South Korea in 1950, the Joint Chiefs of Staff twice said that South Korea was not worth defending in any major war. That view was blessed by President Truman and the National Security Council and made public by Secretary of State Dean Acheson when he excluded that country from the U.S. defense perimeter in Asia. After North Korea invaded, the Truman administration intervened merely for the purpose of a demonstration to friends and foes alike.[35] Likewise, according to eminent cold war historians, the United States did not intervene in Vietnam because it feared communism, which was fragmented, or the Soviet Union, which wanted détente with the West, or China, which was weak, but because it did not want to appear timid to the world.[36] The behavior of the United States in both Korea and Vietnam is typical of imperial powers, which are always concerned about their reputation, prestige, and perceived resolve.

Wars and Empire Lead to Increased Domestic Spending

So although internal changes may cause imperial behavior, as the end of congressional domination in the late 1800s indirectly contributed to the Spanish-American War, external threats—both real and exaggerated—also lead to big government at home. And the larger the perception of the threat, the bigger the government will grow to combat it. Proponents of American empire—neoconservatives, for example—might argue that imperial wars to police the realm are usually far away from the home country, thus minimizing the perceptions of threat at home. Alternatively, they might argue that defending forward on the periphery of the empire nips threats in the bud before they snowball into dangers to the homeland. The terrorist attacks on September 11 should put both of those arguments to rest. Combating "threats" that have little chance of snowballing in backwater, nonstrategic regions of the globe could well lead to fierce animosity and concomitant retaliatory terrorist attacks that endanger the U.S. homeland. For example, Osama bin Laden and al Qaeda attacked the United States because of the American military presence in the Islamic holy land of Saudi Arabia and U.S. support for the corrupt Arab governments and Israel. Thus, the ill effects of even faraway imperial forays can raise the perceptions of threat at home to a fever pitch. In the wake of the September 11 attacks, the Bush II administration urged Congress to pass the PATRIOT Act, which significantly curtailed civil liberties, and increased federal domestic discretionary spending at a faster rate than any administration since Lyndon Johnson's Great Society initiative.

Obviously, much higher spending for the military, homeland security, and foreign aid are required for a policy of global intervention than for a policy of merely defending the republic. For example, after the cold war, the security bureaucracies began looking for new enemies to justify keeping defense and intelligence budgets high.

But when a major war is afoot, or in its aftermath, government activities outside the security realm increase too. Oftentimes, the effects of wars fall disproportionately on the poorer classes. After a conflict ends, that reality often spurs an increase in social welfare programs.[37] Filling the military's enlisted ranks are often less educated people, who do most of the suffering during wars and demand compensation for their sacrifices or those of their relatives.

Like prior wars, Bush II's "war on terror" has led to increases in both security and nonsecurity spending. Even as a portion of GDP, federal outlays have increased under the wartime presidency of Bush II (see Figure 3.1). Some conservatives are bemoaning the Bush record of profligate government largesse. Stephen Moore, president of the conservative Club for Growth, skewered George W. Bush's spending record: "We are now seeing the biggest expansion in government since Lyndon Johnson was in the White House. It is pretty much an across-the-board mushrooming of government. We have the biggest education, foreign aid and agriculture bills in history, and bigger expansions are on the agenda."[38]

Similarly, Brian Riedl, a budget analyst at the conservative Heritage Foundation, has noted that per household government spending in fiscal year 2003 ($20,301) was the highest since World War II ($26,445, as measured in 2003 dollars). According to Riedl, although the Bush II administration tries to pass off the spending increases as necessary for strengthening the military and guarding against terrorist attacks domestically, about 55 percent of the spending increases since 2001 have gone to nonnational security programs.[39] Also, Daniel Mitchell, an economist with that same organization, opines that the ballooning of government under the Bush II administration is "very troubling for conservatives." He estimated that domestic (nondefense) spending has increased by about one percentage point of the GDP and noted "that is quite discouraging, particularly since we made so much progress under Clinton in reducing the size of government."[40]

Moore's, Riedl's, and Mitchell's allegations are borne out by Figure 3.2, which shows that nondefense spending increased more during the wartime presidency of George W. Bush than during any other

FIGURE 3.1: FEDERAL OUTLAYS UNDER THE REPUBLICAN CONGRESS, PERCENTAGE OF GDP

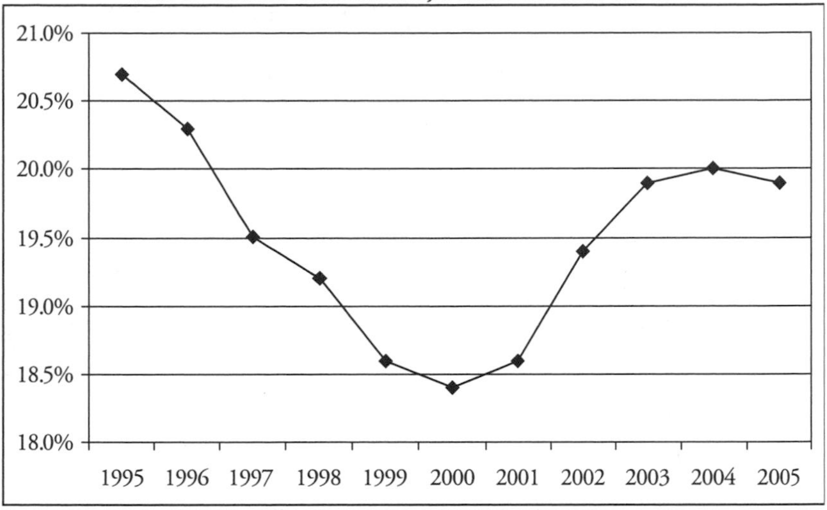

Source: Congressional Budget Office, January 2004. FY2004 and FY2005 are estimates. Reprinted from Veronique de Rugy, "The Republican Spending Explosion," *Cato Institute Briefing Paper* Number 87, March 3, 2004, p. 2.

comparable period since the wartime administration of Lyndon Johnson. The administration of Richard Nixon, also a wartime administration, came in third. The nondefense spending increases during administrations in which warfare was sporadic or nonexistent (Carter, Reagan, Bush I, and Clinton) were all lower than during the three administrations in which major long-term wars were being fought.

Both Moore and Mitchell maintain that the growth of government was much more constrained under President Clinton, in part because Clinton faced off with a Republican Congress. But if the Republican Party is truly the party of small government—a dubious claim when one looks at the history of federal budget deficits—then one would expect a Republican president with a Republican Congress for most of his term to be even more fiscally conservative than a Democratic president with a Republican Congress. What a difference a permanent "war on terror" makes.

During Bush's war on terror, the number of full-time employees working on government contracts and grants has escalated sharply.

FIGURE 3.2: CUMULATIVE REAL NONDEFENSE DISCRETIONARY SPENDING INCREASES IN FIRST TERM

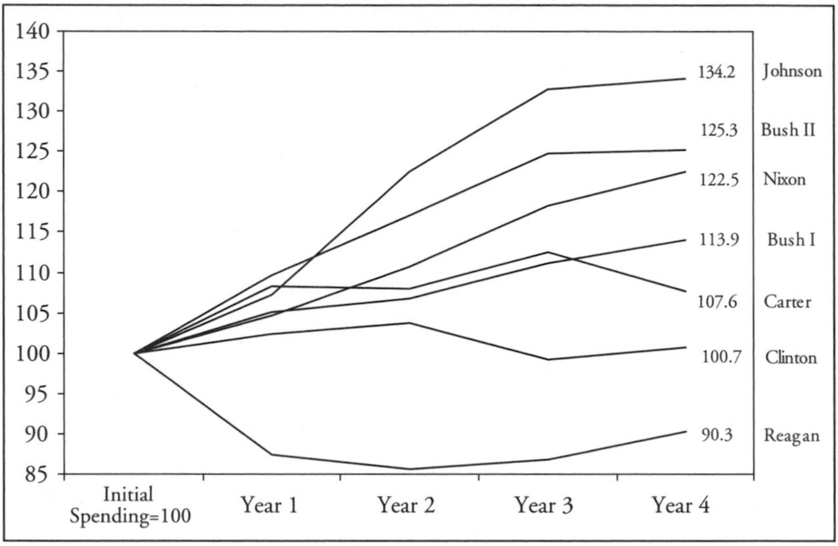

Source: Calculations based on Budget of the U.S. Government FY2005. FY2004 and FY2005 (Years 3 and 4 for Bush II) are estimates. Reprinted from Veronique de Rugy, "The Republican Spending Explosion," *Cato Institute Briefing Paper* Number 87, March 3, 2004, p. 5.

That increase occurred in nondefense agencies, as well as at the defense and homeland security bureaucracies. Paul Light, an expert on the federal bureaucracy, noted that using employees under contract and grant, instead of permanent federal workers, "reflects a deliberate strategy by both Congress and the president to disguise the true size of government."[41] That disguise is needed by the Bush II administration to attempt to avert a revolt, which has already begun, by fiscally minded conservatives.

In an example of how presidents abuse foreign policy crises to increase spending on unrelated items, President Bush justified shoveling "pork" to farmers, an important Republican constituency, by making the preposterous claim that because people had to eat, beef subsidies were required for national security.

Even much of the massive post–September 11 increase in the defense budget (the largest in a decade) was spent on items that had little to do with fighting the war on terror. To avoid increasing anti-

U.S. terrorism generated from rage about high-profile and irrelevant military actions (such as the invasion of Iraq), most of the war on terror should be fought in the shadows with intelligence and law enforcement resources. When the rare military intervention is needed, the United States already has adequate forces and modern weapons to carry out small brushfire wars against unsophisticated opponents. The rout of the Taliban in Afghanistan is proof of that bone-crushing capability. Yet the Pentagon keeps spending billions on buying weapons better designed for use against the Soviet Union during the cold war. For example, the U.S. Air Force is still buying the overbuilt and costly F-22 fighter, which was designed to counter Soviet fighters that were never built, and the U.S. Navy is still building new submarines, even though the Russian submarine fleet is rusting in Russia's ports.[42]

In short, war's effects—direct or indirect—were the primary cause of government growth in the twentieth century. Therefore, to reduce the size of government at home—an important goal of most conservatives—unnecessary wars and overseas military adventures must be stopped.

HIGH DEFENSE SPENDING HURTS ECONOMIC GROWTH

When many conservatives rail against profligate government spending, they seem to disregard massive defense expenditures. (See Table 2.1 for a comparison of the huge U.S. defense budget with the much smaller military budgets of the other great powers.) But defense spending has the same ill effects on the economy as any other federal spending. In a defense industry that is rife with socialism, industrial policy, and excessive regulation[43] and produces no goods beneficial to consumers, every dollar spent on research, development, and production is taken away from the much more productive and efficient equivalent in the commercial sector. In fact, the workers and capitalists in the commercial sector have to support workers and capitalists in the non productive defense sector by producing consumer goods for them.[44]

Curiously, many conservative and neoconservative hawks admire Milton Friedman and other free market economists, but seem to be Keynesians when it comes to defense spending. They somehow believe that defense spending is good for the economy, but that other forms of government spending are not. That belief may be rooted in the common misconceptions that World War II brought the United States out of the Great Depression and that overseas conflicts (certainly not wars in the homeland) are good for the economy. In fact, real nondefense GNP grew more slowly during World War II than it did during the last years of the Great Depression.[45] Ronald Reagan's favorite saying, "there ain't no free lunch," also applies to his and other conservatives'—for example, George Bush II's—sacrosanct, exorbitant defense spending.

And increased government spending is not the only aspect of government growth during times of war. Past examples of expanding government power in wartime include rent control, the income tax, income tax withholding, and corporate welfare. Also, the recent examples of wars in Iraq and Afghanistan show that people begin to ask why the Afghans and Iraqis are getting schools and health care when the United States has its own needs in such areas.[46]

PAYING THE COSTS OF WAR

President Reagan's "there ain't no free lunch" slogan should also be used to rein in neoconservatives who advocate using other peoples' lives (those of the U.S. military and innocent civilians in the targeted country) and money (U.S. taxpayer dollars) to conduct social engineering projects at gunpoint in the developing world.

Even if a war does not cause costly destruction on the home soil, it has to be paid for somehow. Wars can be paid for by an increase in taxes or increased government borrowing; thus, "paying the piper" can lead to a significant drag on the economy or the bidding up of interest rates that causes a crowding out of private borrowing, respectively. Even worse ways of financing conflict are the inflationary printing of money and the coercive government confiscation of resources and people (including military conscription) with no compensation or compensation at below-market rates. Yet according to Joseph Salerno, an economist at Pace University, the latter two methods are often used because they hide the true cost of war. For example, the government may commandeer people, factories, or natural resources so that it doesn't have to take the politically unpopular step of raising people's taxes to pay for such items at market prices. Governments want to disguise such costs because public support for the conflict may evaporate when its true costs are known.[47]

War also eats a nation's capital stock. Not only does war cause a conversion of resources allocated to consumer goods to state-directed war production (a horizontal transfer), it also causes resources to be shifted from the nation's capital goods stock (intermediate goods and equipment used to manufacture future goods) to present war production. The nation's industrial and agricultural equipment is thus worn out and not replaced. War-induced inflation also consumes the nation's capital.

If the government tries to control the inflation via price controls, the shortages and inefficiencies caused by the controls can often lead to further controls. Those controls are usually on production, distribution, and labor and multiply until the market economy is effectively replaced by a fascist economy—that is, nominal private ownership of the means of production exists but crucial production decisions are made by the government.[48] In fact, according to Bob Higgs, during the last two years of World War II, the U.S. economy—mobilized to fight fascism—itself became a "garrison economy."[49] Others would use the term *fascist economy.* During war, we become a little more like our enemies.

In conclusion, whatever the means of financing war, conflict causes a reduction in real wealth and real income in the economy.[50] The ill effects of war on the economy, including the impairment of international commerce, can be seen by looking at figures on the growth of worldwide per capita GDP. During the first age of "globalization" prior to World War I (1870 to 1913), the average growth of global per capita GDP was 1.3 percent annually. From 1913 to 1950—the era of World War I, a Great Depression at least partially caused by the irreparable trade patterns emanating from the Great War, and World War II—the average growth of worldwide per capita GDP sunk to .91 percent. After the wars, the growth of global per capita GDP skyrocketed to 2.93 percent from 1950 to 1973 and was a respectable 1.33 percent from 1973 to 1998.[51]

Thus, in contrast to conventional wisdom, encouraged among the public by Keynesian economists, war and related effects undermine the prosperity and well-being of American society—what should be the principal goal of the U.S. or any other government. For example, during World War II, the American GNP figures spiked as the government initiated a command economy to wage total war. But the portion of the GNP going to civilian consumers and investors declined precipitously. So "wartime prosperity" was a myth to the average citizen. Also, Keynesian economists feared that the end of the war and declining government spending would throw the United States back into depression, but a postwar boom, which included soaring industrial production and low unemployment, ensued instead.[52]

HOSTILITIES RESTRICT FREE FLOW OF INTERNATIONAL COMMERCE

The domestic economy is not the only thing distorted by war. It disrupts and destroys international commercial relationships that are difficult to rejuvenate after the conflict is over. Many analysts have correctly noted that the Great Depression and World War II were, in part, caused by restricted international commerce. But what caused those restrictions has often been ignored. As a result of the quest of nations for autarchy during World War I, immigration and trade flows became very constricted, ending the first period of commercial "globalization."[53] It is ironic that the large navies and "security" treaties of the great powers prior to World War I, justified to "facilitate and protect" international commerce, ended up causing the very wars that undermined and destroyed it.

Interventionists Are Really the Isolationists

It is also ironic that those who advocate an activist U.S. foreign policy overseas accuse the proponents of a more humble foreign policy of being "isolationists." The use of that term—originally coined by Alfred Thayer Mahan, a prominent naval strategist and advocate of American empire—is an attempt to smear, with a one-word label, people who merely want to use coercive economic and military intervention as a last resort. Contrary to the smear, many proponents of military restraint have no problem with free trade, financial flows, immigration, or diplomatic and cultural exchanges among nations. They are also proud that America has the largest and one of the most free economies on the planet and that the dollar is the world's dominant currency.

In fact, an activist foreign policy usually entails attempts to isolate "problem countries." War is not the only means that a powerful empire has to coerce such nations. The United States—as the world's most powerful state and policeman—is the foremost user of economic coercion as a foreign policy tool. Currently, America has economic sanctions against at least twelve countries.[54] Those sanctions aim to change the target country's policies that are objectionable to the United States by isolating it from trade, investment, lending, or cultural contacts.

Is Economically Isolating a Foe Likely to Be Effective?

Since World War II, the United States has imposed such commercial restrictions on countries as diverse as Cuba and South Africa. Curiously, during the cold war, the left tended to argue that sanctions against the apartheid government of South Africa were effective and should be continued but that commercial restrictions against communist Cuba were not and should be terminated; the right argued exactly the opposite.

Those positions should raise suspicion that there is a hefty amount of politics in the debate surrounding the use of economic coercion. In reality, regardless of whether the regime targeted is on the left or the right, economic sanctions are either a useful foreign policy tool or they are not. In the vast majority of instances, they are not.

Most economists would agree that free international commerce among peoples, companies, and nations makes everyone better off. People in one country can specialize in what they are relatively good at producing and sell it to people in other nations, who are relatively good at producing different items. Such specialization and exchange increase economic efficiency, wealth, innovation, and the range of goods produced. One reason the eastern Roman empire survived while the western part of the empire perished to barbarian attacks was that it had more resources available from higher levels of international trade. Similarly, in China, the Ming Dynasty's decision to turn away from international commerce led to imperial decline and weakness ripe for exploitation by the western powers.[55]

Because of the mutual benefits of international commerce, people have spontaneously traded with each other for millennia, despite economic restrictions and even wars. Trade is so mutually advantageous to individuals and companies that when a government tries to turn off the spigot for political reasons, traders just attempt to evade the restrictions. High premiums will be paid by people inside and outside the target country to those who will take the risk of smuggling goods into and out of its ports and airports. Therefore, in the short term, comprehensive, multilateral sanctions can have a devastating effect on the target economy (though even that outcome is unlikely when the more frequent partial or unilateral U.S. sanctions are used), but, over the long term, their economic potency will naturally erode as evasion becomes more rampant.

But ultimately, sanctions are an economic means of coercing the target government to comply with the imposing nation's political wishes—that is, an economic means to achieve a political end. Even if the target economy can be strangled for some time, it is far from certain that the coercion will bring political compliance. For example, from Saddam Hussein's invasion of Kuwait to the U.S. invasion of Iraq, the most comprehensive multilateral sanctions in world history failed to make Iraq withdraw its military forces from Kuwait or give up all efforts to acquire chemical, biological, or nuclear weapons. That U.S.-led policy, for a time, had a devastating effect on the Iraqi economy but ultimately was a failure in achieving the desired Iraqi policy changes.

When an external great power attacks a target nation or tries to strangle it with economic restrictions, the target government is given a powerful tool to shore up its own popularity at home. For example, for more than forty years, Fidel Castro has taken advantage of the "rally around the flag" effect from U.S. sanctions to shore up his standing with the Cuban populace and thus keep himself in power. Even if people do not like their leader, they are usually willing to support him or her in the face of coercion from a foreign enemy. Besides, changing a country's foreign policy from afar by coercion with sanctions is hard enough, but changing a regime's internal policies and form of government by such means is even harder.

Economic Sanctions May Lead to War

When the target nation is willing to endure the intense pain of sanctions instead of modifying the objectionable policy, war is the only more severe threat that great powers can use to achieve compliance. Some advocates of a more restrained U.S. military policy argue that sanctions can be used as an alternative to war. But the usual failure of embargoes to ensure the target's compliance can sometimes even lead to pressure in the sanctioning nation for going to war. For example, Athenian economic sanctions against Megara, a Spartan ally, and blockade against Potidaea, a city-state in revolt from Athens that was seeing the support of a Spartan ally, ultimately led to the Peloponnesian War between Sparta and Athens.[56] Before World War II, U.S. attempts to strangle Japan economically with sanctions to counter its quest for empire led to the desperate Japanese attack on Pearl Harbor. In 1989, the Bush I administration's embarrassment about the failure of stringent U.S. financial sanctions to bring down the Noriega government in Panama probably contributed to the decision to invade that nation and oust the dictator. U.S. sanctions hurt ordinary Panamanians, but Noriega was unfazed. The imposition of sanctions inadvertently helped raise the stakes and reduced U.S. alternatives to the use of force.[57] Similarly, pressure for war built in 1990 and early 1991 when comprehensive multilateral sanctions did not cause Saddam Hussein to withdraw Iraqi forces from occupied Kuwait.

Economic Coercion Can Kill

Using economic sanctions to induce a foreign people to put pressure on their government can also be as immoral as attacking the civilians militarily. Many have criticized the intentional allied bombing of civilians in Japan and Germany during World War II—carried out to attempt to get those citizens to demand that their governments end the war—especially late in the war, when the allies were sure to win. Intentionally targeting civilians to get them to pressure their government to make political changes is what many analysts call "terrorism." Yet when used to attempt to change a government's policies, economic sanctions are also blunt instruments. They are not as rapid in killing civilians as aerial bombing, but over time they may have the same effect. A tyrannical government targeted even by "surgical" sanctions can merely deflect the pain to the poorest in society, while keeping the security forces and other pillars of the regime fat and happy. Of course, comprehensive sanctions blatantly target the whole society. Given the well-documented history of sanctions, the U.S. government should be aware of such well-known effects.

Killing innocent civilians by embargoing food, medicine, spare parts to fix sewage, water, electrical power systems, is no more moral than killing them with bombs. During World War I, the British hunger blockade of Germany was illegal under international law because it targeted, among other things, civilian food products.

Although Saddam Hussein was a brutal, autocratic thug, he killed—in the worst estimate—fewer Iraqis than the five hundred thousand children that UNESCO estimated were killed by the comprehensive U.S.-led sanctions (not to mention the adult Iraqis killed by sanctions and all Iraqis killed in the two Persian Gulf wars).[58]

Economic Sanctions Are "Doing Something"

So if sanctions have a poor record of strangling the target government's economy in the long term (while hurting the most vulnerable in the target society in the short term) and inducing the target government to comply with the sanctioning nation's political demands, why do great powers—particularly the United States—continue their profligate use as a policy tool? The reason is that sanctions are always effective in one major respect. The sanctioning government can show pro-sanctions interest groups and any interested members of the public that they are doing something about an international problem. Oftentimes, a diplomatic protest is deemed too soft a response to a target country's objectionable actions; at the same time, military and covert action are perceived as too drastic a reaction or too secret for the desired public relations effect, respectively. So policymakers choose the mid-range option of sanctions, knowing full well that they probably will not coerce the target to comply. They are instead costly symbols to mollify domestic interest groups and to signal the empire's displeasure with actions of the target government. For example, sanctions against apartheid South Africa in the 1980s satisfied the congressional black caucus and protectionist groups worried about competition from South African coal, steel, textiles, and agricultural products. Sanctions against Cuba's communist government mollified the powerful anti-Castro Cuban lobby in Florida and symbolically showed U.S. displeasure with Castro's totalitarian government. In short, the American empire uses economic coercion as one of several available tools to manage uncooperative countries overseas and domestic interest groups at home. But the use of such commercial restrictions may inadvertently make the world less safe.

Commerce between Nations Lowers Probability of War between Them

Commerce between two nations probably does lessen the probability of war between them. Business interests in each nation that favor bilateral trade are likely to oppose the march to war. For example, prior to the Spanish-American War in 1898, large portions of the U.S. business community dragged their feet in the march to combat because of fears that the disruptions of conflict would nix the recovery from the (economic) panic of 1893.[59] In addition, the best way to tame despotic regimes, such as Castro's Cuba, may be to open them to the new ideas inevitably accompanying trade and investment, rather than to isolate them. As noted earlier, the isolation of Cuba with economic sanctions has been a disaster because of the "rally around the flag" effect. In contrast, although China remains an authoritarian state, foreign trade and investment and market reforms probably have forever mellowed the more extreme totalitarian communist system. There is still a long way to go, but the average Chinese citizen is now freer, both economically and politically, than ever before.

A caveat is needed here: the proliferation of global trade and financial linkages does not guarantee world peace or the end of all dictatorships. Although high levels of trade and financial interactions between any two nations will increase the wealth of both countries, provide incentives to avoid disruptions to such wealth generation, and thus reduce the chance of war between them, the globalization of commerce means that each of the countries also has more sources of capital, imports, and markets for exports in the event of war. Therefore, if one nation develops a dispute with another, it may be easier for them to go to war than in the past because they can each redirect their trade and financial flows to other countries more easily, thus reducing the economic costs of war.

But even when the costs of war cannot be reduced, nations may go to war anyway. Adam Smith wrote in *Wealth of Nations* that "defence is of much more importance than opulence." [60] World War I, one of the most horrific wars in history, was fought in a "globalized" economy. In 1910, even as the world moved toward war, Norman Angell wrote the international bestseller *The Great Illusion,* which predicted that war would become prohibitively uneconomical for both the victor and vanquished.[61] He was proved terribly wrong four years later and throughout what would become by far the world's most bloody century.

Furthermore, despite free market economic reforms often creating a "culture of liberty," autocratic countries that open their economies to the world may not all necessarily become liberal democracies, as did Taiwan, Chile, and South Korea. The regime in China is freeing its economy and opening it to the world in hopes of maintaining power. Whether China goes down the path of those other nations toward democracy or maintains its authoritarian status is an open question. Even if China does become a democracy, the "democratic peace theory" is suspect, and thus the Chinese could remain nationalistic and wage war with other democracies.

But even with the caveat, free trade and financial flows among nations make everyone more prosperous and may even reduce the chances of war and undermine dictatorships. Therefore, any cutoff or restriction of such commercial linkages with despotic governments could increase the chances of war with them. But then the following question arises: Doesn't the American empire contribute to the stability needed to maintain the globalization of commercial links worldwide, and therefore to American security and prosperity?

EMPIRE IS COUNTERPRODUCTIVE FOR SECURITY AND PROSPERITY

Ironically, at the turn of the last century, high-level American policymakers essentially accepted what would later become a Leninist argument that capitalist countries created excess production and capital that had to find markets, profits, and investment opportunities overseas.[62] Those policymakers also believed that if foreign markets were not opened to American goods and investment, the U.S. economy would suffer and create domestic political instability.

Even if the above theories were true (and they are not), the U.S. government would not necessarily need to adopt mercantilist policies by augmenting military forces to open overseas markets at gunpoint. Yet those policies were adopted. In 1898, during the Spanish-American War, America's first imperial adventure, the supposedly nonimperialist United States created a Philippine colony and acquired a military presence in the Pacific. Under the Open Door policy facilitated by that new military presence, the United States used its military to help the European colonial powers carve up China and open Chinese markets to western goods. Thus the first stirrings in the American heart for an overseas empire were born.

Free Commerce Is Better than Imperialist Mercantilism

Yet the need for such government intervention—in this case, indirectly subsidizing international commerce using U.S. military power—had already been discredited by free market economists (classical liberals). During the 1800s, the imperial lobby in Great Britain had maintained that the British empire was economically beneficial to the home country's populace. Richard Cobden and John Bright, followers of Adam Smith, had persuasively opposed that argument. They suggested that overseas trade and investment were mutually beneficial to the parties involved—that is, represented a non-zero-sum game—and so would occur without the need for an empire. And even if some governments of other countries refused to open their markets to foreign goods and investment, Cobden and Bright believed that no empire was needed to force them open. In other words, even unilateral free trade would be beneficial to Great Britain. British consumers would pay less for goods that were imported, and the foreign competition made British companies stronger. With the repeal of the Corn Laws in 1846, those free traders got the British government to adopt unilateral free trade. Unfortunately, believing the false premise that foreign commerce is a zero-sum game, the United States has never accepted unilateral free trade as beneficial and has thus demanded a reciprocal opening of markets.[63]

Conservative economist Robert Lucas notes, "In common with many British thinkers from Adam Smith onward, I think of imperialism as almost an opposite of liberalism—a system based on paternalism and coercion rather than on autonomy and free exchange." Such British classical liberals also realized that reaping the benefits of uncoerced, mutually beneficial trade with other nations without incurring the high costs of ruling them was much more cost-effective than maintaining an empire. Curiously, John Mearsheimer rejects that argument and maintains that conquest sometimes pays dividends by confiscating industrial plants or economic output, imposing taxes, or extracting resources.[64] Mearsheimer seems to ignore all the costs of conquest: maintaining a large military, colonial administration and security, economic distortions and loss from preferential commerce within the empire, the costs of providing military and economic aid, etc. British liberals realized that taking resources, land, markets, and people by force is analogous to devising a plan to burglarize a secure store that is more expensive than simply buying the store's goods honestly.

The sheltered trade between the center and the periphery in an empire tends to make the center's companies sluggish and uncompetitive compared to the alternative of unbridled competition with the firms of all nations. Britain entered a self-defeating retreat into imperial markets between 1883 and 1914.[65] In short, empire led to a decline in the British economy, which, when combined with two unaffordable world wars, led to the demise of Britain as a world power.

(Such economic costs of empire, when combined with the cogent realist analysis summarized in Chapter 2 demonstrating that democracies do war against each other, cast much doubt on the U.S. policy, endorsed by both left-wing and right-wing Wilsonians, of spreading democracy and free markets at gunpoint. Furthermore, as the next chapter will show, the United States is not usually successful in spreading either—for example, in Iraq, the United States is avoiding the democratic elections supported by many Iraqis and handing out reconstruction contracts without competition.)

A cursory review of human history quickly shows that people have conducted cross-border and intercontinental commerce for many centuries, even during wars and sometimes even between citizens of the belligerent nations. You don't need Economics 101 to reach the conclusion that foreign trade and investment are mutually beneficial to the parties involved. Otherwise, international commerce would not have been so popular over the millennia.

The idea that unilateral free trade is harmful and that markets must be opened reciprocally—either through treaty or by force—persists because of special interest politics, not because economists believe it. Politically powerful industries that either export goods or are threatened by foreign imports pressure the U.S. government to use access to the large U.S. market as leverage to gain entry to foreign markets. The exporters hope such negotiations succeed in opening the foreign market to their goods, and the industries threatened by imports hope that the demand for the opening of foreign markets will cause the negotiations to fail, keeping all markets restricted. But the interest of the general population—that is, of American consumers—is never hurt by unilaterally opening the U.S. market. Customers benefit from lower-priced and higher-quality imports, and American industry even gains a long-term advantage by becoming stronger via more intense competition against foreign firms. Voluntary global free trade is the best outcome for people in all countries. Foreign governments that close their markets to foreign trade and investment are ultimately hurting only their own consumers, industries and economy.

Despite the refutation in the 1800s of the imperialist, mercantilist path to prosperity, prominent advocates of this view still exist today. Thomas Friedman, a prominent liberal foreign-policy columnist for the *New York Times,* succinctly sums up the modern mercantilist or neomercantilist argument as follows: "The hidden hand of the market will never work without a hidden fist—McDonald's cannot flourish without a McDonnell Douglas, the builder of the F-15. And the hidden fist that keeps the world safe for Silicon Valley's technologies is called the United States Army, Air Force, Navy and Marine Corps. . . . Without America on duty, there will be no America Online."[66]

William Cohen, then-Secretary of Defense, who had a vested interest in the matter, similarly argued that "economists and soldiers share the same interests in stability." He further opined that "when you have stability, you have at least the opportunity to enjoy prosperity because investment flows. . . . When they [businesses] find a secure environment, they will invest." He concluded: "Business follows the flag."[67]

Friedman's and Cohen's views are common and at the same time curious. The American economy became world-class in 1830 and the planet's largest during the 1880s, but the United States did not have a large peacetime military to "provide security" until 1950. In making the Herculean assumption that profligate U.S. military interventions overseas increase rather than decrease stability, Cohen also implies that economists would endorse the muscular inducement of such stability. As noted earlier, however, classical liberal economists long ago debunked the notion that empires were cost-effective.

Of the U.S. military services, the Navy uses the "protection of commerce" justification the most to advocate building more weapon systems. The service argues that the more expansive web of international trade produced by globalization requires more ships to protect it. Certainly, the U.S. Navy should protect any U.S. civilian cargo ships that come under attack from other nations or pirates, but the bone-crushing world dominance of the American fleet is overkill on a grand scale for that mission. The United States has twelve very large supercarriers, and no other navy has even one functioning counterpart. In addition, for that mission, the Navy should be purchasing more destroyers and frigates to use as escorts rather than supercarriers to attack nonexistent naval competitors or land targets. Most important, with globalization, if certain waters are dangerous because of an ongoing regional war or piracy, the United States can simply trade with increased numbers of alternative suppliers or buyers rather than paying the exorbitant cost of maintaining a huge navy. In other words, trade in a globalized world can simply redirect itself around wars or instability more easily and thus requires less naval protection.

Staying Out of Wars Is Advantageous

Of course, the U.S. military also makes an even broader argument: that stability—presumably ensured by the global military power of all of the U.S. armed services—in certain important countries, regions, and even the world will facilitate commerce. All other things being equal, stability probably will facilitate international commerce. As noted earlier, however, international trade is a natural phenomenon and will flow even during wars, both large and small. The question then becomes whether the expenses of the large U.S. military pay for themselves in increased trade via enhanced stability.

According to professors Eugene Gholz and Daryl Press, even using worst-case assumptions about the extent of fighting that would occur without a global U.S. military presence and about the vulnerability of the American economy to wartime dislocation, the overextended U.S. defense perimeter is much more expensive than the costs to the American economy of a major war if America remained neutral. They concluded that only a minimal economic effect of war on neutrals arises because they can increase trade in war materiel with the belligerents, take over the overseas markets abandoned by the belligerents as they focus on war production at home, lend money at higher interest rates, and act as a safe haven for capital fleeing the zone of conflict. So the adverse economic effects on neutrals of even a major conflagration may be less than believed. In fact, in some cases, neutrals may be better off economically than before the war started. Gholz and Press found that as a neutral nation for most of World War I, the United States profited from trade and capital flows with belligerents and other neutrals. Japan and Sweden—both neutral in that war—also prospered. They also report that A.F.K. Organski and Jacek Kugler reached a similar conclusion in another study, that neutral countries' GNPs were not substantially affected in the medium term or long term by World Wars I and II.[68] The finding of the Organski and Kugler study is even more remarkable because World War II was a much larger war than even World War I.

From their study, Gholz and Press concluded that the world economy is resilient and flexible and thus adaptable even to large wars. Even if a major conflagration occurs, trade and investment patterns will adjust, but the adverse economic effects on neutrals from lost trade and higher interest rates are small.[69] Furthermore, wars and their associated costs may or may not happen, but the expensive U.S. military presence around the globe is not a contingent expense.

And the short-term economic advantages of being a neutral country are eclipsed by the long-term benefits. Nations trying to change the international system often miscalculate and come to realize that the costs of doing so outweigh the benefits. Third parties on the periphery often profit from their mistakes. Wars can weaken the belligerents and make them vulnerable to conquest by an outside power.[70] For example, the Peloponnesian War between Athens and Sparta and subsequent conflict between Greek city-states weakened the Athenian Empire and the city-state system, thus facilitating the conquest of Greece by the Macedonians.[71] Also, during the Thirty Years' War (1618–48), fighting between Sweden and the Hapsburg Austrians over Germany left the German countryside devastated. With a weakened Germany, the big winner was France under Louis XIV (the "Sun King"), who then began a rampage of conquest that plagued Europe for the following 35 years.[72]

Furthermore, Wilsonians of both the left and right give the illusion that the world will fall apart if the benevolent superpower fails to be the sheriff. Yet, for example, in the nineteenth century, the United States did not get involved in European politics, but long periods of peace among the great powers nevertheless were common because of a balance of power among them.

U.S. Intervention Is Often Counterproductive

Of course, heretofore, this analysis has assumed that the U.S. worldwide military presence and profligate military, economic, and covert interventions have had a positive effect on global stability and then has assessed their cost-effectiveness. In many cases, U.S. military presence and interventions may reduce stability in the long term. Fredrick Hayek, the famous Nobel Laureate and free market economist, argued against government intervention in any domestic economy. He stated that the economy's complexity was so great that the government almost always did the wrong thing. Analogously, managing the world is much more complex than even managing a domestic economy, and government intervention overseas is liable to produce unpredictable and unpleasant outcomes (for example, the aforementioned rise of Louis XIV). Similarly, historian Joseph Stromberg has postulated Stromberg's First Law, which states that "there is virtually no situation anywhere in the world that can't be made worse by U.S. intervention." His corollary is that "the more U.S. interference and 'help' a country receives, the bigger the anti-American explosion down the line (e.g., Cuba, the Philippines, Nicaragua and Iran)."[73]

Vietnam was an example of a U.S. war that accomplished exactly the opposite of its intended goals by igniting more than ten years of inflation, weakening the U.S. military, reducing support at home for America's worldwide activism, creating tensions in the NATO alliance, and inviting Soviet global mischief in the 1970s. Similarly, Japan invaded China in the 1930s to create an autarkic military-industrial base but became caught up in a quagmire that devoured that base by diverting industrial investment into current military consumption. The invasion of China also antagonized the powerful United States. Japan needed that eroding industrial base to fight this more industrially capable foe. In the end, Japan's entire industrial base was destroyed by the cataclysmic war.[74]

To provide further evidence supporting Stromberg's First Law of war's unintended consequences and his corollary, recalling a recent chain of events is important. In 1953, Prime Minister Mossadegh nationalized U.S. and British oil interests in Iran, whereupon the CIA sponsored a coup to bring back the Pahlevi throne. As a client of the United States, Shah Reza Pahlevi then ruled that nation with an iron fist and used oil revenues to buy excessive amounts of U.S. weaponry instead of allowing his people to prosper. The Iranian population became so restive under that oppression that they overthrew the Shah in 1978 and replaced him with a radical theocratic Islamic regime under the Ayatollah Khomeini. Hatred of America in Iran, generated because of the close superpower-client relationship between the United States and the reviled Shah, was so rabid that the U.S. embassy was captured and U.S. diplomats held hostage from 1979 until 1981. That hatred continues until the present day.

Having created a monster, the United States, in an attempt to cage it, was about to create another one. In the late 1960s, it sponsored a coup in Iraq to bring the Baath Party to power. Using lists provided by the CIA, the Baathists eliminated hundreds of leftist professionals, including doctors, lawyers, teachers, and political activists. In 1980, Saddam Hussein, the Baathist ruler of Iraq, had attacked Iran because the Khomeini regime was stirring up ethnic groups within Iraq. The United States desperately feared that radical Iran would win the bloody conflict that lasted from 1980 to 1988. To contain Iran, the United States, although ostensibly neutral in the war, secretly helped Saddam win the war. The U.S. government provided Iraq with key intelligence, military planning, and billions of dollars in loans—some of which Saddam used to try to build a nuclear weapon—and looked the other way when Iraq used chemical weapons, produced with technology and materials purchased from Western nations, on the Iranians and the Iraqi Kurds.

After Saddam won the Iraq-Iran War, he became ascendant in the region. Saddam could now invade Kuwait only because the balance of power in the region had been altered in favor of Iraq by its U.S.-assisted victory over a now weakened Iran.[75] Strangely, between the end of the Iraq-Iran war in 1988 and Saddam's invasion of Kuwait in August 1990, the United States continued its support for his regime, rather than balancing its power against him. In fact, a month before Iraq's attack on Kuwait, the United States was planning joint military maneuvers with the Iraqi armed forces that were to be conducted later that year. Saddam invaded Kuwait because he became angry at Kuwait's slant drilling into oil reserves under Iraqi soil and its not forgiving the Iraqi war debt incurred in leading the "Arab cause" against Iran. Saddam's invasion of Kuwait triggered two U.S. wars with Iraq, connected by twelve years of hostility, economic sanctions, and low-level conflict. The long-term effects of U.S. policy: wars galore and hostile relations with both Iraq and Iran.

A final example of the American cure being worse than the original problem is that of U.S. intervention in Afghanistan. Although it seemed like a good idea at the time, a U.S. attempt to entrap the Soviet Union in an unimportant backwater led to one of the biggest threats to the U.S. homeland in the history of the republic. In an ultimately successful attempt to enmesh its cold war rival in a Soviet Vietnam-style quagmire, the Carter administration aided the radical Mujahadeen opponents of the Soviet-supported Afghan government. With glee, the even more anti-Soviet Reagan administration continued shoveling aid—including arms, cash, and training—through Pakistan to the most radical Islamic groups fighting against the Soviet invaders. After the Soviets withdrew, the radical Islamists not only won control of Afghanistan, but also then used it as a sanctuary and training base from which to launch terrorist attacks against U.S. targets at home and abroad. Unintentionally, the United States had helped train and fund those who attacked the U.S.S. Cole, the U.S. embassies in Kenya and Tanzania, and, of course, the World Trade Center and Pentagon on September 11, 2001. In the end, the ultimate consequences of the remedy, namely, U.S. intervention, were far worse than the original malady—the Soviet invasion of a remote, nonstrategic country.

So the unintended consequences of fifty years of U.S. intervention in the Persian Gulf/Central Asian region lend credence to Hayek's concerns about government intervention into complex situations. Instead of having the seemingly minor problems of a nationalized oil company in Iran in 1953 and Soviet domination of a remote and poor Afghanistan in the 1980s,[76] the United States helped generate the threat of catastrophic terrorist attacks by al Qaeda against U.S. targets abroad and in its homeland, three hostile adversaries (the Taliban, Iran, and Iraq), five wars, and two military occupations. Those conflicts included the Iran-Iraq War, two Persian Gulf wars, low-level conflict enforcing the no-fly zones in Iraq in between those wars, and the U.S. invasion of Afghanistan to oust the Taliban and al Qaeda. The U.S. military occupations in Afghanistan and Iraq are rapidly turning into quagmires of spiraling violence and chaos. Much of the conflict in the Persian Gulf/Central Asian region can be attributed to past U.S. interventions.

Doing nothing is doing something—and it is often a better solution. Although neoconservative Robert Kaplan argues that an American empire is needed to safeguard U.S. security in an "age of collapsed distances,"[77] the advent of nuclear weapons and their long-range delivery systems actually have made the chances of any attack on the United States even more remote. Other nations, even those few with nuclear arsenals or long-range bombers, have a home address and can be deterred from attacking the United States by the threat of massive conventional or nuclear destruction in their homeland. In addition, American geography still presents a formidable barrier to any foreign invasion. Amphibious assault is difficult even across small bodies of water—for example, the assaults in Normandy in 1944 and Inchon in 1950—let alone across vast oceans in an age of satellite reconnaissance and precision munitions. In sum, America's advantages in geography (being far away from most zones of conflict, having two large oceans as moats, and residing between two weak and friendly neighbors) and nuclear weaponry (presiding over a globally dominant nuclear force of thousands of warheads) make it intrinsically more secure than most countries in the world.

Less subject to deterrence are terrorists—the only true threat to U.S. security at the present time. But less U.S. involvement in foreign civil and ethnic wars abroad would dramatically reduce the chances that such groups would attack the United States. Interventionists argue that the United States needs to go in and fix failed states so that they will not become breeding grounds for terrorists. In fact, getting embroiled in "somebody else's civil war" is the best way to paint a bull's-eye on America for retaliatory terrorism. The September 11 attacks resulted because the United States has become involved in a civil war within Islam.

The U.S. foreign policy elite, which thrives on American intervention and empire-building around the world, tries to obscure the link between that activist foreign policy overseas with blowback terrorism against U.S. targets, but the American people have finally realized the connection. According to a poll conducted by the University of Maryland, about 64 percent of the American people believe that U.S. military presence in the Middle East increases the likelihood of terrorism, and 54 percent of the public say that the United States has been too assertive in its foreign policies. A separate ABC News poll produced similar results. About 48 percent of Americans thought that the war in Iraq has increased the threat of anti-American terrorism, while 40 percent thought it had reduced the risk.[78] Recent revised data from the U.S. State Department showing an increase in terrorist attacks bear those fears out.

The American public is only now realizing what has been obvious to others around the world for quite some time: the American empire and U.S. intervention into the affairs of other nations, particularly in the Middle East, lead to the hatred that spawns anti-U.S. terrorist attacks. In poll after poll of Arabic and Islamic nations, respondents say that they like U.S. culture and freedoms—both political and economic—but dislike U.S. foreign policy toward the Islamic world.

In sum, the American empire is not a cost-effective way to preserve U.S. prosperity and security and, in fact, actively undermines them both. Conservatives should even be leery of empire for reasons of "national greatness." If the United States continues to pursue empire, it may not, in the end, even retain its status as a great power.

MAINTAINING AN EMPIRE COULD LEAD TO AMERICA'S DECLINE

Deepak Lal, a proponent of American empire, analyzes the British, Indian, Ottoman, Chinese, Greek, Roman, Mongol, Austro-Hungarian, and Arabic Abbasid empires and admits that "most of these empires have ultimately declined. Given the existing technology and the inevitable predatoriness of the state, most of them overextended themselves."[79]

The same could be said for the Spanish, Soviet, Nazi, and Japanese empires. Great conflicts tend to destroy empires, sometimes even if the empire wins the war. Some empires expand too far and meet their end at the hands of more powerful states that balance against them; for example, in World War II, the U.S., Soviet, and British coalition defeated the Nazi and Japanese empires. World War I destroyed the losing Ottoman and Austro-Hungarian empires. The Carthaginian empire met its end in wars with the more powerful Roman empire. The Spanish empire finally collapsed in the early 1800s as a result of Spain's demise in the Napoleonic wars. Defeats in the Russo-Japanese War in 1905 and World War I contributed heavily to the Czarist empire's collapse in Russia in 1917.

But World War II even destroyed the winning British and French empires, through the depletion of resources. Many such empires overextend by bankrupting themselves with endless security commitments and wars to maintain the realm, both of which make the costs of empire rise faster than the benefits. Because of losses in war and overextension, Jack Snyder, a prominent researcher on empire, maintains that security through expansion usually fails.[80]

Robert Gilpin hypothesizes a reason that all empires have declined. He argues that when equilibrium between the costs and benefits of imperial expansion is achieved, the costs for the empire to maintain the resulting status quo rise more rapidly than its ability to pay for it. Maintaining the empire requires increased military spending, financing of allies, distribution of foreign aid, and maintenance of international economic institutions. Such protection and related costs are not productive investments and drain the economy of the dominant power, thus leading to the decline of the empire.

Gilpin also ominously notes that imperial decline has accelerated over time. He notes that in premodern times, the Byzantine and Chinese empires lasted a thousand years. In contrast, the nineteenth-century British empire lasted only a hundred years and Pax Americana is under strain after only a few decades.[81]

Economic Problems Exacerbated by Militarism Lead to Decline

In his comparative study of declining empires, Carlo M. Cipolla notes, "Whenever we look at declining empires, we notice that their economies are generally faltering. The economic difficulties of declining empires show striking resemblances." He also noticed that public consumption—that is, government spending on public works, the military, and the extravagant tastes of the rulers—in mature empires rises sharply. Thus, a common feature of autumnal empires is heavy taxation. The mature empire develops resistance to the change needed for economic growth and technological advancement. The reasons for that phenomenon are the large number of sclerotic institutions and regulations supported by vested interests.

Cipolla then gives examples of expanding government crowding out the productive power of private enterprise and causing imperial decline. He notes that the late Roman empire quadrupled the armed forces and dramatically enlarged the civil service. Taxes to support that expansion of government became so heavy that peasants left the land. The Roman economy ceased to be innovative and weakened Rome in the face of the barbarian onslaught. One of the reasons for the Spanish empire's decline was excessive bureaucracy. In the 1500s, Spain (as well as Italy) had heavy taxes. Bloated bureaucracies also afflicted the mature Byzantine and Arab empires.

Excessive government spending also leads to runaway inflation. The late Roman, Spanish, and Byzantine empires all experienced de facto taxation from the debasement of currencies caused by inflation.[82]

Adolf Wagner, a mid-nineteenth-century economist, had the same view. He postulated Wagner's Law, which states that public expenditures rise faster than the economy.[83] The implication: rising warfare and welfare expenses sap the economies of mature empires, leading to relative decline.

From 1937 to 1941, rapid imperial expansion drained the Japanese economy, just at the time strength was needed to fight the nation with the largest economy on the planet—the United States. The Japanese military dominated Japanese decision making and developed a grand strategy that was too ambitious for Japanese resources.

Another particularly good example of imperial overextension was that of the Dutch empire of the mid-1600s. The Dutch were the economic leaders in Europe, and thus Amsterdam was the foremost capital market in Europe. But to deal with enemies, the Dutch had to increase military spending and concomitant taxation. They were gradually surpassed as a great power by a more efficient and geographically secure English competitor.[84]

At the root of the Russian and Soviet empires was a bias toward expansion. They declined both because of frequent costly wars or cold wars with other powers (leading to backwardness vis-à-vis the Western powers) and because of territorial overextension with insufficient resources to protect and rule the vast expanse and many peoples within their borders. In the 1980s, the costs of the expensive Soviet empire increased at the same time that oil revenues dropped, resulting in an imperial collapse.[85] Also, the Soviet bias toward expansion led to the militarization of society. The nonviable communist economy collapsed under the weight of excessive military spending.

The Roman empire, in its later stages, also became excessively militarized. As Rome waged foreign wars of conquest, rival Roman legions became kingmakers, each attempting to have its general elevated to emperor. This phenomenon led to the growing political influence of the military, which it used to enrich itself. The resulting enormous military sapped the empire's economy through excessive taxation, thus weakening the people's allegiance in the face of attacks by the barbarians.[86]

In the 1600s, the Hapsburg empire (Spain and Austria) overextended, and thus declined, by getting enmeshed in frequent wars. The empire spent more on the military than its economy could bear.[87]

Not only is an overextended empire's economy sapped, but its technology and skills flow to potential competitors, especially in a global market economy. The diffusion of Roman military skills to the German barbarian tribes was a major factor in Rome's demise. Similarly, the backward Mongols adopted the metallurgical techniques of the superior Chinese and then defeated them. Thorstein Veblen spoke about the "advantages of backwardness." Imitating countries have lower costs and can use technologies more efficiently than mature empires, which have greater expenses to research and develop technology initially and "vested interests" that prevent the introduction of the latest version of the technology.

When Macedonia, Rome, Britain, and the United States were rising, they were each close enough geographically to the leading nation of the time to absorb its technology, far away enough to be protected from its power by the "loss-of-strength gradient," and endowed with less developed institutions that were more inclined to accept new ideas. They were also in zones of peace devoid of constant war.[88] (The loss-of-strength gradient refers to the lessening ability of a great power to project military force as the distance to the target increases.)

Yes, Decline Could Happen to the United States Too

Despite the decline of past empires, according to Cipolla, flourishing empires delude themselves that what has transpired throughout history cannot happen to them. Cipolla concludes that history provides no instance of an indestructible empire.[89]

Victor Davis Hanson seems to be a typical proponent of that viewpoint. Admitting that overextension has led to the demise of many empires, he states, "Most empires chafe at the cost of their rule and complain that the expense is near suicidal. Athens raised the Aegean tribute often and found itself nearly broke after only the fifth year of the Peloponnesian War. The story of the Roman Empire is one of shrinking legions, a debased currency, and a chronically bankrupt imperial treasury. Even before World War I, the Raj [India] had drained England."[90] Curiously, however, Hanson doesn't think that the same fate could befall the United States. He continues, "In contrast, America today spends less of its GNP on defense than it did during the last five decades. . . . The remarkable fact is not that we have twelve massive five billion dollar aircraft carriers but that we could easily build and maintain twenty more yet choose not to do so. So our military is enormous not because of our skewed priorities of guns over butter but simply because the vast size of the present-day American economy allows more soldiers and weapons with a 4 percent GNP investment than most other countries could field with 50 percent."[91]

In contrast, neoconservative Robert Kaplan acknowledges that the American empire is likely to be short-lived, but wants the United States to pass its legacy to a utopian world civil society with new international institutions and responsible like-minded regional powers. Such an unrealistic goal could also have come from the Wilsonian liberals. Kaplan writes,

> No doubt there are some who see an American empire as the natural order of things for all time. That is not a wise outlook. The task ahead for the United States has an end point, and in all probability the end point lies not beyond the conceptual horizon but in the middle distance—a few decades from now. For a limited period the United States has the power to write the terms for international society in hopes that when the country's imperial hour has passed, new international institutions and stable regional powers will have begun to flourish, creating a kind of civil society for the world. . . . There will be nothing approaching a true world government, but we may be able to nurture a loose set of global arrangements that have arisen organically among responsible and like-minded states.[92]

In fact, Jim Garrison, a Wilsonian liberal, espouses a similar empire leading to a utopian world, though he, like Kaplan, is careful not to endorse world government:

> America must consciously view itself as a *transitional empire* [emphasis in original], one whose destiny at this moment is to act as midwife to a democratically governed global system. Its great challenge is not to dominate but to catalyze. It must use its great strength and democratic heritage to establish integrating institutions and mechanisms to manage the emerging global system so that its own power is subsumed by the very edifice it helps to build. . . . If it attains this level of greatness, it could become the final empire, for it will have bequeathed to the world a democratic and integrated global system in which empire will no longer have a place or perform a role.[93]

Similarly, but more realistically than Kaplan or Garrison, John Adams, the second American president, astutely realized that even the most dominant nations in the world can and have declined:

> All that part of creation that lies within our observation is liable to change. Even mighty states and kingdoms are not exempted. If we look into history, we shall find some nations rising from contemptible beginnings and spreading their influence, until the whole globe is subjected to their ways. When they have reached the summit of grandeur, some minute and unsuspected cause commonly affects their ruin, and the empire of the world is transferred to some other place. Immortal Rome was at first but an insignificant village, inhabited only by a few abandoned ruffians, but by degrees it rose to a stupendous height and excelled in arts and arms all the nations that preceded it. But the demolition of Carthage (what one should think should have established it in supreme domination) by removing all danger, suffered it to sink into the debauchery, and made it at length an easy prey to Barbarians.[94]

At the height of the British empire in early 1918, few Brits would have believed that involvement in India and getting dragged into two world wars would take their great empire to its knees in less than fifty years. According to Niall Ferguson, a British historian and cheerleader for the British empire, the staggering cost of fighting the German, Italian, and Japanese empires ultimately ruined the British empire.[95] The empire lasted as long as it did because Britain kept its army and defense expenditures small and relied on its navy to police the world's first global realm.[96] The British empire, at its peak, maintained a global empire for fifty to a hundred times less than the cost of the American empire's defense spending at the beginning of the cold war in the 1950s and early 1960s.[97] The British stationed fewer military forces overseas during peacetime than the United States does now. Unfortunately, however, having far-flung security commitments all over the world meant that Britain could be more easily sucked into great wars among other powers. For most of its imperial history, Britain consciously and wisely tried to limit its involvement in expensive and draining land wars by either appeasing opposing powers or finding continental allies to provide the vast bulk of the land forces to use against them when war broke out. For example, Lord Palmerston, the British Prime Minister, thought about expanding the Crimean War into a world war to snuff out Russian power forever, but his cabinet allies and neutral states forced him to seek a compromise.

In contrast, when Britain failed to avoid the costly World Wars I and II, and its economy buckled as result, the empire was lost.[98] The economy could not support those large and expensive wars because the sheltered trade in the British empire had made British firms less competitive between 1893 and 1914. In 1947, the British economy was so weak that Britain could not provide aid to Turkey and Greece against communist subversion. The United States had to take the lead in containing communism in Europe and filling the power vacuum left by a declining British empire in the Middle East and East Asia.

According to Niall Ferguson, in order to have preserved their empire, the British should have stayed out of costly World War I, which ultimately led to World War II.[99] (The Spanish empire in 1600, the post–World War II French empire, and many others have also declined because far-flung commitments exceeded resources.) Britain's expansive world empire also impeded the marshalling of resources when a major threat to the home island's existence—Hitler's Germany—arose. And when World War II began, the empire dissipated Britain's resources around the globe to defend colonial possessions against German, Italian, and Japanese attacks.[100]

The Soviet Union, the principal enemy of the United States during the cold war, dissolved, allowing the United States to scale back defense spending as a percentage of GDP from 6 to 3.5 percent. (Unbelievably, in absolute real terms, the United States is still spending ten percent more on defense than it did during the cold war.) The expansion of the American empire to take advantage of its powerful foe's demise, however, means that defense expenditures as a percentage of GDP could skyrocket again if the United States gets involved in a major war or wars in its attempt to police the globe. The U.S.-dominated NATO alliance has expanded into the sphere of influence of the former Soviet Union and former Soviet territory. By allowing former Soviet satellites and the new republics of the former USSR to join the alliance, the United States is explicitly guaranteeing their security against any resurgence by Russia. To contain China, the United States has strengthened ties with Asian friends and allies.[101] In order to contain Russia or China, the United States also used the "war on terror" to acquire a military presence in the Philippines, Georgia, and the Central Asian republics of the former Soviet Union. A policy of containing those two countries could eventually result in a renewed cold war or even a hot war with either or both, causing U.S. security expenditures to skyrocket.

Unfortunately, unlike the British empire, the American superpower is unwilling to limit its foreign exposure by accommodating certain problem nations or limiting its influence in nonstrategic areas of the world. In the post–cold war era, the Clinton and two Bush administrations have regarded the entire world as their playground, intervening haphazardly all over with no apparent strategic plan.

The U.S. Army alone operates in a hundred and twenty countries,[102] creating the potential to be sucked into many nonstrategic brushfire wars. Even such "small" wars can be expensive. The Vietnam War started modestly but ended up costing $500 billion in today's dollars. The Bush II administration is already bogged down in potential quagmires in Iraq and Afghanistan that are projected to cost more than $200 billion during the 2003–2005 period alone. If violence persists in those countries, the potential for escalation of those already eye-popping costs is great.

U.S. Empire Is in Auto-expansion Mode

Enlarging empires can create the dynamic of continuous further expansion. On the extreme, that dynamic is manifested in the "expand or die" mentality of Catherine the Great, who declared, "That which ceases to grow begins to rot."[103] Expanding empires often believe they need to secure recently acquired territory by acquiring more resources or by "stabilizing" lands even farther afield that border on the new area—this is the "turbulent frontier" thesis.

Examples of that phenomenon are the U.S. invasion of Cambodia during the Vietnam War and the Soviet empire's invasion of Afghanistan to guard against an Islamic insurgency in its Moslem regions.[104] Also, the Austro-Hungarian empire's worries about Serb attempts to destabilize the newly acquired Bosnia-Herzegovina led that empire to use a Serbian's assassination of Archduke Ferdinand as a pretext to confront Serbia. That confrontation led to World War I.

Furthermore, with the conquest of Egypt and the pushing of the Roman empire's frontier to the Rhine and Danube rivers by 12 BCE, Emperor Caesar Augustus thought the empire to be complete. But he soon feared that the territory between the Rhine and Elbe rivers (now southwestern Germany), which was still outside the empire, could become an invasion route for barbarian tribes. So he decided he must conquer that territory too. But the Roman army sent to do so was massacred at the Teutoburg Forest.[105]

After the Spanish-American War, the United States annexed Puerto Rico so as to avoid having a Spanish military base near Cuba, a strategic island that also had been taken from Spain during the conflict. Even more egregious were the policies of interwar Japan and Germany. Their slender resource bases and industrial capabilities should not have permitted wholesale expansion. Yet the more they expanded, the more they needed to expand farther to obtain the resources to defend what they had already taken.[106]

Britain gradually absorbed India to quell disturbances on its empire's frontier. Then the British took Egypt and South Africa to guard the routes to India, which had become the crown jewel of the empire. They then had to take Sudan and the upper Nile to protect Egypt and the bulk of sub-Saharan Africa to guard South Africa.[107]

More recently, to take advantage of the retraction of Soviet power in Europe, the United States expanded the NATO alliance to add three new former Warsaw Pact nations. That expansion was done in part to ensure that instability or war in Eastern Europe would not destabilize Western Europe. Western Europe is the core of the alliance and an area of great economic and technological power. Now NATO has expanded again to the borders of Russia, in part to better protect Western Europe and the newly admitted Poland, Hungary, and the Czech Republic. The further expansion of NATO satisfied powerful lobbies in the United States that did not want those three new members to be on the frontline of NATO. Similarly, NATO bombed Serbia over Kosovo in 1999 to safeguard its investment in Bosnia and prevent the instability in Kosovo from spreading either near a new NATO member (Hungary) or near future NATO members (Romania and Bulgaria). Historically, following that "expansion breeds expansion" pattern, many empires eventually overreach and collapse.

After the Spanish-American War, William Graham Sumner, considering the new possessions of Hawaii and the Philippines acquired during that war, best expressed the faulty logic of the turbulent frontier thesis:

> We were told that we needed Hawaii in order to secure California. What shall we now take in order to secure the Philippines? No wonder that some expansionists do not want to "scuttle out of China." We shall need to take China, Japan, and the East Indies, according to the doctrine, in order to "secure" what we have. Of course, this means that, on the doctrine, we must take the whole earth in order to be safe on any part of it, and the fallacy stands exposed. If, then, safety and prosperity do not lie in this direction, the place to look for them is in the other direction: in domestic development, peace, industry, free trade with everybody, low taxes, industrial power.[108]

Put the Economy, Not the Military, First in Foreign Policy

Since economic power is what military, cultural, and political power ultimately rest on, sometimes it's better to "keep your powder dry" to ensure that you remain a global power for years to come. In the last five hundred years, changes in the global military balance have followed shifts in the world's economic balance, and the side with the biggest economy has always won major wars.[109]

Even before that period, the Byzantine empire (eastern Roman empire) lasted a thousand years because the scale of the empire was reduced to match the resources available to defend it. The empire withdrew from Rome's exposed and vulnerable western provinces and consolidated in the eastern provinces, which were cheaper and easier to defend.[110] And defense of the lands already held was the purpose of the empire, not expansion. The strategy worked despite attacks from many enemies. Nearly six hundred years after separating from the western Roman empire, Byzantium still ruled the Balkans south of the Danube and nearly all of Asia Minor (what is now Turkey).[111]

Similarly, the United States became a great power in the first place by resisting excessive foreign commitments that would drain the economy. In the 1800s (even after the Civil War), the United States kept its military modest, which allowed it to concentrate on becoming the world's dominant economy. A small government and low taxes enabled the U.S. economy to expand rapidly from the fourth largest in the world in 1830 to the second largest in 1850 to the largest in the late 1880s. Even during the first half of the twentieth century, the peacetime U.S. military remained small, and there was still reluctance to get dragged into foreign wars and permanent alliances. When the United States entered wars, there was public pressure to demobilize military forces rapidly after their end.

Recent American history, however, does not signal much hope that the leaders of the U.S. empire know how to conserve American power in the long term. U.S. policymakers have forgotten that the United States is so dominant today only because other empires decline as a result of either losing wars (Italy, Germany, and Japan) or winning wars but becoming overextended overseas past what their frail economies would allow (Britain, France, and the Soviet

Union). The United States may now be falling into the same trap that caused the latter three empires to decline or collapse.

After the buildup for the Korean War in 1950, U.S. forces were not demobilized in the traditional manner when the conflict ended. During the cold war, for the first time in its history, the United States retained a large peacetime military. Even if the argument is made that such a policy was needed during that period (a debatable proposition), the U.S.-Soviet rivalry has now been over for more than a decade. Since the demise of the rival Soviet superpower, the now unconstrained American military juggernaut has been used to police the world.

Beginning during the cold war and continuing to the present, military considerations have eclipsed the economic considerations that were paramount in traditional U.S. foreign policy. During that time, the realist school of foreign policy, which emphasizes military power in international relations, became dominant in the international affairs field and enthralled U.S. policymakers.[112] But even John Mearsheimer, a proponent of that school, admitted that "the rise and fall of great powers over the past two centuries has been due in good part to changes in the distribution of wealth among the major actors in the international system."[113]

Any withdrawal from the overextended U.S. defense perimeter would be seen by the American security bureaucracies as "appeasement" or "decline," when such a retrenchment is likely to do more to preserve American power into the future than any other policy. A vague awareness exists in the security bureaucracies that their ultimate livelihood depends on a strong economy, but getting bigger budgets in the short term usually makes them act contrary to the nation's long-term interests. Only when the American mindset is changed and the economy is reinstated as the number one priority for the nation and the nation's security can U.S. power be preserved for the long haul.

China has learned that lesson from the collapse of the overextended and military-heavy Soviet economy, but the United States has lost sight of the principle. The lesson for U.S. policymakers should not have been that the Reagan military buildup and support for anti-Soviet insurgencies in places like Afghanistan, Nicaragua, and Angola vanquished the Soviet Union. Undoubtedly, Reagan's buildup and "rollback" strategy put added pressure on the Soviet Union, but his policy was only incrementally more activist than all the other Cold Warriors who sat in the White House in the post–World War II era. The Soviet Union collapsed because its nonviable economic system could not support its overextended foreign and military policies. It would have probably collapsed even without the activist policies of Reagan and the others. During the cold war, most of the areas of active competition between the United States and the Soviet Union were backwater areas not worth having, for example, Korea, Vietnam, Cambodia, Laos, Nicaragua, and Chile. The GDP and technology housed in those areas was miniscule.

A more sophisticated U.S. policy during the cold war might have been to let the Soviet Union conquer, occupy, and administer all the backwater areas (exempting the European and East Asian regions of substantial GDP and technology) of its choice in the hope of overextending and exhausting it more quickly. That way the United States could have engineered the demise of its great rival, while at the same time saving the lives of American soldiers and hundreds of billions of dollars in defense expenditures that were wasted during the cold war. The same strategy could be used against any future rising power. Unfortunately, the opposite approach is being taken by the advocates of American empire and the security bureaucracies all too willing to support them. The United States is still pursuing huge and increasing military budgets and expanding global security commitments, even in the absence of a great power rival.

Historians Stephen Ambrose and Douglas Brinkley claim that an overextended United States is exhibiting "American hubris," writing, "The experience of the Cold War gives Americans a sense that they can run the world because their military power is so much greater than that of any other nation or group of nations. But the nation's economic base is smaller than ever, so resources do not support expectations."[114]

The overextension of the American empire can be demonstrated by calculations showing that the United States accounts for nearly 40 percent of the world's military spending but only about 30 percent of global GDP.[115] Some calculations of the U.S. share of world GDP are even lower.[116] The United States has bone-crushing military dominance but no longer has the economic dominance to match, which is usually a symptom of a declining power (for example, the Soviet Union). The Center on Budget and Policy Priorities discovered that broadening the definition of U.S. security spending budgets to include the Defense Department, the Energy Department's nuclear weapons, and the Department of Homeland Security reveals that spending has increased from 3.4 percent of GDP in 2000 to 4.7 percent in 2004.[117] Robert Higgs argues that the security budget is even larger. To the categories of the Center on Budget and Policy Priorities, he adds expenditures for the State Department's foreign assistance programs (which pay off potential adversaries and reward friendly nations for battling perceived threats), veterans' programs to compensate past military service, and interest on the national debt attributable to spending on security. Higgs cogently asserts that when all security-related expenditures are made explicit, the actual national security budget is about twice the stated budget for the Department of Defense.[118] Thus, the real security budget would represent about 7 percent of the U.S. GDP.

As high as U.S. defense spending is, it is lower than that needed to fulfill current U.S. requirements for military forces. Those requirements, in turn, do not measure up to the vast security commitments that the United States has undertaken around the world. (The military commitments today are greater than they were during the 1960s, when the United States had a much greater share of the world's GDP.) Those comparisons are widely known, undisputed, and used by the military services, defense industries, and their advocates in

Congress to attempt to hike the already massive (in absolute terms) U.S. defense budget. A much better alternative, of course, would be to reduce far-flung overseas commitments and force requirements.

Thus, the assertion that 3.4 percent of U.S. GDP[119] is spent on national defense is misleading. Moreover, that number could quickly skyrocket if the United States gets dragged into even small brushfire wars in its role as the world's policeman. Martin Van Creveld has noted that in today's world even the small wars of Vietnam and Afghanistan nearly bankrupted the American and Soviet superpowers, respectively.[120] As noted earlier, the decade-long Vietnam War cost the United States almost $500 billion (in 2004 dollars).[121] More frightening, only the first two years of what promise to be long quagmires in Iraq and Afghanistan have cost the United States $166 billion. To fight such brushfire wars and an amorphous and open-ended "war on terror," the U.S. defense budget (in absolute terms) has skyrocketed in recent years.

The bottom line is that the United States does not have the economic power to police the planet and is already overextended. For all the talk about America being the "lone remaining superpower" or even a "hyperpower," those labels do not apply to the economic sphere—the factor that will ultimately determine a nation's other indices of power. The EU alone has a GDP greater than that of the United States, and Japan, China, India, and Russia are also formidable economic powers. The common wisdom that the United States is a hyperpower is a military-centric view. In economics, the world is more multipolar than in the military sphere.

In the Longer Term, Rivals Could Overtake the United States

U.S. defense spending as a percentage of GDP needs to be compared with equivalent statistics from current economic and potential military rivals. Although 3.4 percent of GDP, the official U.S. total for military spending, may seem manageable, the United States spends huge amounts on defense relative to other nations. U.S. defense spending is equivalent to the expenditures of the next thirteen highest nations combined.[122] And such exorbitant U.S. spending defends allies that are rich enough to defend themselves and are economic rivals.

Allied Nations

Allied nations could plow the amount saved through U.S. subsidization of their defense back into productive sectors of their economies to achieve growth rates that surpass that of the United States. Meanwhile, heavy U.S. defense spending could constrain U.S. growth rates and long-term U.S. power. Over time, even a difference in growth rates of only a percentage point or two can allow other powers to catch up economically to the United States or at least close the gap.[123] A country with long-term productivity growth only one percent less than other nations—for example, imperial Britain—can turn from the global economic leader into a middle economy.[124] Since Spain's formal direct rule of its empire proved more durable than Britain's formal indirect rule (ruling with the help of local elites), the informal empire of the United States—with even looser control than either the Spanish or British empires—may be more fragile than either country. Also, historically, the prosperity and technology of the empire diffuse to other countries and hasten their ascendancy as a threat to imperial goals.[125]

As noted earlier, the countries of the EU already have a total GDP that exceeds the United States, but their combined spending on defense is only about half of what the U.S. spends (see Table 2.1). The EU relies heavily on the United States to subsidize its defenses, while at the same time invoking protectionist measures against U.S. exports to its market. Japan has a GDP of about 40 percent of the United States but spends only about 13 percent as much on defense (about one percent of GDP); it also has a market that is less open to foreign goods than that of the United States. The same situation exists with lesser U.S. allies. So what does the United States get out of that situation? The ability to deter other rich nations from challenging U.S. military power—but only for the short term.

In the long term, such profligate defense spending is a short-sighted strategy to maintain U.S. power. If other nations use the U.S. shield to increase their growth rates and increase their economic power, as post–World War II Japan and Europe have done, then all they have to do is decide to build the military forces to challenge the United States.

G. John Ikenberry argues that the other great powers are now more concerned with the United States discontinuing its provision of security and stability than they are with American desires to rule the globe.[126] This preference for continued U.S. involvement (overstated in the cases of China and Russia) may have something to do with the United States being geographically remote, and therefore less intrinsically threatening, and the sweet deal the allies receive in getting their security heavily subsidized. But if U.S. allies become dissatisfied with the way the United States is managing the world—for example, if more anti-Western catastrophic terrorism is generated from reckless U.S. invasions, such as the one in Iraq—both Japan and the EU already have the economic power to challenge the United States militarily. Even the imperialist Charles Krauthammer admits that President Bush's "axis of evil" approach to the world may be causing hostility in formerly friendly nations and may end the grace period without opposition that the United States has heretofore enjoyed.[127] The U.S. invasion of Iraq has already contributed to enhanced efforts for a common European defense.[128]

Since the GDP of the EU is slightly greater than that of the United States, it could raise military expenditures to equal that of the American defense budget and still spend less as a percentage of GDP. To raise defense expenditures to the level of U.S. military spending, Japan would need to raise the funding of security to 7.5 percent of GDP—certainly a substantial increase over the current level, but well within the capabilities of a modern industrial economy. To think that those nations would not do so because they are fellow democracies is to fall victim to the fallacy of the democratic peace theory discussed earlier.

China, India, or Russia

In the long term, the United States is likely to face economic—and maybe military—competition from China, India, or a resurgent Russia. Of the three nations, China is the most likely to challenge U.S. economic power. In purchasing power parity terms (equalizing the cost differences in various economies), the Chinese GDP is the second largest of any individual state in the world—surpassing Japan and second only to the United States—and growing rapidly. Recent Chinese economic growth rates have dwarfed those of all Western nations. From 1978, the year China began its experiment with capitalism, to 1995, its average annual growth in per capita GDP was 6.04 percent, compared with 1.47 percent in the United States and 1.48 percent in Europe. Since 1995, Chinese growth has been at least that spectacular. Even if China's annual growth rates slow because gains in population attenuate or because the easiest economic reforms have already been made, China probably can still sustain a 5 or 6 percent growth rate.[129] Even if China's growth slumps to those rates per year, it will surpass the United States before 2020 as the world's largest economy (in terms of purchasing power parity).[130]

China has been the center of the world for two of the last three thousand years, the exceptions being the period of the Roman empire and the last six hundred years of dominance by the Spanish, British, and American empires.[131] Now China has a huge population, rapid growth and prudent restraint in relations with its neighbors (with the possible exception of Taiwan) and in military spending. Defense expenditure is the lowest of four major priorities behind industry, science, and agriculture and began increasing significantly after the United States bombed Serbia during the war over Kosovo. Thus, China has the best chance of any non-U.S. ally of challenging U.S. economic and military power.

The relatively unentangled Chinese have taken a lesson from the demise of the Soviet Union. They have realized that becoming overextended in foreign and military policy, with excessive commitments and bloated military spending, is a recipe for collapse. Although there are disputes about how much China spends on defense, even with recent increases, the authoritative *Military Balance* picked a midrange number of $51 billion for 2002.[132] That relatively low number (compared to the United States at about $400 billion) indicates that rapid economic growth remains China's highest priority. Perhaps the thoroughly entangled United States, which has retained outdated cold war alliances, overseas military deployments, and high levels of defense spending, should learn the same lesson.

Over the long haul, India or a resurgent Russia could also rise to contest U.S. power. Both have large populations and have undertaken some economic reforms. In the long term, despite Russia's possession of thousands of nuclear warheads, India may be more likely to become a potential competitor of the United States. Although the Indian economy still needs much reform, its per capita growth rate from 1978 to 1995 was 2.53 percent, which substantially exceeded the figures for the United States and Europe cited above.[133] Next to China, India is currently experiencing the fastest annual economic growth rate in the world—almost seven percent.[134]

Can Potential Rivals Overcome Their Limitations?

Of course, Japan, the EU, China, India, and Russia all have current limitations that probably keep them from challenging the United States in the near term. Despite heavy government involvement in the U.S. economy, the economies of all of those other nations or group of nations face even greater government interference, thus slowing their potential rate of growth.

In Asia, though, the economic crisis of the late 1990s has helped to reduce the cronyism, protectionism, and excessive government regulation that hampered economic progress in the past. The crisis caused a greater reliance on markets, democracy, the rule of law, and foreign financial institutions, which are better than the corrupt and creaky Asian ones. Nicholas Kristof, a columnist for the *New York Times* and an expert on Asia, predicts that "partly because of this forced restructuring Asia is likely to wrench economic, diplomatic, and military power from the West over the coming decades." Kristof bases this belief on a virtual unanimity of economic forecasts that show Asia dramatically increasing its share of world GDP; for example, the World Bank predicts a gain from 33 percent in 1998 to 55 to 60 percent by 2025. Asia is also increasing its population from 60 percent to two-thirds of the world total by midcentury (North America comprises only five percent of the world's people). If those predictions were to hold true, Asia would again be much richer and more advanced than Europe, as it was for the great majority of last few thousand years. During most of that period, Asia accounted for at least two-thirds of the world's GDP.

In addition to a rapidly growing China, the future may also see economic growth accelerating in India, a potential South Asian powerhouse. India has reduced protectionism, bureaucracy, and barriers to foreign investment and has reformed its banking sector. As India opens its markets, it looks increasingly like East Asia did in the past. The Indian economy will benefit from a high savings rate and a young, working-age population that will grow twice as fast as the population of dependents. (China and Europe will have the problem of aging populations.) Although uncertainty exists in projections of future growth rates, some projections show that by the middle of this century both China and India will have larger economies than the United States.[135]

Most of America's potential future competitors, however, also face inefficiencies in defense spending. In the EU, defense spending as a percentage of GDP is low, and its national militaries and defense industries have redundant and incompatible capabilities. China, India, and Russia all need to modernize and downsize large, obsolescent forces. Japan would need to spend more on defense and add offensive power projection capabilities to its already modern, defensively oriented force.

Of course, things could change rapidly. Any of those potential competitors could further enhance their economic power by initiating wholesale economic deregulation or augment their military power by accelerating and making more efficient their defense spending. The United States, like many past empires, believes that assertive international behavior (such as U.S. interventions in Kosovo and Iraq) will attract allies and inhibit balancers—that is, lead to "bandwagoning." In reality, that belief contravenes the well-established principle in international affairs of countries balancing against a state that is too strong.[136] For example, China is increasing its defense spending (partly in response to the U.S. bombing of Serbia in 1999), and the Europeans are creating their own rapid reaction force, have signed an agreement for mutual assistance in case of attack, and are setting up a cell to plan military operations independent of the United States (all in reaction to the U.S. invasion of Iraq). Those European efforts could be the germ of a future independent European military force.

Proponents of American empire, both neoconservatives and liberal interventionists, exhibit excessive confidence that the United States can indefinitely stay on top by policing all regions of the world, protecting allies to keep them from augmenting their own military forces to compete with the United States and deterring awestruck enemies from doing the same. Other empires—such as the Roman, British, Nazi, and Soviet—had visions of perpetual glory and dominance, only to be consigned to the dustbin of history by becoming overextended in entanglements and wars that either destroyed them or sapped their strength. The same fate could befall the United States if it does not abandon its costly and potentially entangling empire and retract its defense perimeter to more sustainable dimensions. In other words, instead of following those overextended empires, the United States should take its cues from the long-lived Byzantine empire.

In the twentieth century, nine empires—the Ottoman, Austro-Hungarian, French, Dutch, British, Nazi, Imperial Japanese, Soviet, and Chinese—came tumbling down because of imperial overstretch, a lack of reform, and economic rigidity that made them susceptible to exhaustion by wars, many of which they caused. The same is likely to happen to the United States if it doesn't willingly abandon its empire.[137] Nicholas Kristof argues that U.S. power has in fact been declining for decades: "To Americans, proud and content as they dominate the globe, United States leadership in everything from nuclear weapons to Internet sites may seem so overwhelming that it is difficult to imagine Asia chipping away at this preeminence—although of course that is precisely what has already happened for more than half a century. America has been in relative decline, measured by its share of GDP or even by its share of global nuclear weapons, since 1945."[138]

In addition to demise by overextension—either running into opposition from powerful states or becoming bankrupt from excessive commitments or wars—empires can also corrode from within. Moreover, the first effect can cause the second. For example, at the height of the Roman empire during the reign of Marcus Aurelius, wars occurred on its frontiers. Such conflicts led to the rise of the massive provincial armies with their top generals competing for the office of Roman emperor, resulting in the total militarization of the empire and the establishment of a police state. Thus, the treasury was drained, and the competing regions foreshadowed the division of the empire. Distant frontiers began to be overrun by "barbarians." Threats to the frontier led to further militarization and civil wars.[139] Similarly, the U.S. empire is undermining the pillars of American society.

WAR AND EMPIRE DISTORT THE CONSTITUTION

Conservatives pride themselves in trying to restore the role of government to what the founders had intended in the U.S. Constitution. Yet the Constitution makes no mention of attacking countries, occupying them, and governing their populations—whether unilaterally (as in the case of Iraq) or with American power veiled with a multilateral fig leaf (as in Somalia, Bosnia, and Kosovo)—with no representation in the U.S. Congress. U.S. experience with British colonial rule and the sentiments expressed in the Declaration of Independence should remind us of the problems of foreign rule without representation.

Many conservatives support the U.S. empire (and the profligate wars needed to maintain it), despite the fact that it continues to erode the checks and balances contained in the Constitution, the foundation of American self-government. President George Washington best summarized that problem in his 1796 Farewell Address: "Overgrown military establishments are under any form of government inauspicious to liberty, and are to be regarded as particularly hostile to Republican liberty."[140]

War and the Rise of the Imperial Presidency

During the peaceful decades between the end of the Civil War in 1865 and the Spanish-American War in 1898, the Congress was dominant over the executive branch, just as the founders had intended. But as the nation went through the Spanish-American War, World War I, the Great Depression, and World War II, the presidency became much stronger. Because the nation was on a permanent war footing during the ensuing cold war and the perception was that decisions needed to be made quickly, presidential power ballooned into a full-blown imperial presidency. One leader, not a legislature with hundreds of members and opinions, best executes wars and the preparation for them. Thus, in wartime, power flows to the president. When the president handles the war badly, some power can revert back to the legislature (for example, during the 1970s after the disaster in Vietnam). But then new wars arise—many caused by the government's own policies—leading to further expansion of executive power. So the trend over time has been the concentration of authority in a powerful chief executive, a development that the founders would have found alarming.

The founders' position on executive power was nicely summed up by John Adams, the second president of the United States: "Ambition is one of the more ungovernable passions of the human heart. The love of power is insatiable and uncontrollable. . . . There is danger from all men. The only maxim of a free government ought to be to trust no man living with power to endanger the public liberty."[141]

James Madison, the father of the U.S. Constitution, commented on why war contributed to the expansion of executive power and why that had to be restrained by the extensive congressional war powers:

> War is in fact the true nurse of executive aggrandizement. In war, a physical force is to be created; and it is the executive will which is to direct it. In war, the public treasuries are to be unlocked; and it is the executive hand which is to dispense them. In war, the honors and emoluments of office are to be multiplied; and it is the executive patronage under which they are to be enjoyed; and it is the executive brow they are to encircle. The strongest passions and most dangerous weaknesses of the human breast; ambition, avarice, vanity, the honorable or venal love of fame, are all in conspiracy against the desire and duty of peace.[142]

At the Constitutional Convention, Madison explained why such wartime executive ambition is a threat to liberty at home: "Constant apprehension of War has the . . . tendency to render the head too large for the body. A standing military force, with an overgrown Executive will not long be safe companions to liberty. The means of defense agst. Foreign danger, have been always the instruments of tyranny at home."[143]

With European monarchs of the day in mind, the founders designed the American system of checks and balances to keep the leader from conducting wars of aggrandizement at the expense—in blood and treasure—of the citizens. Although the founders gave the president the power to command the armed forces (and the militia when it is called to serve the federal government), they clearly vested most of the war powers with Congress. Yet in examining the events leading up to wars after World War II, that congressional preeminence is not apparent. During the post–World War II period, Congress has forfeited those powers or constrained itself in exercising them.

The U.S. Constitution gives Congress the following major war powers:

- to provide for the common defense,
- to declare war and to grant letters of marque and reprisal (which approve situations short of all-out war),
- to raise and support armies and fund them,
- to provide and maintain a navy,
- to regulate the land and naval forces,
- to provide for calling forth the militia to execute federal laws, suppress insurrections, and repel invasions,
- and to provide for organizing, arming, and disciplining the militia and governing the parts of it employed by the federal government.

Debates at the Constitutional Convention in 1787 clearly indicate that the founders intended that the president have a right to take defensive action if the country was under imminent or actual threat of attack. Even then, however, the founders felt that the Congress should meet to declare a state of war at the earliest possible time. For offensive warfare (a designation that fits all major wars in U.S. history except the War of 1812 and World War II), the founders intended that a declaration of war would be needed before hostilities began. Unfortunately, starting with the Korean War during the first years of the cold war, this vital safeguard against presidential aggrandizement of power went out of fashion. No congressional declaration of war has been issued since World War II. The executive branch has spent more than fifty years usurping Congress's war powers. As a result, the common belief now among policymakers, legislators, and the media is that the president, as commander in chief, can take the country to war without congressional approval.

Demonstrating the erosion of the congressional war power subsequent to World War II, presidents have conducted many U.S. military actions without getting even a congressional resolution of support (a lesser means of approval than a formal declaration of war). Before the first Gulf War, President George H.W. Bush asked the Congress for a resolution approving the conflict. He claimed, however, that he had all the authority needed to make war, even without such approval, and that he was only seeking it as a courtesy. President Clinton did not see fit to get Congressional approval for this bombing of Serbia and Kosovo or his threatened intervention of Haiti.

Presidents have also taken it upon themselves to wage secret paramilitary wars via the CIA and military Special Forces—in many instances without getting approval of the full Congress. For example, several presidents carried out paramilitary action in Tibet against communist China for twenty years.[144] Secret or overt, war is still war. In fact, for a republic, secret war without public or full congressional approval may be the most threatening to the liberties of the people. Yet some conservatives, such as Robert Kaplan, openly advocate that the U.S. empire be even more evasive of constitutional checks and balances than it already is: "Covert means are more discreet and cheaper than declared war and large-scale mobilization. . . . There will be less and less time for democratic consultation, whether with Congress or with the UN."[145] But after the end of the cold war, and even during that era, what threat is (was) so menacing that the republic needs to be destroyed in order to save it?

Even Congress's all-important power of the purse is rarely used to rein in executive branch warfare. Obviously, if funding for a military operation is cut off, the armed intervention has to cease. Once in a great while, Congress gets fed up with an unpopular military adventure and shuts off the funding, as in the Vietnam War. Even when Congress cuts off funding for an imperial foray, the executive branch sometimes ignores it. For example, in the Iran-Contra affair, Oliver North circumvented a congressional ban on funding to the Nicaraguan Contras by selling arms to the state sponsors of terrorism in Iran and using the proceeds to finance the Contras. (This flouting of the congressional power of the purse cuts to the core of the American constitutional system of checks and balances, and was therefore probably a more severe abuse of presidential power than Watergate.) In most cases, however, Congress comes up with the cash—sometimes after grumbling about the costs or holding extensive hearings to register its displeasure.

Members of Congress Have No Incentive to Rein in Presidential Warmaking

Why is Congress so shy about reasserting its constitutional authority to declare war or to disapprove of certain military interventions by refusing to fund them? At the time that the Constitution was drafted, the founders believed that a system of checks and balances would work because the president would assert his prerogatives, and members of Congress would push back by defending that institution's powers. Very few members of Congress, however, stand up for institutional prerogatives. Instead, the members are more concerned about their own reelection. They know that when the president sends American troops into battle—whether the reason is good or not—the public usually, at least initially, rallies to support his decision. They also know that the initial groundswell of such "patriotism" among the public will allow the president to use his office as a powerful "bully pulpit" to paint anyone opposing the war, or even asking questions about it, as unpatriotic. If the conflict goes well, the president will remind voters in the next election of who opposed the war. For example, after the crushing U.S. victory against Iraq in the first Gulf War in 1991, those members of Congress who had opposed going to war had the unenviable position of trying to defend their stance in the next election. Antiwar members had that public relations problem despite the fact that General Colin Powell, the Bush I administration's Chairman of the Joint Chiefs of Staff, had expressed in internal administration debates before the conflict a reluctance to conduct the military action.

With that unpleasant experience in mind, many fewer members opposed George W. Bush's invasion of Iraq in 2003, even though much information in the public domain prior to the conflict called into question Saddam Hussein's alleged links to the September 11 attackers and the Bush administration's characterization of Iraq as an imminent threat that required a preemptive war. Instead of challenging a president still basking in high poll numbers from the September 11 attacks, members of Congress lay in the weeds waiting for an opening. When the American occupation of Iraq turned into chaos, congressional critics saw their chance and began to attack not only the occupation but also the need for the war itself.

Although better late than never, such postintervention criticisms of unnecessary wars—that is, Congress pointing its finger to the wind before openly opposing the president—do not comport well with Congress's constitutional responsibilities to act as a check against the locomotive of presidential warfare. The cold war thus led to a perversion of the U.S. Constitution (which continues to this day) that has allowed the president to imitate the kings of eighteenth-century Europe. He can conduct war for his or the government's purposes without the proper consent of the representatives of the people, imposing costs in blood and treasure on those very citizens. Some of the lost treasure is in the form of international commerce forgone because of the war.

The next chapter is directed mainly toward those on the left, but also has relevance to some on the right who are defenders of civil liberties. Among other issues, the chapter examines how overseas military and covert action carried out to maintain the American empire can subvert republican government at home.

4

Why Liberals Should Be Against Empire

Today, more liberals than conservatives oppose the American empire. Those liberals are the same new (or "McGovernite") left that protested U.S. imperial policing in Vietnam. The new left astutely realizes that assigning the United States the role of being the world's policeman in conflict-prone areas will only legitimate the use of American imperial power. For example, author Gore Vidal perceptively observed, "We have neither the money nor the brains to monitor every country on earth."[1] But the old left, Wilsonian to the core, still has to be convinced.

Bill Clinton was a Wilsonian who believed in making the world more like the United States by enlarging the universe of nations with democratic governance and free markets and by conducting interventions for ostensibly "humanitarian" purposes—all at gunpoint. Clinton sold the policy of enlarging the number of free market democracies in the world with the slogan "engagement and enlargement," in which "engagement" was many times a euphemism for the use of American military power. Clinton's Secretary of State, Madeleine Albright, termed this liberal version of imperialism "assertive multilateralism." This policy is strangely similar to that of President George W. Bush, who stated, "The United States will use this moment of opportunity to extend the benefits of freedom across the globe. We will actively work to bring the hope of democracy, development, free markets, and free trade to every corner of the world."[2] Same policy, different party.

LEFT-WING AND RIGHT-WING WILSONIANISM BOTH EQUAL EMPIRE

Many liberals think that George W. Bush has flexed U.S. military muscle too much by invading Iraq and taking out its government. But in terms of the numbers of military interventions (not necessarily the scale of such actions), Bill Clinton is the modern-day champion. He intervened in Somalia, Haiti, Bosnia, and Kosovo, bombed Iraq, and fired cruise missiles at Afghanistan and Sudan.

For those liberals who believe that George W. Bush's foreign policy is different in kind rather than degree from that of Bill Clinton, David North, chair of the editorial board of the World Socialist Website, notes: "The election of Bill Clinton did not produce any significant change in the increasingly aggressive attitude of American military planners. Under the slogan, 'Shaping the World Through Engagement,' the 1990s saw the emergence of a political consensus within both the Democratic and Republican parties that saw military power as the principal means by which the United States would secure long-term global dominance."[3]

Chalmers Johnson, a liberal foreign policy scholar, notes that the left and right strands of American imperialism, which have now converged, both originated at the turn of the last century.

> With Woodrow Wilson, the intellectual foundations of American imperialism were set in place. Theodore Roosevelt and Elihu Root had represented a European-derived, militaristic vision of imperialism backed by nothing more substantial than the notion that the manifest destiny of the United States was to govern racially inferior Latin Americans and East Asians. Wilson laid over that his own hyperidealistic, sentimental, and ahistorical idea that what should be sought was a world democracy based on the American example and led by the United States. It was a political project no less ambitious and no less passionately held than the vision of world Communism launched at almost the same time by the leaders of the Bolshevik Revolution. As international-relations critic

> William Pfaff puts it, "[The United States was] still in the intellectual thrall of the megalomaniacal and self-righteous clergyman-president who gave to the American nation the blasphemous conviction that it, like he himself, had been created by God 'to show the way to the nations of the world how they shall walk in the paths of liberty.'"[4]

These two slightly varying strands of left and right Wilsonianism have come to dominate U.S. foreign policy in the post–World War II world. During and after the cold war, despite all of the harsh rhetoric between the two parties for electoral purposes, they both peddle slightly differing versions of military interventionism to retain U.S. worldwide preeminence.

Johnson and Andrew Bacevich have both noted the rise of militarism in the United States and the desire for military supremacy. Neither party now has a major antimilitary faction. According to Bacevich, the military fervor contrasts greatly with the suspicion of militarism at the nation's founding and continuing through World War II. In this more traditional U.S. view, the Americans were different from Europe in their disapproval of war, of costly military competition, and of standing armies that could threaten liberty.[5] Yet since World War II, the aberration from the customary antimilitarism has become the norm.

Although many Wilsonian liberals would like to forget the heritage of their viewpoint, Wilsonianism preceded President Wilson and was rooted in the desire of Christian missionaries to save "savage and inferior peoples" and vanquish "evildoers." (Similarly, the "Just War Doctrine" began much earlier with a desire to elevate the wars of Christian kings to a higher moral plane.[6]) For example, before Wilson ever took office, the "progressive" movement—originating from a rising tide of Protestantism—ostensibly fought the Spanish-American War in 1898 to stop the Spaniards from committing atrocities against Cuban rebels but ended up brutalizing a Philippine insurgency after the United States took the Philippines from Spain.[7] Historian Paul Johnson writes that for the Philippines, U.S. moral imperialism was rationalized by the perceived "white man's burden" (Rudyard Kipling's phrase) of modern civilized nations to bring religion to "lesser breeds" (also Kipling), much like the Spanish and Portuguese justifications for their empires in the new world. The consensus now is that the do-gooder missionaries and colonial technocrats did great harm to Cuba, Guam, Panama, Puerto Rico, and the Philippines during America's first imperial foray. In Puerto Rico, for example, the United States displaced indigenous farmers with U.S.-owned sugar plantations.

And modern Wilsonianism is even more ambitious than Wilson's original goal. Wilson wanted to make the world safe for democracy. Today's Wilsonians want to make the whole world democratic.[8]

Recently, many Wilsonian liberals have criticized the Bush II administration for running an aggressive foreign policy, engaging in "preemptive" (really preventative) attack, ousting leaders from sovereign nations, and promoting empire-building. Yet they are willing to excuse the Clinton administration for the same imperial policies. In fact, the United States has been engaged in profligate preventative worldwide military deployments, alliances, and interventions—in short, empire-building—since the cold war began.

International Institutions Veil, Rather than Constrain, U.S. Power

The old left is not protesting the post–World War II American empire as much as it is protesting the perceived arrogance with which the more unilateralist Bush II administration is going about preserving and expanding it. The liberal Wilsonian penchant for promoting international organizations and multilateralism causes Wilsonians to be angry when the Bush II administration foreign policy blatantly marginalizes both. The Bush II administration received widespread criticism among liberals for sidestepping the United Nations in its march toward the invasion of Iraq. But in 1999, when the United Nations refused to endorse Bill Clinton's attack on Serbia over Kosovo, he merely used another multilateral organization, the U.S.-dominated NATO alliance, as a fig leaf and did it anyway. In fact, unlike Bush II in the second Iraq war, Clinton failed even to get congressional approval for the bombing of Serbia and Kosovo or the threatening of Haiti with invasion. But the congressional okay for the exercise of U.S. military power seems to be less important to Wilsonian liberals than the approval of international organizations.

Unlike the formal imperialism of the British empire, the United States uses the United Nations, World Bank, International Monetary Fund, and other international bodies to legitimize imperial interventions into the political and economic systems of developing nations. Rather than using such institutions to constrain U.S. power, Wilsonian liberals astutely use them to veil it. For example, Robert Cooper, director general for external affairs at the European Union and senior advisor to Prime Minister Tony Blair of Britain, advocates a "new kind of imperialism" in which Western states, acting under the guidance of the United Nations, take responsibility for zones in conflict.[9] But the veiled nature of this liberal version of imperialism is exposed: on security issues, the United Nations does the bidding of the five great powers that are permanent members of the UN Security Council. Political scientist John Mearsheimer best sums up the reality of the politics of international institutions, writing that "what's most impressive about international institutions is how little independent effect they seem to have on great power behavior."[10]

U.S. Foreign Policy Has Been Imperial under Many U.S. Post–World War II Presidents

Clinton's foreign policy, although much the same as Bush II's, provoked far fewer protests, because unlike Bush, he was usually astute enough to get some sort of multilateral approval or to adopt Wilsonian rhetoric to disguise what amounted to an effectively unilateral and imperial policing action. The Clinton administration's euphemistic "engagement and enlargement" policy was a much more subtle echo of the controversial Bush I administration's plan, drafted in 1992 by then-Undersecretary of Defense Paul Wolfowitz, to prevent the rise of any rival power center. That neoconservative "in-your-face" muscle flexing was as unpopular then as it is now, in an even more blatant form, during the Bush II administration. Clinton's more veiled "mailed fist" got much less opposition but was essentially the same policy. Joseph Nye, an Assistant Secretary of Defense for Clinton and advocate of "multilateral" military interventions, revealed his administration's covert neoimperial agenda when he praised the British empire: "The U.S. can learn a . . . useful lesson from the period when Britain held primacy among the global powers."[11]

Although the Bush II administration ousted the government of a sovereign country—that is, Iraq—by an invasion, the Clinton administration threatened to invade Haiti to successfully do the same thing. Clinton got far less domestic dissent over Haiti than Bush II did over Iraq because he justified the threatening deployment of troops near Haiti with the Wilsonian rhetoric of restoring Bertrand Aristide, the elected president who was deposed by the Haitian military. In reality, Clinton ousted the Cedras military dictatorship in Haiti to staunch the flow of poor Haitian refugees that were streaming to the United States. In contrast, Bush II relied mainly on very thin evidence that Iraq's nuclear, biological, and chemical programs were an imminent threat to the United States and the false implication that Saddam Hussein had some role in the September 11 attacks. The Wilsonian arguments that the invasion was needed to end Saddam's perpetration of human rights violations and to democratize the Middle East were only emphasized after the war when the United States failed to find the "superweapons."

Bush's less unilateralist father also received less domestic dissent than his son for his interventionist foreign policy because he either employed Wilsonian rhetoric or used multilateral fig leaves to cover effectively unilateral military actions. Although American policymakers of both parties often make foreign policy for reasons of realpolitik, they usually justify it by the Wilsonian rhetoric of saving a group of people or humankind from some nefarious end. Such rationale appeals to the idealism in American culture.

Like Clinton and Bush II, Bush I ousted the leader of a sovereign nation, Manuel Noriega of Panama, on shaky security grounds. In order to appeal to the moral values of the American public, Bush I emphasized that Noriega was a corrupt, drug-running thug. Strangely, other leaders in Latin America at the time fit that same description. And like Clinton, Bush I used a multilateral coalition—with the vast bulk of the military muscle provided by the United States—as a fig leaf to cloak an American attack on a sovereign nation to roll back its military aggression against a neighboring country. Even by the standards of liberal Wilsonian interventionists, Bush I's 1991 attack to remove Saddam Hussein's brutal military occupation from Kuwait could be regarded as less questionable than Clinton's 1999 bombing of Serbia and Kosovo over Serb human rights violations in Kosovo. Although Clinton had nominal help from NATO allies, he failed, like Bush II, to get the UN Security Council resolution of approval that Bush I enjoyed, but attacked anyway. Furthermore, Clinton was forcing the Serbs to abandon part of their sovereign territory rather than rolling back an invading army from occupied territory. Finally, the Bush I administration obtained at least some sort of congressional authorization for its offensive against Iraq, whereas the Clinton administration failed to do so for its aerial bombardment of the Serbs.

Bush II has also been criticized for his policy of "preemptively"—more accurately preventatively—attacking sovereign nations (for example, the invasion of Iraq), but many recent presidents pursued preemptive and preventative threats and attacks. For example, although the Eisenhower administration's nuclear doctrine in the 1950s was called "massive retaliation," evidence indicates that after the Soviets developed a small nuclear arsenal, U.S. policy likely was to preemptively attack nuclear-armed Soviet bombers before they took off during any crisis. When the Reagan administration bombed Libya in 1986, the government's justification was "self-defense against future attack"[12]—a preposterous charge, since Reagan provoked Moammar Qaddafi by ordering U.S. naval forces to enter Libyan-claimed waters and air space. The conventional wisdom is that Reagan's bombing of Libya in 1986 was in retaliation for Libya's bombing of a German nightclub frequented by U.S. military personnel. But the historical record shows that Reagan's provocations against Libya began in 1981, shortly after his presidency commenced. Reagan provoked Qaddafi because he felt that the Libyan leader was a pawn of the Soviet Union. In response, Qaddafi, who had been sponsoring terrorist attacks against European targets, began to attack American targets. A tit-for-tat battle between the United States and Libya then ensued.[13]

Also, Bush I invaded Panama without a legitimate self-defense rationale and used military force to compel Iraqi withdrawal from Kuwait and apparently to preempt any possible Iraqi invasion of Saudi Arabia (although evidence indicates that such a threat was very unlikely). In 1994, Clinton threatened preventative war with North Korea unless it froze its nuclear program. In 1998, he launched cruise missile attacks against a Sudanese factory and terrorist training camps in Afghanistan—allegedly to preempt future attacks by al Qaeda. (Since none of the targets hit would have preempted al Qaeda cells already in the field poised for another attack, those strikes were really to prevent longer-term threats.) Also in 1998, Clinton launched air strikes against Iraqi unconventional weapons facilities to prevent Iraq's eventual acquisition of such weapons and punish it for obstructing the work of international arms inspectors. In 1999, Clinton bombed Serbia and Kosovo ostensibly to prevent the Serbs from escalating their ethnic cleansing of the Kosovar Albanians, but the attack had the opposite effect.

All this is not to defend Bush II's empire-building but to note that both right-wing (Bush I) and left-wing (Clinton) Wilsonians used mulitlateralism and idealistic rhetoric to hide the same underlying policies of empire. Bush II's military actions are not a quantum leap in aggressiveness above his predecessors' military interventions. Rather, Bush II's major problem is the public perception that his policy is much more aggressive. Such a perception exists because his foreign policy is more unilateral and less embellished with the Wilsonian veneer. After large-scale public protests over the invasion and occupation of Iraq, maybe the Bush II administration will learn that Americans like to avoid being confronted with their empire directly and prefer it sheathed in more idealistic garb. Perhaps that lesson will lead the administration and future administrations to ensure that Wilsonian justifications for future military action are always developed.

Unfortunately, many liberals (particularly the Wilsonian left in the U.S. foreign policy establishment) supported taking out the despotic Saddam, but objected to Bush II thumbing his nose at the United Nations. Many would like to restrain the unilateral use of American power by enhancing a UN-centered system of world security,[14] but overlook the reality that the United States often gives the UN the choice either of providing a cover for U.S. imperial muscle flexing or of becoming irrelevant as a result of a reduction in the superpower's enthusiasm for the organization. So in foreign policy circles, where interventionists dominate, the debate on the invasion of Iraq came down to whether to do it with or without multilateral blessing, rather than the more crucial question of whether to do it all. On the streets, it was a different story. Some on the McGovernite new left questioned the need for attacking Iraq at all, as illustrated by actress Susan Sarandon's provocative but unanswered question, "What has Iraq ever done to us?"

And some on the left are torn over or are inconsistent about U.S. military interventions overseas. Some liberals—most notably Democratic presidential candidate Howard Dean—opposed the American removal of a despotic leader of a sovereign Iraq but a few months later supported a never-implemented U.S. military intervention to oust the thuggish Charles Taylor from a sovereign Liberia. In 2004, some liberals also supported a Bush administration intervention to stabilize Haiti. Many liberals often support military interventions portrayed as defending human rights or humanitarian ends, but those rationales were used as at least one of the justifications for invading Iraq and have been used many times by past presidents to justify questionable military actions.

Wilsonians of Both Left and Right Are Aggressive

Neoconservative "hard" Wilsonians and old-left "soft" Wilsonians both support military interventions overseas in the crusade for the spread of democracy and free markets. Thus, the two camps each implicitly support the American empire. In the Christian crusader tradition that is their legacy, they both maintain that the world will fall apart without intrusive American management—a dubious historical claim, since the United States was not in existence for most of recorded human history. The following example of such reasoning comes from the neoconservative Robert Kaplan, but could have been written by the Wilsonian liberals: "By sustaining ourselves first, we will be able to do the world the most good. Some two hundred countries, plus thousands of nongovernmental organizations, represent a chaos of interests. Without the organizing force of a great and self-interested liberal power, they are unable to advance the interests of humanity as a whole."[15] Of course, in reality, military actions are usually undertaken for the benefit of the "self-interested liberal power" and rhetorically justified as "advancing the interests of humanity as a whole."

The left and right Wilsonian condescension toward other countries and peoples—the assumption that they need to be "saved" by an enlightened superpower—recalls what Senator Albert Beveridge of Indiana said in 1900 after the Spanish-American War about U.S imperial expansion: "He [God] has given us the spirit of progress to overwhelm the forces of reaction throughout the earth. He has made us adepts [sic] in government that we may administer government among savage and senile peoples. . . . And of all our race He has marked the American people as His chosen nation to finally lead in the regeneration of the world."[16]

Both camps have no problem attacking sovereign countries without provocation for often bogus "humanitarian" ends, thereby flouting an important international norm, now enshrined in the UN charter, against violating the sovereignty of other nations except in self-defense. That norm has contributed to global stability since its original inception in the Treaty of Westphalia in 1648. The two camps differ only on whether U.S. military interventions should be unilateral (the preference of neoconservatives) or carried out with a multilateral veneer in which the superpower pretends to allow the international community some say in the matter (the choice of the old left).

Andrew Bacevich best summed up the post–World War II continuity in U.S. foreign policy, even as power has been transferred between American political parties.

> Like Eisenhower in 1953, George W. Bush in 2001 by and large embraced the policies of his predecessor. As in 1953, Republicans vigorously denied that such was the case, and Democrats found it expedient to minimize similarities. But those similarities far outweighed the differences. As a result, although the rhetoric changed, the overarching grand strategy—aimed at creating an open and integrated international order dominated by the United States—emerged from the transfer of power intact. This was the case prior to September 11, 2001. And it continued to be the case after that date.[17]

As Bacevich implies, the two key tenets of the U.S. foreign policy consensus since the Truman administration have been (1) ensuring an open world commercial order and (2) doing so with U.S. military supremacy. Wilsonian liberals rhetorically cloak support for overseas military interventions more in terms of serving "humanitarian" ends than neoconservatives do. But a closer historical examination of humanitarian interventions—even under Democratic administrations—indicates that such rhetoric usually veils imperial motives.

HUMANITARIAN INTERVENTIONS ARE OFTEN NOT GENUINE OR EFFECTIVE

Many liberals questioned Bush II's invasion of Iraq but supported Clinton's wars in Somalia, Bosnia, Haiti, and Kosovo. Many conservatives exhibited diametrically opposed opinions. Such skepticism of the other side's wars may be pure politics—that is, reluctance to support the wars of an ideologically incompatible president and skittishness about criticizing the wars of a more "friendly" president—or it may be a result of suspicions about the motives of an "unfriendly" leader. Although the rationales for wars by conservative presidents are equally suspect, this chapter is designed to convince liberals that the motives even of leaders considered friendly should be questioned when war is afoot. The chapter also tries to convince liberals that the U.S. government's attempts to defend human rights or achieve humanitarian ends using military means usually are not sincere or effective, and are often counterproductive.

As Chalmers Johnson, a liberal foreign policy scholar, perceptively notes: "The United States has been inching toward imperialism and militarism for many years. Our leaders, disguising the direction they were taking, cloaked their foreign policies in euphemisms such as 'lone superpower,' 'indispensable nation,' 'reluctant sheriff,' 'humanitarian intervention,' and 'globalization.'"[18] This chapter tries to unmask the real motives behind the interventions of recent U.S. administrations, including those of the Clinton administration.

Hidden Motives in "Humanitarian" Wars

Because the American public is idealistic, politicians often justify wars conducted for ulterior motives on the basis of achieving moral ends. For example, the Spanish-American War was justified on the grounds of freeing Cubans from Spanish oppression. Yet Cuba, the Philippines, and Puerto Rico did not achieve genuine independence after the war. In fact, in Puerto Rico, the United States replaced an autonomous, elected government with press censorship and military rule. And after defeating the Spanish in the Philippines, the United States conducted a brutal war against Philippine insurgents that rivaled or exceeded the original brutality of the Spanish against the Cubans. The U.S. government also ran a neomercantilist policy, whereby Philippine and Cuban resources were essentially stolen using military means.

During the cold war, both Democratic and Republican presidents, using the veneer of fighting communism in part as a disguise, preserved the American empire by supporting petty tyrants in backwater regions of the world.[19] For example, the United States supported Ferdinand Marcos in the Philippines, General Suharto in Indonesia, Chiang Kai-Shek in Taiwan, and despotic rulers in South Korea, South Vietnam, Cambodia, and many other countries. In fact, despite U.S. rhetoric about spreading democracy, in Iran and Guatemala the CIA sponsored coups against democratically elected leaders whose policies did not favor U.S. corporations.[20] Similarly, in Indonesia and post–World War II Italy, the U.S. government intervened because those governments were too democratic, allowing participation by parties on the left.[21] In Indonesia, the forces of General Suharto, whom the United States helped into power in 1965, killed hundreds of thousands of people—with the U.S. embassy providing lists of whom to execute.[22] In Argentina, during the 1970s, newly released records indicate that the White House encouraged the right-wing autocratic government to accelerate its human rights violations.[23]

In reality, both Democratic and Republican presidents have often supported political and economic reforms only in unfriendly, closed countries and not in more congenial authoritarian states. In the post–cold war world, the veneer has changed from one of fighting communism to one of promoting humanitarian ends, democracy, and free markets, but the underlying realpolitik is the same. There is no reason to think that the U.S. security bureaucracies—whether under Democratic or Republican administrations—would alter their ruthless pursuit of what they have deemed to be "U.S.

vital interests" overseas. With the Soviet enemy gone, other moral justifications for U.S. imperial policies have had to be found. According to liberal Chalmers Johnson, the term *empire* is deliberately avoided:

"If empire is mentioned at all, it is in terms of American soldiers liberating Afghan women from Islamic fundamentalists, or helping victims of a natural disaster in the Philippines, or protecting Bosnians, Kosovars, or Iraqi Kurds (but not Rwandans, Turkish Kurds, or Palestinians) from campaigns of 'ethnic cleansing.'" But Johnson argues that self-declarations of humanitarian intervention like those of the United States in Somalia or Serbia are merely veiled imperialism: "Positing a new, unilateral 'responsibility to protect' that is to be the sole responsibility of the world's last great power and then assuming it only when that superpower finds it convenient to do so may actually worsen relations among states."[24]

Bill Clinton used the humanitarian rationale for interventions in Haiti, Bosnia, Kosovo, and Somalia. In the first three instances, that rationale was dubious; the fourth episode was an abysmal failure. Despite the idealistic rhetoric often used to justify U.S. military actions, in the last hundred years, the only truly humanitarian mission in which American forces have died was that of Somalia in 1992 and 1993.[25]

As noted earlier, Americans are idealistic by nature (probably more so than the people of many other nations) and thus prefer to have moral justifications for what the U.S. government does overseas. So if presidents are smart, they will drape policy made for reasons of realpolitik in idealistic rhetoric. Bill Clinton was smart.

Haiti

In 1994, a flood of poor Haitian refugees were arriving on U.S. shores in makeshift boats. Clinton realized that this flow would be a burden to Florida. Under the justification of restoring the ousted, democratically elected Jean-Bertrand Aristide, who was also a thug, Clinton assembled a U.S. military force offshore that threatened to invade Haiti if the dictatorial regime of Raoul Cedras did not leave power. That rhetoric was hypocritical, because the United States had previously undermined Haiti's nascent democracy after the 1990 election. In fact, in the 1980s and early 1990s, senior members of the military junta's tools of terror in the army and paramilitary forces were on the CIA's payroll. And the United States restored Aristide in 1994 only after he agreed to adopt policies of the U.S.-backed candidate, who had received only 14 percent of the vote in the 1990 election.[26] Thus, even Democratic presidents support democracy only when it is convenient—usually to lambaste an unfriendly autocratic foreign leader but never a foreign despot who does U.S. bidding.

Of course, the wealthy United States could have assimilated the Haitian refugees without threatening a potentially bloody invasion of Haiti, but that was a politically unacceptable solution. Despite the killing, torture, and mayhem engulfing Haiti, the U.S. Coast Guard turned back the boat people into the frightening chaos. In the end, Clinton's threat worked and the Cedras regime departed without the need for a U.S. invasion. A great victory was declared for human rights and democracy without examining whether an alternative to the threat of force would have been a better policy. After U.S. forces eventually left Haiti, that country remained corrupt, violent, and one of the poorest nations on earth. Neoconservative Max Boot, normally a proponent of such brushfire interventions (but maybe less so if a Democratic president conducts them), noted that holding an election and then leaving achieved little in Haiti.[27]

The 1994 episode was only the latest of many U.S. military interventions in Haiti since the beginning of the last century, but the country never seems to get any better. In fact, the United States has made things worse. One of the reasons Haiti is a chronic, turbulent basket case is that it has no civil institutions because the United States, during its military occupation from 1915 to 1934, dissolved parliament, declared martial law and created the Haitian Army, which later was used to terrorize the Haitian population.[28]

U.S. meddling continues to this day. In 2004, in the wake of violent opposition to the corrupt and thuggish Aristide, the Bush II administration initially made known its preference that the Haitian president should step down, implicitly supporting an opposition supported by the dark forces from Haiti's authoritarian past. Then the U.S. government reversed course and decided that Aristide should finish out his term in office but allow the opposition to be part of his cabinet. Then the administration reversed itself again and successfully pressed for Aristide's ouster.

Bosnia

In 1995, the United States intervened militarily in Bosnia, ostensibly for humanitarian reasons. Bush I had avoided U.S. intervention, but Clinton had criticized him for that stance in the 1992 presidential campaign and advocated a more activist stance. After taking office, however, Clinton initially adopted Bush I's policy of inaction. But this ethnic conflict was not a brushfire war in the developing world; it was a minor conflict in Europe. The Europeans also had been reluctant to take military action because they already had lightly armed troops on the ground in a peacekeeping role.

But then in 1995 Clinton decided to reverse course. According to Andrew Bacevich, this change was not "to stop ethnic cleansing or in response to claims of conscience, but to preempt threats to the cohesion of NATO and the credibility of American power, each called into question by events in Bosnia." In short, according to Bacevich, "it was not Bosnia itself that counted, but Europe and U.S. leadership in Europe."[29]

As noted earlier, Korea and Vietnam were not considered strategic, either, but wars there were justified by the same perceived need to maintain and demonstrate the "credibility of American power." Such "demonstration" and "credibility" arguments are usually made by an empire trying to maintain its position in the world.

Clinton apparently believed that the United States had an interest in settling the conflict by using force so that no incentive would be given to the Europeans to enhance their own armed-power projection capabilities and thus challenge the American empire in Europe. The United States wanted to continue its post–World War II domination of that continent, and to do that it had to keep American forces stationed permanently there. With the demise of the Soviet superpower, it became harder and harder to justify a continued American military presence unless the NATO alliance had a new mission outside its traditional—and newly obsolete—role of defending Western Europe. Thus, the new, offensive, "out-of-area" mission was born to give NATO something to do. Eventually, not only the alliance's mission but also its territory was expanded. Proponents of such expansions openly warned that NATO would need to "expand or die."

Cloaking all this realpolitik was the justification of stopping the killing in a bloody ethnic civil war. That war could, the Clinton administration implied, mushroom into a European-wide conflagration and humanitarian disaster much like World War II. Of course, the conditions in Europe during 1995 were much different than they were prior to World War II. In contrast to the economic depression and hostile relations between European great powers before World War II, modern-day Europe features prosperity in many countries, progress toward that goal in others, and amicable great-power relations within a European Union. With little potential to spread to the rest of Europe, the ethnic conflict in Bosnia was in such a backwater area that the Europeans were even reluctant to get involved in it. (Thus, the conflict probably would not have generated a greater European defense effort, but to the American empire, any instability could have a domino or snowball effect that would adversely affect its position.) In fact, it can be argued that the European Union's early support for the independence of Croatia and Slovenia from Yugoslavia helped trigger the war in the first place.[30] Certainly, conflict in the remote region did not affect U.S. security, but it did have the perceived potential to undermine the American empire.

The ostensible humanitarian goal of U.S. and NATO intervention in Bosnia was to stop ethnic cleansing (the forced resettlement of peoples). All three groups in Bosnia—the Serbs, the Croats, and the Moslems—engaged in ethnic cleansing. Western rhetoric, however, was belied when the United States ignored the forced expulsion of a hundred and fifty thousand Serbs from the Krajina region of Croatia by Franjo Tudjman—NATO's Croatian ally who was every bit as thuggish as Slobodan Milosevic, NATO's Serb adversary. The expulsion in Krajina was arguably the single largest instance of ethnic cleansing during the Bosnian conflict.[31] The United States looked the other way in that human catastrophe because policymakers saw Milosevic and the Serbs as the strongest party in the conflict and the biggest threat to stability in the Balkans. U.S. officials wanted to weaken the Serbs in any way possible.

Moreover, the United States, after sitting on the sidelines for years watching all of the ethnic cleansing in Bosnia, finally provided air power through NATO to those same Croatians when their reconstituted army started beating the Serbs on the ground.[32] That Croatian army, trained by the United States, obviated the need for the United States to endanger its own forces by inserting them on the ground. (To lessen the costs of empire by reducing American casualties during U.S. overseas military adventures, the same model using U.S. airpower to support indigenous forces on the ground was followed later in Kosovo and Afghanistan.) The combined NATO-Croatian campaign forced the Serbs to accept the Dayton peace accord. Furthermore, U.S. bombing was supposed to help the Bosnian Muslims, the weakest group in the tripartite civil war. Yet in the long period when the United States was on the sidelines, it supported an arms embargo that denied the Muslims the means to defend themselves. If such arms sales had been allowed, U.S. military intervention might have been avoided.

Also showing the thinness of the Clinton administration's humanitarian impulses was Secretary of State Madeleine Albright's obsessive focus on stability in Europe when much more tragic events were occurring in the African nation of Rwanda. Brutal tribal genocide eventually killed five to eight hundred thousand people there. The term *genocide* is overused—usually to pressure the U.S. government to undertake military intervention in a particular country—but in this case was warranted. Politically, Albright knew that the United States could not intervene in both places, so she chose to do so in Europe, which she and many others in the administration believed was more strategic than Africa. So much for the humanitarian veneer on the U.S.-led NATO intervention in Bosnia.

These episodes also point out the inconsistency of such humanitarian interventions. Often the United States does not intervene in the most horrific civil wars—for example, those in Rwanda, Sudan, Sierra Leone, the Congo, and Cambodia—because they do not affect its perceived imperial interests. Instead, the United States meddles in areas that are more central to those interests.

Kosovo

In 1999, U.S. intervention in Kosovo was a classic case of a self-expanding empire intervening to ensure stability in contiguous areas even farther afield to preserve its initial investment in new territory. That intervention then becomes yet another new investment that requires policing at the frontiers and so on until the empire is in autoexpansion mode.

Although Clinton promised that the U.S. forces would only be in Bosnia for one year to police the coerced Dayton accords between the Serbs, Croats, and Moslems, no one took him seriously. And justifiably so, because at this writing American troops have been there nine years and counting.

No longer tied down supporting the Serbs in Bosnia, Slobodan Milosevic, the Serbian leader, was free to use his forces to beat back the militant Kosovar Albanians of the Kosovo Liberation Army (KLA). The KLA was attacking the minority Serbs in the Albanian-dominated Kosovo province of Serbia. Before becoming U.S. allies against Serbia, the KLA was considered by some in the

U.S. State Department to be a "terrorist" group. The KLA began attacking Serbs in Kosovo in hope that Milosevic would overreact with violent means that would radicalize the Albanian population, then supporting the nonviolent pursuit of Kosovar independence from Serbia. Milosevic obliged them and began to eject Albanians from Kosovo.

With an expanding NATO alliance in East Central Europe and thousands of American forces in Bosnia, the United States wanted to preserve NATO's investment in the Balkans and U.S. predominance as the guarantor of security in Europe. Many in the U.S. foreign-policy community believed that the simmering unrest in Kosovo was a bigger threat to the stability of southeastern Europe than the ethnic conflict in Bosnia had been. They also justified the U.S.-led military action as preserving "NATO's credibility" (in the words of then-NATO commander Wesley Clark)—really the credibility of the United States in the eyes of "rogue state" threats to the empire around the world.[33]

Again, as in the U.S.-led NATO intervention in Bosnia, the humanitarian veneer was raised as a justification for another U.S.-dominated military action, only to be discredited by the actual facts. To justify intervention in another Balkan civil war, Secretary of State Albright estimated that 100,000 Kosovar Albanians had been killed in the Serbs' initial ethnic cleansing in response to the KLA's attacks. In fact, in the year before the NATO bombing campaign, the number of Kosovar Albanians killed by Serbs was only about 2,500. In contrast, during the eleven weeks of allied bombing, with no longer anything to lose, the Serbs slaughtered 10,000 Kosovar Albanians. More than 260,000 additional Kosovar Albanians were "cleansed" from their villages and 200,000 more were made international refugees.[34]

To maintain support for the war at home, the Clinton administration made the decision to bomb only at high altitude to reduce U.S. casualties. That decision, which reduced the accuracy of U.S. air strikes, condemned greater numbers of Serb and Kosovar civilians to death.[35] As noted earlier, another method of limiting the costs in American lives and money of imperial excursions is to use foreign, U.S.-backed allies on the ground (supported by U.S. air power), much as empires of the past used mercenaries or troops raised from imperial possessions. For example, in recent conflicts, the United States has relied on the KLA in Kosovo, the Croatians and Bosnians in Bosnia, and the Afghani Northern Alliance in Afghanistan. After the NATO victory in Kosovo and a withdrawal of Serb military forces from the province, Kosovar Albanians conducted reverse ethnic cleansing on the Serbs. So not only was the humanitarian justification for the NATO intervention built on grossly inflated estimates of the human carnage, but the medicine of a U.S.-led bombing campaign made the sickness worse by accelerating Serb ethnic cleansing of Kosovars and by leading to a Kosovar reverse ethnic cleansing of Serbs after the allied victory. Clearly, as with U.S. military actions in Haiti and Bosnia, underlying realpolitik drove a military intervention in Kosovo that was then justified with humanitarian rhetoric.

Andrew Bacevich cogently describes the real motivations behind the U.S. intervention in Kosovo:

> Assertions that the United States and its allies acted in response to massive Serb repression of Kosovar Albanians simply cannot survive close scrutiny. Operation Allied Force was neither planned nor conducted to alleviate the plight of the Kosovars. When Slobodan Milosevic used the start of the bombing as a pretext to intensify Serb persecution of the Kosovars, that point became abundantly clear: NATO persisted in a bombing campaign that neither stopped nor even retarded Serb efforts to empty the province of Muslims. To the extent that General Wesley Clark, the SACEUR [Supreme Allied Commander, Europe] modified the script of his original campaign plan, he did so not by providing protection to the victims of Serb repression but by victimizing Serb civilians.

Indeed, some members of the Clinton administration actively sought a showdown with Slobodan Milosevic: Secretary of State Madeleine Albright designed the so-called Rambouillet peace conference in February and March 1999 so as to ensure that the Yugoslav president would reject any negotiated settlement of the Kosovo issue. Effective diplomacy would have precluded NATO action. But military action was what the United States wanted: a demonstration of what a new, more muscular alliance under U.S. direction could accomplish in thwarting "creeping instability." The intent of Operation Allied Force was to provide an object lesson to any European state fancying that it was exempt from the rules of the post–Cold War era. It was not Kosovo that counted, but affirming the dominant position of the United States in a Europe that was unified, integrated, and open. As Clinton himself explained on March 23, 1999, just before the start of the bombing campaign, "if we're going to have a strong economic relationship that includes our ability to sell around the world, Europe has got to be a key. . . . That's what this Kosovo thing is all about."[36]

So like the U.S. intervention in Bosnia, the war over Kosovo was not about saving people but about preserving and demonstrating the credibility of the NATO alliance and the informal U.S. empire in Europe.

Chalmers Johnson best summarizes the sincerity of U.S. military interventions, under both Democratic and Republican administration, after the cold war ended:

> After the collapse of the Soviet Union, we began to wage at an accelerated rate wars whose publicly-stated purposes were increasingly deceptive or unpersuasive. We were also ever more willing to go to war outside the framework of international law and in the face of worldwide popular opposition. These were de facto imperialist wars, defended by propaganda claims of humanitarian intervention, women's liberation, the threat posed by unconventional weapons, or whatever current buzzword happened to occur to White House and Pentagon spokespersons.[37]

The U.S. intervention in Somalia may have been one of the few cases where purely humanitarian concerns were the motivating factor. But this episode shows that using the military to perform social work, social engineering, or nation-building is usually ineffective and sometimes even counterproductive.

Humanitarian Interventions Are Ineffective and Immoral

At the time of this writing, more than twenty wars are raging worldwide. Even the U.S. superpower does not have the resources to use its military to stop them all and rebuild those societies. How does the U.S. government decide in which countries to intervene? Domestic interest groups often have a role in such decisions. For example, the Florida congressional delegation pressured both the Clinton and Bush II administrations to intervene militarily in Haiti to stop or prevent, respectively, an outflow of Haitian refugees to the shores of that state.

In many cases, wars do not free more people than they subjugate. Even in the classic "good vs. bad" war, World War II, more people may have been enslaved than liberated. Despite the well-publicized liberation of Western Europe and Japan, Eastern Europe was enslaved under Soviet totalitarianism. Furthermore, during the war, Japanese forces terrorized and therefore radicalized China's inherently conservative peasants, helping to bring a communist party to power that killed thirty million people in the Great Leap Forward and brutalized Chinese society during the Cultural Revolution.[38]

In general, wars tear at the social fabric and often cause subsequent wars, civil wars, or instability. World War I led to the Bolshevik revolution in Russia and destabilized and embittered German society, making it ripe for subjugation by Adolf Hitler. Woodrow Wilson had idealistic intentions in leading the United States into World War I, aiming to establish a world order that would make war obsolete, but he ended up planting the seeds for the most catastrophic conflict in world history—that is, World War II. Wilson, in order to encourage democracy, insisted on the removal of the Kaiser, thus removing a major roadblock to the later ascent of

Hitler. Such unpredictable, unintended and adverse long-term consequences of wars—even of wars undertaken for idealistic reasons—should cause American policymakers to be leery of short-term "fixes" using U.S. military intervention. Near-term stability achieved with American military power may create instability or tyranny over the long haul.

David Rieff, an authority on "humanitarian" interventions, noted, "If anything should be clear from the Kosovo crisis, and, for that matter, from the unhappy experiences that outside intervention forces, whether serving under their own flags, the UN's or NATO's, have had over the past decade in places like Somalia, Rwanda, and Bosnia, it is that ad hoc responses to state failure and humanitarian catastrophe are rarely, if ever, successful."[39]

In 2004, renewed mayhem in Kosovo and Haiti demonstrated that outside military interventions do not solve the underlying problems causing the violence in the first place. U.S. or international peacekeepers are often just barely keeping their fingers in the dike (for example, in Kosovo) or have to come back repeatedly to "restabilize" the situation (for example, in Haiti).

George Kennan, a famous foreign policy theorist, has cautioned that the United States overestimates its ability to right the wrongs of the world.[40] Even Max Boot of the Council on Foreign Relations, a staunch proponent of military intervention for spreading democracy and free markets, admits that imposing liberal democracies by force in the developing world has been less than successful (yet he still advocates attempting to do so).[41] Boot admits that rebuilding nations is difficult and instead advocates "state-building." As the case of Somalia shows, creating even a viable state at gunpoint is a Herculean task. Even where the United States has had colonies or repeated military interventions—for example, in the Philippines, Haiti, Nicaragua, Cuba and even Puerto Rico—it has not been successful at imperialism. Central America, in particular, has been an American playground. All of the Central American countries have no real democracies and are some of the most destitute nations on the planet.[42] In short, the United States tries to use short-term intervention to institute political and economic freedoms in nations with no experience with them. The United States itself, even with some prior experience, took centuries to perfect those freedoms.

In fact, Amy Chua notes that often democracy and free markets do not mix well in the developing world. Sudden empowerment of a poor, indigenous majority via democracy often leads to confiscation of assets and the killing of an economically dominant minority, rather than peace and prosperity. So in the developing world, democracy can prove a potent threat to the market. She also notes that despite Western triumphalism, which claims that more and more countries are being converted to democracies, many of the converts are in name only.[43] Thus, democracy should not be imposed on developing nations by force. The experiences in Chile, Spain, Taiwan, and South Korea show that precursor economic reforms, which create powerful middle classes and civic institutions, will likely lead to peaceful pressures for more gradual, homegrown, and voluntary moves toward democracy. But the United States never seems to learn, as shown by the following failed episodes of peacekeeping, nation building, and humanitarian intervention.

Disaster in Lebanon

In 1982, after the Israelis invaded Lebanon, the Reagan administration sent U.S. forces, as part of a UN-sponsored multinational force, to separate the warring Lebanese factions and oversee the withdrawal from the country of U.S.-backed Israeli forces and Soviet-backed Syrian forces. Initially (perhaps *ostensibly* is a better word) neutral, the United States then gradually became embroiled in the Lebanese civil war essentially by helping one side in the conflict. U.S. military began training and arming the armed forces of the Lebanese government, which was dominated by the Israeli-friendly Christian minority. Making things worse, the U.S. Marines and Lebanese Army then began conducting joint patrols. Later, the United States supported the Lebanese Army with gunfire from its ships and also provided heavy equipment—armored vehicles and howitzers—for that force. When the Lebanese Army disintegrated, the Marines even took up their positions. Naturally, the majority Muslim factions in the civil war then became increasingly hostile to the United States. The Marines were also fighting the Syrian Army and fundamentalist Islamists sponsored by Iran.

Hezbollah, an Iranian-sponsored group, launched the suicide-bomb attack against the Marine barracks in October of 1983, killing 241 American military personnel. Those well-publicized battle deaths, like the ones in Somalia ten years later, led to public pressure to withdraw U.S. forces without fulfilling their mission.

Failure in Somalia

Similarly, "mission creep" had disastrous consequences for the United States in Somalia in the 1990s. In Somalia, the original intention by the Bush I and Clinton administrations was to use military power to provide a secure environment for the delivery of food aid to civilian victims of a civil war. Although the Clinton administration has been criticized for expanding the mission to try to kill or capture Muhammad Farah Aidid, the dominant Somali warlord, the disarming of factions and other forms of mission creep had already begun in the twilight of the Bush I administration.[44]

Of course, that mission creep is typical in humanitarian or peacekeeping missions. In the case of Somalia, relief supplies were being stolen by the various warring factions and not getting to the civilians in need. So disarming the factions was thought to be necessary. Yet in doing so, the United States began selectively attacking Aidid's dominant faction—which was abiding by a ceasefire—and used excessive force in doing so.[45] The collateral killing of innocent civilians by U.S. forces ended up making a Somali population initially supportive of the intervention turn toward backing the warlord. The newly hostile population eventually killed U.S. servicemen and dragged their bodies through the streets. Those horrible television images caused a buildup of pressure in the United

States for a rapid withdrawal of U.S. forces, leaving Somalia in much the same sad shape as when U.S. forces had arrived.

Because Somalia was probably the United States' only true humanitarian intervention in the last hundred years, there was no perceived national interest to keep U.S. forces there when the going got tough. Although high-flying rhetoric usually surrounds U.S. military interventions, they are often commenced for underlying reasons of realpolitik. So in Somalia, an always-short U.S. attention span got even shorter.

According to Captain Huchthausen, U.S. Navy (retired), the mistakes made in Lebanon were repeated in Somalia a decade later.[46] Lebanon and Somalia should teach us several things about peacekeeping or nation-building interventions. First, peacekeepers can rarely remain neutral, even if they are scrupulous about it. Peacekeeping forces are usually donated by one or more outside nations and often act in their national interests, not neutrally or in the interest of humanitarian ends. Arguably, the behavior of U.S. forces in Lebanon fits that scenario. Second, one faction in the conflict can attack the peacekeepers and give the appearance that another faction is to blame. That ploy is often an attempt to provoke an attack on the latter faction by the peacekeepers, thus destroying their neutrality. Alternatively, a faction can kill its own civilians and blame it on the peacekeepers. The population then may turn against the peacekeepers. Aidid used that tactic effectively in Somalia. Thus in any ethnic conflict or civil war, peacekeepers should probably expect to end up getting dragged into fighting for one side or the other.

SHAKY PUBLIC SUPPORT FOR MILITARY SOCIAL ENGINEERING OVERSEAS

In the wake of Vietnam, Lebanon, and Somalia, it has become evident that the U.S. population does not genuinely support wars where U.S. security is not perceived to be at stake. Even when prewar polls indicate public support for intervention, that approval is often a chimera. If the intervention results in well-publicized casualties or takes longer than expected, the public and press can very quickly start asking why the U.S. military is fighting in faraway country X. Well-publicized casualties caused failure in both Lebanon and Somalia. More recently, because no nuclear, chemical, or biological weapons were found in Iraq, the Bush II administration had to fall back on a humanitarian rationale for removing Saddam Hussein from power. Yet the failure to pacify the country and mounting U.S. casualties from the guerrilla insurgency have magnified the shaky prewar justifications for the conflict and eroded American public support for continuing it.

America's notoriously short attention span is reflected by the conduct of its leaders in overseas military adventures—even in wars that are perceived to be vital to U.S. security, such as the one eradicating al Qaeda and removing the Taliban regime from Afghanistan. Over time, the Bush II administration diverted its attention and resources to removing Saddam Hussein from power in Iraq and allowed Osama bin Laden, al Qaeda and a resurgent Taliban to destabilize one-third of Afghanistan and operate out of Pakistan. In Bosnia and Kosovo, the American government and public lost interest long ago. An average of $1.5 billion spent per year on both combined will hardly make a dent in reconstructing their societies.[47] In fact, such reconstruction is likely to be an impossible task for any outside power or organization. In relation to Somalia, with no perceived national interest at stake, the U.S. attention span was even shorter. U.S. forces withdrew abruptly after the first major setback, leaving the country in chaos. How many Americans—even informed ones—know what is now going on in any of those remote countries or others like them?

America's leaders—be they Democrats or Republicans—know that popular support for non-national-security-related military actions is fragile. But instead of ceasing such interventions in the wake of debacles in Vietnam, Lebanon, and Somalia and failed attempts to build viable nations elsewhere, policymakers instead resort to "war on the cheap"—at least cheap for the United States. Unfortunately, that strategy results in the use of military tactics that reduce fatalities among U.S. service personnel—preserving fragile domestic political support for the war—but increase casualties among civilians in the nation being "helped." The use of heavy U.S. air and ground firepower results in the moral equivalent of "killing people to save them." Thus, military interventions for "humanitarian" purposes usually achieve quite the opposite and are morally questionable.

David Rieff, criticizing half-hearted, non–national-security interventions of governments that do not have the genuine support of their people, writes: "It is to be hoped that in the wake of Kosovo, the realization that this kind of geostrategic frivolity and ad hoc–ism, this resolve to act out of moral paradigms that now command the sympathy but do not yet command the deep allegiance of Western public opinion—at least not to the extent that people are willing to sacrifice in order to see that they are upheld—will no longer do."[48]

While Western publics are unwilling to give up much for humanitarian interventions in faraway countries about which they know little, advocates of humanitarian military interventions *are* willing to sacrifice lives and money—others' rather than their own.

In the Kosovo campaign, to reduce U.S. combat deaths in the wake of the debacle in Somalia and thus maintain fragile popular support for the war, the Clinton administration ruled out the use of American ground forces and restricted the U.S. air services to bomb from only a high altitude. When then-NATO commander Wesley Clark gave orders to his officers before the Kosovo campaign began, his first priority was to avoid allied aircraft losses.[49] Even with modern precision weapons, bombing from high altitudes kills substantial numbers of civilians, more than bombing from lower altitudes. Because the American intervention in Kosovo was sold on humanitarian grounds, it is both ironic and tragic that U.S. policies were then adopted that knowingly killed more civilians.

In the Kosovo campaign, such strategic bombing somehow may have had some effect in getting Milosevic to withdraw Serb forces from Kosovo (other explanations were that Russia, a Serbian ally, pulled the diplomatic rug out from under Serbia or that a U.S. threat of a ground attack was transmitted through Russia to Milosevic[50]). But killing enemy civilians from the air often just makes the enemy fight more ferociously. For example, strategic bombing against German and Japanese civilians during World War II seems to have had that effect. The Clinton administration may have been lucky in the Kosovo air campaign, but when the United States is fighting on the ground against guerrillas in the developing world, it is dangerous to anger the local population, because guerrillas are critically dependent on civilians for shelter and support. Yet to reduce casualties among U.S. forces, Americans frequently use excessive firepower from the air and ground that does exactly that—as in, for example, the Vietnam War.

Even if the dubious proposition that the wars Vietnam, Kosovo, and Iraq II were fought for moral reasons ("just wars," by Thomas Aquinas's religious standards), rather than for strategic or material gain, is accepted, it must be remembered that the cruelest tactics are often used by moral crusaders. For example, the Spanish conquest of the Americas under the banner of converting heathens to Christianity inflicted more suffering than "salvation" on Native Americans.[51] After the Spanish-American War, the same brutality came from the United States after the call went out to "Christianize" an already Christian people in the Philippines. In short, when the cause is perceived as so lofty and important, questionable means normally out of bounds are often excused to advance it.

The American political and military leadership routinely argue that they are not purposely trying to slaughter civilians, but that some "collateral damage"—a euphemism for the killing of innocent civilians—is inevitable during war. But those leaders have a choice of tactics. More important, even the accidental killing of civilians is morally questionable if the war is unneeded to legitimately safeguard U.S. security. Thus the killing of innocent civilians was morally questionable in the Bush I administration's invasion of Panama, the Clinton administration's interventions in Somalia, Bosnia, and Kosovo, and Bush II's invasion of Iraq. The use of air power somehow makes the slaughtering of civilians from afar less morally objectionable to U.S. policymakers, military personnel, and the American public than gunning them down in person on the ground.

Of course, factions in unstable countries know that the Achilles' heel of the American empire is public opinion back home. So they have a huge incentive to try to launch a spectacular attack that will cause enough American casualties to prompt pressure back home for a U.S. military withdrawal.

Alternatively, U.S. adversaries can capitalize on the possibility that even well-trained American soldiers can lash out and commit atrocities among civilians when fighting enemy guerrillas, who can maddeningly strike and then melt back into the general population. The Mi Lai massacre in Vietnam and the excessive use of force in Somalia are examples of such overreactions by U.S. forces. Or the enemy can simply kill civilians and blame it on the American invaders. Both of those scenarios can turn the local population against U.S. forces and the likely squeamish American public against the war.

Third, like the North Vietnamese and the Viet Cong, the adversary can attempt to drag out the conflict and hope the American public gets exhausted and pressures the U.S. government to bring the troops home.

A fourth alternative is to simply lay low and wait for the peacekeeping forces from nations with short attention spans to leave. Arguably, the factions in both Bosnia and Kosovo are merely laying low and waiting for the Western nations to tire of retaining peacekeepers there. If U.S. and NATO peacekeepers left, fighting among the factions would probably begin again.

In any of the aforementioned alternative scenarios, U.S. forces and the peacekeeping or nation-building mission that they are trying to perform are very vulnerable to such tactics, and thus to failure.

Nation-Building Has Not Succeeded

Even if the U.S. military is not forced to leave in disgrace, rebuilding or restructuring the institutions, economies, and societies of strife-torn nations is a Herculean task prone to failure. U.S. forces occupied and then left Haiti, but that nation remains poor, corrupt, undemocratic, and an economic basket case. Similarly, despite a lengthy foreign occupation and injections of substantial amounts of aid, Bosnia has made little progress in establishing a civil society that would be sustainable and allow the population to prosper. In fact, hard-line factions have recently won elections in Bosnia, Croatia, and Serbia, making a positive outcome even less likely and illustrating that forcing elections before countries are ready for democracy can be counterproductive. Kosovo also has made little progress in creating a civil society. Thus, as David Rieff states, "Kosovo is probably a lost cause; it is certainly ruined for a generation, whatever eventual deal is worked out, as Bosnia, whose future is to be a ward of NATO, America, and the European Union, probably for decades, probably has also been ruined for a generation, Dayton or no Dayton."[52] In sum, advocates of international social work at gunpoint may (or may not) have good intentions but can list very few instances of success.

Whenever proponents advocate the latest installment of imperial nation-building, they usually compare their efforts with Marshall Plan, which by common wisdom resuscitated Europe and Japan after World War II. The Bush II administration made that wishful comparison to put the best spin on the chaotic and inept attempt at nation-building in Iraq.

In fact, Americans probably take too much credit for making postwar Japan and Germany success stories. Although political and economic revitalization took place, the Germans and Japanese probably deserve most of the credit themselves. The Germans provided 80 percent of the capital and 100 percent of the labor for Germany's reconstruction. Some economic historians have noted that the European economic recovery would have occurred sooner or later even without Marshall Plan aid and that it played only a modest role in the resuscitation. Furthermore, in Germany, every recovery program for the democratization of education, labor relations, and industry sponsored by the U.S. Joint Chiefs of Staff failed or was aborted. In Japan, almost all of the economic and cultural programs by the U.S. military occupation were cancelled, co-opted, or evaded.[53] Despite the common wisdom, the U.S. military probably had no better luck at imperial nation-building in Japan and Germany than it has had in Iraq.

Moreover, the Iraq episode illustrates that most attempts at nation-building occur in nations dissimilar to postwar Japan and Germany—that is, in underdeveloped nations racked by civil strife and long histories of tyranny, political corruption, and excessive economic regulation. Before they were bombed into rubble during the war, Japan and Germany were developed, industrial nations with highly educated work forces. They were fairly wealthy nations before the war because of the way their economies and societies were organized. Despite horrific damage to the physical infrastructure during the conflict, the fighting did not destroy those cultures of efficient socioeconomic organization. And in spite of their turn to authoritarianism prior to the war, the Germans and Japanese both had some earlier experience with democracy that they could refer back to during the postwar rebuilding. Most importantly, after World War II, German and Japanese societies retained a sense of national unity and avoided the civil strife that occurs after many external wars.

Unfortunately, attempts at nation-building in the twenty-first century usually center on developing nations that have none of those advantages. Even Max Boot, an avid proponent of imposing liberal democracies at gunpoint, admits that doing so in the developing world has been less successful than doing so in developed countries, such as Japan and Germany.[54]

In addition to failing to improve the targeted developing country, imperial nation-building could enmesh the United States in a shooting war that becomes a quagmire—for example, the U.S. occupation of Iraq. As international financier George Soros noted, an ignominious withdrawal from the Iraq trap could lead to a "catastrophic reversal similar to what happened in Vietnam."[55] Thus, extreme care should be exercised in employing the U.S. military overseas in the first place.

Curing "Failed States" with Military Force Is a Failure

Given the shaky record of using armed intervention to remold entire societies in the developing world, proponents of imperial nation-building have taken advantage of the more security-conscious post–September 11 era to develop security arguments for fixing "failed states" with military force. That development is ironic because the imperialism of the nineteenth and twentieth centuries helped cause the targeted states to fail in the first place. In the current political climate, some on the left know that justifying military interventions overseas by arguing that they enhance U.S. security is more marketable to the public and Congress than arguments for fixing states simply because they are experiencing social strife. The new liberal Wilsonian argument is that poor countries with ethnic or civil conflicts are breeding grounds for anti-American terrorists. (The Bush II administration adopted the argument and has used it to justify intervention in Georgia, the Philippines, and Yemen and the continued occupation of Iraq and may use it in the future to justify military interventions in other "failed states." This should be a warning to liberals that the "failed state" rationale for military intervention is ripe for abuse.)

Using the security argument is merely a politically expedient way for liberal Wilsonians to justify increasing government spending on foreign aid. An honest debate should be held about whether increased U.S. foreign aid will help the unstable countries in question, but the security argument is a red herring. If terrorism were caused by poverty, almost all terrorists would be citizens of sub-Saharan Africa, which houses the poorest countries in the world. Although there have been some major acts of terror in sub-Saharan Africa—for example, the simultaneous bombings of the U.S. embassies in Kenya and Tanzania—the perpetrators are usually from outside that region. More generally, out of the vast multitudes of poor people around the world, only a minuscule number resort to terrorism. On September 11, 2001, most of the perpetrators were well-educated and at least middleiclass. Gregory Clark of the *Japan Times* perceptively notes that remedying the problem of poverty will not solve the problem of terrorism: "If people in the Third World want to use force against the governments of the West, that is because of perceived injustice." He believes such attacks will continue as long as America continues "meddling" abroad and supporting autocratic dictatorships.[56]

Intense ethnic conflicts often do breed terrorism, but the security argument assumes that terrorist groups spawned by those conflicts would automatically train their sights on the United States, no matter what U.S. policy toward those countries was adopted. Most of the failed states are half a world away from America and of no intrinsic strategic value to U.S. security. If the United States refrained from getting embroiled in foreign civil wars, the terrorist groups involved in those conflicts would have no incentive to strike U.S. targets. The September 11 attacks on the U.S. homeland ultimately resulted from unnecessary U.S. involvement in "somebody else's civil war"—the war conducted by militant Islamic fundamentalists who believe that many secular governments in Islamic countries are corrupt. (A more detailed discussion of those topics is included in the next chapter.)

Thus, intervention by the U.S. military to fix a particular failed state will probably be ineffective (as in Haiti and Bosnia), may unintentionally make things worse (as in Lebanon, Somalia, and Kosovo), and will inevitably reduce—not increase—U.S. security.

Moreover, U.S. military interventions overseas are often advocated by people who are willing to expend others' lives (both U.S. military lives and civilian lives in the country that is "helped") and money (public resources that could be used for other societal purposes) on their pet projects. For example, Wilsonian Max Boot makes the following shocking remarks: "If the U.S. is not prepared to get its hands dirty, then it should stay home" and "Any nation bent on imperial policing will suffer a few setbacks. . . . This did not appreciably dampen the British determination to defend and expand the empire; it made them hunger for vengeance. If Americans cannot adopt a similarly bloody-minded attitude, then they have no business undertaking imperial policing."[57] But Boot's blood will not be spilled to conduct military social engineering in maintaining the empire.

Besides, safer and more effective options exist to help strife-torn nations.

HUMANITARIAN ALTERNATIVES TO "HUMANITARIAN" MILITARY INTERVENTIONS

Understandably, many on the left believe that people in the wealthy United States should help the less fortunate in the developing world. Curiously, though, some on the left who are suspicious of the military, and who opposed military action in places like Vietnam and Iraq, encouraged social work at gunpoint in places like Somalia, Bosnia, Kosovo, and Liberia. But imperial nation-building is much the same and has much the same chance of success—very low—no matter what country is the recipient and no matter what president does the honors.

Heavy-handed U.S. military intervention to do social work, or create the conditions to facilitate its undertaking, rarely works because of the onset of mission creep (as in Lebanon and Somalia), the creation of enemies in some or all of the population as a result of taking sides or using excessive force (as in Lebanon, Somalia, and Iraq), the exacerbation of original problems (for example, the ethnic cleansing in Kosovo), or the loss of public support at home (as in Lebanon, Somalia, and Iraq).

Strangely, in the post–cold war world, U.S. foreign policy has become militarized. The Pentagon has more influence on the formulation of U.S. foreign policy than the State Department and many more resources to carry it out. In fact, at times, the Pentagon has been criticized for carrying out its own foreign policy—for example, when U.S. special forces train despotic countries' militaries in counterinsurgency tactics even as the U.S. government is condemning those same governments for human rights violations.[58] But other means besides reflexively employing the American military can be used to help destitute and unstable countries.

In the rush to increase foreign aid budgets, it is often forgotten that developing countries would benefit more from the United States ending import restrictions on the developing world's raw materials and manufactures (for example, textiles), as well as terminating subsidies to American farmers. Those subsidies allow the American farmer to lower the price of exported crops and compete unfairly with the farm products of the developing world. To demonstrate how important the ending of those subsidies is to agriculture in developing regions, the South African ambassador to the United States recently offered to give up U.S. foreign aid to his country if the United States would terminate domestic farm subsidies.

Liberals often discount such free market alternatives because they are, with some justification, suspicious of American capitalists. Large U.S. businesses often try to get hidden subsidies by having the U.S. government defend their overseas investments; for example, the U.S. military's unnecessary defense of Persian Gulf oil (see Chapter 6) is a subsidy to large oil companies. U.S. intervention in Iran in 1953 and Guatemala in 1954 to prevent the nationalization of Western companies is another example. But such subsidized mercantilism should not be confused with voluntary, private, mutually beneficial commerce between foreign people and companies and U.S. citizens and firms.

If rapid assistance from the United States is deemed necessary to alleviate a humanitarian emergency in a particular country, the supplies should be dropped from the air to those who need it. Putting U.S. forces on the ground to guard it or facilitate its transport will merely inflame certain segments of the local population and risk the entire mission. If protection on the ground is needed, armed local guards should be hired.

If local security is insufficient and peacekeepers are needed, a force from the region should be organized. Peacekeepers from a particular region know much more than a U.S. force about the culture and the problems of the area, and are not perceived as being from a faraway invading neocolonial superpower. A regional great power or organization—for example, the EU, the Association of Southeast Asian Nations (ASEAN), or the Economic Community of West African States (ECOWAS) in West Africa—could provide them. Also, Edward Olsen of the Naval Postgraduate School has proposed a standing force of UN peacekeepers that would exclude forces from major powers that are permanent members of the Security Council. The UN General Assembly would make the decision to deploy such peacekeepers, but volunteers from Security Council states could be integrated into the force. This arrangement would take great power politics, including veiled empire-building and maintenance, out of international peacekeeping.[59]

But care must be taken in any peacekeeping mission, no matter who does it. Although the natural impulse of the international community is to commission peacekeepers to immediately rush in, enforce a ceasefire, separate the parties, and start rebuilding the particular country, this may in the long run cause a greater number of deaths. If ethnic, religious, or nationalist factions around the world that are dissatisfied with their governments know that they can provoke civil wars with those governments, internationalize the conflict by luring international peacekeepers, and thus win autonomy or independence, more will attempt to do so. There will be more civil wars and thus more innocent victims. Guerrilla groups often attack their governments, hoping for an overreaction to help them garner support from the international community. The KLA started attacking Serbs in Kosovo to provoke a Serb overreaction and thus international intervention. The KLA was successful in recruiting U.S.-led NATO aircraft to be its air force against the Serb onslaught. Kosovo thus won autonomy, but probably will not stop until it achieves eventual independence. But it may take another war to achieve that end.

The KLA's successful effort to gain international support for its rebellion is likely to be a model for other separatist groups around the world. Clinton's undermining of the principle of national sovereignty in the Kosovo campaign (as well as Bush's undermining of it by invading Iraq) has grave implications for the future. The principle of the inviolability of sovereignty—that nations should not intervene within the borders of other countries to meddle in internal developments there—while not perfect, has dampened international conflict since the 1600s. Even the Bush II administration's limited U.S. intervention in Liberia—demanding the ouster of President Charles Taylor and providing support for the international peacekeeping force—provided de facto support for the country's rebels and thus undermined the principle of sovereignty.

In the long run, if separatist movements are encouraged by such international interventions, more civil wars and rebellions will result and more people will probably die than would have without the intervention of the international community. Unfortunately, in the rush to "do something" about a tragic civil war, the long-term implications of international interventions are rarely considered by U.S. policymakers and the international community.

There are plenty of strife-torn countries in which the parties are exhausted by war and want to make peace. The international community should focus its efforts on assisting those nations. Waiting to assist countries until the violence ends may be hard to stomach but may also save more lives worldwide in the long term by providing a powerful incentive to stop the fighting.

Many liberals praise international law and the United Nations but advocate—knowingly or unknowingly—violating provisions of Article 51 of the UN Charter in order to use military force to prevent human rights violations in a particular country. Article 51 prohibits violating the sovereignty of a country for reasons other than self-defense. Each time the charter is violated, this important restraint on cross-border aggression is undermined. The international norm against illegitimate, aggressive war that violates national sovereignty has ensured some semblance of global stability and at least limited occurrences of violence in the turbulent world. Since no permanent, forced change of borders since 1945 has been internationally recognized, the norm appeared to be strengthening until it was undermined by the lone remaining superpower's profligate post–cold war military interventions without legitimate security justifications.

In particular, the U.S. invasion of Iraq—as any attack on one nation by another, particularly an assault by a superpower, could be expected to do—gave other countries and groups around the world a cover for committing violent acts on neighbors. India and Pakistan, both possessing nuclear weapons, almost went to war after a group that India associated with Pakistan attacked India's parliament building. Russia escalated its own war on "terrorism" in Chechnya. Palestinians stepped up suicide bombings against Israeli targets, and the Israelis answered back with military interventions into Gaza and the West Bank.[60]

Instead of using military force, the United States could always open its borders and take in refugees from countries in turmoil. Recently, in contrast to its earlier role of melting pot, the United States has had an abysmal record of taking such basic steps to relieve human suffering. Instead, America often reflexively threatens or conducts military action. For example, the United States took in few Jews being persecuted in Nazi Germany prior to World War II and, in 1995, turned back Haitians trying to flee the violence and economic devastation of their home country. In both cases, the United States eventually resorted to military threats or action to oust the offending foreign government. This contradiction once again casts doubt on the humanitarian motives for U.S. wars. Even in the rare case in which a war needs to be fought, the U.S. government should be honest about its real reasons for fighting and not neglect to open U.S. borders for refugees from the conflict.

If one side in a war is slaughtering the other, it may even be humane, in the short term and as a last resort, to sell arms to the weaker side so that the right of self-defense can be exercised. The United States declined to do so in the conflicts in both Rwanda and Bosnia. In fact, in Bosnia, U.S. support for the UN arms embargo helped the stronger Serbs conduct an ethnic cleansing campaign against the weaker Muslims. Liberals shy away from the option of arms sales, but that may have a better chance of success than many of the failed military interventions by the United States, which has a short attention span. When U.S. attention inevitably wanes, friendly local forces and citizens may end up holding the bag, and conditions in the country may have been made worse by outside intervention. And U.S. citizens are also at risk because of America's imperial wars.

THE GREATEST DRAWBACK TO IMPERIAL WARS MAY BE AT HOME

The founders of the United States astutely realized that the republic was uniquely defined by its liberties and that the nation's foreign policy was meant to defend the U.S. political system, not define it. That is, U.S. foreign policy should not erode the individual freedoms it was designed to protect.[61]

In what should be a caution to liberals concerned about civil liberties, John Quincy Adams, in 1821, summarizing traditional U.S. foreign policy, cautioned that wars, even for good causes, could undermine American independence and liberty at home. Adams, then

President James Monroe's Secretary of State, when confronted with the question of whether the young republic should support—with alliances or military action—the emerging South American republics in their separation from the Spanish empire, stated:

> America does not go abroad in search of monsters to destroy. She is the well-wisher to the freedom and independence of all. She is the champion only of her own. She will recommend the general cause by the countenance of her voice, and the benignant sympathy of her example. She well knows that by once enlisting under other banners than her own, were they even the banners of foreign independence, she would involve herself beyond the power of extrication, in all the wars of interest and intrigue, of individual avarice, envy, and ambition, which assumed the colors and usurped the standards of freedom. . . . She might become the dictatress of the world. She would be no longer the ruler of her own spirit.[62]

War always leads to the "our team versus their team" attitude. Discussions about this high-stakes issue are often seen in black or white, with no gray permitted. Even in a democracy, anyone who finds the government's rationale for war unconvincing, or cautions about the probable ill effects, is looked on with suspicion and is sometimes even accused of being a traitor. Some of the heated rhetoric by supporters of President Bush's Iraq War II, including administration officials, against those who opposed it should be noted.

War undermined democracy in ancient Greece and extinguished the republic in ancient Rome. In the former case, the Athenian fleet's failure to take Syracuse in the Peloponnesian War allowed proponents of oligarchy in Athens to undermine democracy in the name of better conducting the war.[63] Losing the entire war also eroded the Athenian democratic system. In the latter case, the army of the Roman Republic originally was a defense force. Nevertheless, the principal conquests of Rome occurred during the Republican period. In particular, the Punic Wars against the Carthaginians demanded an increasing concentration of power. During and after the wars (ending in 201 B.C.), Rome became a republic only in name. As the locus of Roman power, three hundred aristocratic senators, elected for life, replaced the annually appointed consuls and the popular assembly.[64] More foreign and civil wars transferred power from the oligarchic Senate to a long line of dictators and emperors. Those leaders were backed by armies in a militarized society in which glory and power were obtained through fighting foreign wars. The large armies required to defend a huge empire were not compatible with a republic. In short, conquest destroyed the Roman Republic. In history, imperial republics are prone to authoritarian takeovers.

Liberals in the eighteenth and nineteenth centuries warned that the same could happen in America. In the words of Alexis de Tocqueville, a foreign commentator on the American republic, "All those who seek to destroy the liberties of a democratic nation ought to know that war is the surest and shortest means to accomplish it."[65] James Madison, in this famous quote, elaborated on the consequences of war on liberty: "Of all the enemies to public liberty, war is, perhaps, the most to be dreaded, because it comprises and develops the germ of every other. War is the parent of armies; from these proceed debts and taxes; and armies, and debts, and taxes are the known instruments for bringing the many under the domination of the few. . . . No nation could preserve its freedom in the midst of continual warfare."[66]

Modern liberals also warn about the effect of wars on the American constitutional system. Arundhati Roy, for example, notes that "For the ordinary American, the price of 'New Democracy' in other countries is the death of real democracy at home."[67]

War and Lost Civil Liberties: A History

And those great observers have been proved right. Throughout U.S. history, wars that were usually unnecessary for the security of the American public have eroded the liberties that make the United States unique among nations. In other words, the U.S. government is strangling the nation in order to save it. Some prominent examples should suffice.

After the war for American independence, the young United States fought a quasi war at sea with its former French ally. As a result, in 1798, under the administration of George Washington's successor, John Adams, the Alien and Sedition Acts were passed. Those acts gave the president the authority to deport foreigners and made dissent criminal. Purportedly, the acts were designed to make the nation unified against the French, but they really served to buttress the ruling Federalist Party against its opposition.[68] Fortunately, the subsequent administration of Thomas Jefferson, believing those laws to contravene the principles enshrined in the U.S. Constitution, initiated their repeal.

During the American Civil War, the Union and Confederate governments both encroached on the liberties of their citizens. In the south, freedom of speech about slavery and other issues was curtailed. In the north, Abraham Lincoln suspended the writ of habeas corpus without congressional approval. In the aftermath of the war, the U.S. military governed the southern states. In reaction to this draconian rule, the Posse Comitatus Act was passed in 1878 to keep the military out of domestic police activities. Unfortunately, over time, the act has been diluted to allow military involvement in drug enforcement, border patrols, and now counterterrorism and immigration control.

At the time of the Spanish-American War, the U.S. Secret Service needlessly harassed innocent Spanish and Italian immigrants.[69]

World War I was the first war to mobilize the entire American society and took on the aura of a moral crusade. People were jailed for opposing the war. President Wilson urged Attorney General Palmer to initiate treason charges against any publication that criticized him or his war efforts.[70] World War I also raised suspicions about immigrants. After the war, immigrants were detained in the Palmer raids. Those suspicions also played a role in the trial and execution of Italian immigrants Sacco and Vanzetti for the crime of murder, despite evidence of their innocence.

During World War II, as the federal law enforcement bureaucracy expanded, things got even worse. People were put in detention camps not for what they did but for who they were. Solely because of their ethnic origin, loyal Japanese-Americans were held prisoner without trial and conviction and had their assets confiscated. Also, to promote his secret goal of involving the United States in the war, President Roosevelt, with the help of the executive branch, cooperated with British agents sent to America by Winston Churchill. The mission of those agents was to help drag a reluctant American public into supporting entry into the conflict. The three hundred British agents intercepted mail, tapped phones, cracked safes, kidnapped people, started rumors and smeared U.S. "isolationists."[71] The U.S. government itself censored radio content and newspapers, some of which were banned altogether. The federal authorities also suppressed groups of war dissidents.

During the cold war, Red scares resulted in the McCarthy hearings and the needless ruining of many careers and reputations.

During the Vietnam War, which was supposedly fought to defend freedom, the CIA and U.S. Army both spied on dissenters at home. That spying was exposed during the mid-1970s by congressional hearings.

After the September 11 attacks, the military created a new command—the Northern Command—to defend the United States against terrorism and weapons of mass destruction. Even during World War II, such a centralized command was avoided because of fears that it could lead to a military dictatorship.[72]

Domestic civil liberties are usually restricted in proportion to the perceived severity of the threat. For example, the imperial misadventure against a relatively weak North Vietnam resulted in government spying on dissenters at home, whereas the global war against Axis powers brought the much more severe incarceration of Japanese-Americans for doing absolutely nothing. Thus, in the past, because distant brushfire wars to maintain the empire were not undertaken to stanch a perceived threat to the homeland (which then leads to the larger question of why they needed to be fought at all), their resulting threats to liberties at home, although significant, were probably less severe than the much larger world wars. But the aftereffects of the September 11 attacks indicate that this maxim has changed dramatically.

After September 11, 2001, the American people understandably reviled those who could murder innocent civilians in cold blood. But such feelings of hatred obscured the need to answer a crucial and fundamental question: As immoral as the attacks were, what could have made the perpetrators hate the United States so much that they would travel halfway around the world and give up their lives and fortunes to perpetrate such slaughter on innocents? The short answer is that the September 11 attacks were a result of America's involvement in someone else's civil war.

Islamic radical terrorists, such as Osama bin Laden, blame the United States for supporting corrupt dictatorships in the Islamic world and stationing troops on Islamic soil to ensure "stability," which they read to mean keeping those regimes in power. (The next chapter will present detailed evidence that the United States is attacked by terrorists for what it does, not who it is.) Ensuring stability in the Islamic world has little to do with U.S. security and more to do with propping up despotic client regimes of the American empire. In fact, the core of U.S. security is dramatically undermined when retaliatory terrorist attacks are launched on U.S. soil. Thus, in the age of modern communication and transportation, terrorists can turn even imperial U.S. interventions in backwater countries into dire blowback to the American homeland. And the global reach of terrorists now makes the danger to the continental United States more severe than the more limited threat to it posed by the Germans and Japanese during the cataclysmic conflagration of World War II.

With such a dire self-generated threat to the homeland at hand, American civil liberties are once again under severe assault. In the wake of the September 11 attacks, President Bush advocated and

Congress hastily passed the draconian USA PATRIOT Act, which substantially constricted civil liberties and enhanced government powers of law enforcement. Also, the Bush II administration has taken executive actions that further undermined civil liberties and proposed successor legislation to the PATRIOT Act. Similar to the draconian detention of Japanese-Americans during World War II, the September 11 attacks have led to the arrest and long-term detention without charge, trial, or access to lawyers of people based on ethnicity or country of origin but guilty only of technical immigration violations.[73]

The PATRIOT Act

The centerpiece of the U.S. government's reaction to the September 11 attacks was the PATRIOT Act, which was enacted by Congress in October 2001 at the behest of the Bush administration. The act passed rapidly, with little congressional debate. After any sort of crisis, elected officials want to be seen as "doing something" to prevent another such occurrence. Little consideration, however, was given to whether the proposed measures were actually needed or would be effective in preventing a future catastrophic terrorist attack. After any such crisis, a "cooling-off" period should be observed before any new legislation is passed—to let passions cool and to enable a more objective analysis to be done about the weaknesses in security that allowed the attack to succeed. Coming little more than month after the attacks, the PATRIOT Act failed dramatically in that regard.

In any security crisis, added to the congressional desire to show the panicked voters that measures are being taken to protect them, executive branch law enforcement agencies, like any bureaucracies, seek to use the crisis to garner more general powers. If there is doubt about this assertion, an absurd example should suffice—namely, that of the newly created Homeland Security Department widening its mission to encompass fighting child pornography and other child predators. According to Tom Ridge, the head of the new department, the aftermath of the September 11 attacks had given law enforcement authorities "a vast set of resources" to apply to other threats, including criminals who threaten children.[74] The big mysteries here are why the federal government needs to usurp local and state law enforcement efforts in this area and what the department's new mission has to do with securing the U.S. homeland.

In the wake of the September 11 attacks, the law enforcement authorities succeeded in expanding their powers. Many of the long-sought investigative powers they received in the act applied not only to terrorism, but also to criminal investigations. Those agencies needed to get Congress to enact such expansive powers quickly before the crisis atmosphere passed and the window of opportunity closed. To put even more pressure on Congress to act, Attorney General John Ashcroft even suggested that its members would be responsible for any further terrorist attacks while the act was pending. So both congressional and executive branch interests coincided to work against a more deliberate "good government" approach to improve security in the wake of the attacks. At the least, allowing provisions of the act to sunset (expire after a period of time) would have allowed Congress to reconsider the legislation when the heat of the moment was over. Such expiration, however, applied to only a few of the eavesdropping measures that were, in turn, only a small part of the act.

In the PATRIOT Act's assault on civil liberties,[75] it widened the definition of terrorism to include "domestic terrorism." The definition is now so fuzzy that lawful advocacy groups, such as the environmental group Greenpeace or the anti-abortion group Operation Rescue, could be deemed terrorist organizations and subjected to surveillance, wiretapping, and even criminal prosecution. We could soon be in for a return to the 1960s, when groups exercising free speech were spied on and harassed by the U.S. government.

The Act also permits law enforcement authorities to conduct criminal investigations on U.S. citizens without probable cause of a crime having been committed, provided the authorities say it is for "intelligence purposes." That provision seems to contravene the

Fourth Amendment of the U.S. Constitution, which states that "no Warrants shall issue, but upon probable cause."

The law expanded government authority in both terrorism and criminal cases to conduct secret searches without the knowledge of the party being searched. Such secret searches may have a place in totalitarian or authoritarian states but have no place in a free society.

Under the Act, law enforcement was granted wide powers of phone and Internet surveillance of U.S. citizens in both terrorism and nonterrorism investigations. It was also allowed access, with minimal judicial oversight, to student, medical, mental health, and financial records. The weakened judicial oversight is one more example of increased authority flowing to the already too-powerful executive bureaucracies at the expense of other branches of government in the U.S. checks and balances system.

The legislation allowed the CIA back into the game of spying on Americans, giving the agency wide authority to conduct surveillance in the United States. Apparently, Congress has learned nothing from its own hearings in the 1970s that exposed the abuses of CIA and military spying on domestic groups in the United States during the Vietnam War.

Under the law, the Attorney General can jail noncitizens if he believes they are a "reasonable threat to national security." He can then hold them indefinitely, in six-month installments, with minimal judicial review. Noncitizens can also be denied readmission to the United States for engaging in speech protected by the First Amendment.

The Fifth Amendment to the Constitution states that no "person" (note that sometimes the Constitution uses the term *citizen,* but not here) should be "deprived of life, liberty, or property without due process of law." The Sixth Amendment states, "In all criminal prosecutions, the accused [note that there is no reference to "citizens" here either] shall enjoy the right to a speedy and public trial." The Constitution also states that only the Congress, not the executive branch, can suspend the "Great Writ of Habeas Corpus," which prevents the indefinite detention of prisoners. And Congress can do so only "when in Cases of Rebellion or Invasion the public Safety may require it." Therefore, indefinite detention of even noncitizens on mere suspicion appears to be unconstitutional. The United States is not experiencing an invasion or a rebellion, and, in any case, the Congress has not formally suspended the writ. Finally, even the First Amendment uses the term *people* and so applies to noncitizens.

In addition to the PATRIOT Act passed by Congress at the president's request, the executive branch has acted unilaterally to undermine the Constitution's sacred freedoms.

Executive Branch Infringements of Civil Liberties

Although mouthing the Orwellian words of "fighting for freedom" in his war against terror, George W. Bush has constricted, more than any president in recent memory, those very liberties for people in his own country.[76]

The government interrogated thousands of Arab and South Asian immigrants merely because of their ethnicity or Islamic beliefs and not because it had cause to suspect them of illegal acts. Such interrogations seem to violate the Fourth Amendment provision of "no Warrants shall issue, but upon probable cause" and the spirit of the Fourteenth Amendment, which guarantees "persons" the "equal protection of the laws."

All but a few of the more than one thousand Arab and South Asian men detained secretively and indefinitely (without charges, a trial, or access to counsel) had no connection to terrorism. The detainees were physically and mentally abused while in custody, according to the Justice Department's own Inspector General's office. The Inspector General reported that in detaining those men indefinitely, the Justice Department made little effort to distinguish the few terrorism suspects from the overwhelming majority of detainees, who had merely committed minor immigration violations. The arbitrary (incommunicado) detention of prisoners is a violation of the International Covenant on Civil and Political Rights, to which the United States is a party.[77] Thus, the U.S. policy opens the possibility that other nations could do the same to U.S. citizens detained on their territory. More important, the Constitution guarantees noncitizens, as well as citizens, protection from being detained indefinitely and having their liberty deprived without due process. It also entitles them to equal protection of the laws and a speedy and public trial. In response to the Inspector General's report, the Justice Department remained defiant, stating that it made "no apologies" for using every "legal" means to safeguard the public from future terrorist attacks. At a congressional hearing designed to explore the abuses of detainees noted in the report, Attorney General John Ashcroft had the chutzpah to request even more powers for his department.[78]

Even U.S. citizens have been designated by the Bush administration as "enemy combatants," a status which allows them to be detained indefinitely in military custody without charges, a trial, or access to counsel. That status keeps them in limbo between having their rights fully protected as "prisoners of war" under the Geneva Convention and having their rights protected as regular defendants in the civilian court system of the United States. The label of "enemy combatants" is a convenient, fabricated, and artificial designation that allows the administration to flagrantly exclude those people from any of the traditional republican safeguards against administrative abuse. The American Bar Association recommended that those citizens and legal aliens designated as enemy combatants have the right to judicial review of their status, counsel during such a review, and clear standards and procedures governing their designation and treatment.[79] The U.S. Supreme Court subesquently ruled that such "enemy combatants" do have the right to judicial review of their indefinite imprisonment. A better solution would be to do away with the "enemy combatant" designation altogether and cover the detainees under one of the two other more legitimate categories.

In order to try noncitizens, the Bush administration has set up military tribunals away from American territory and, it maintains, legal authority. Although the administration made some concessions to the public outcry about lack of safeguards for the rights of the defendants facing such tribunals, the deck is still heavily stacked against them. The tribunals feature secrecy on who is eligible to be tried, standards of evidence less than that of a civilian court (including secret evidence), conviction of the defendant by only a two-thirds vote, the absence of the right to appeal to civilian courts, and judges (who also act as jurors) beholden to the President's men. According to the Pentagon's General Counsel, even if the tribunal acquits a detainee, he or she may not be released.[80] The odds are so stacked against defendants that the President of the Association of Criminal Defense Lawyers discouraged civilian defense lawyers from participating in the tribunals.[81]

But, of course, arguing about procedural safeguards in military tribunals is like arguing about what meat to grill as the house is burning down. Although such tribunals were used to try and convict German saboteurs caught on U.S. soil during World War II, they were likely as unconstitutional then as they are now. The Fifth Amendment to the Constitution promises that "No person shall be held to answer for a capital or otherwise infamous crime unless on a presentation of a Grand Jury, except in cases arising in the land or naval forces, or in the Militia, when in actual service in time of War or public danger." The exception for armed forces refers to U.S. troops to be tried in military courts martial, not to people in foreign armies or groups. The standards of military tribunals do not even measure up to that of military courts martial. The Fifth Amendment also says that no "person" should be "deprived of life, liberty, or property without due process of law." Military tribunals in no way provide adequate safeguards for due process. And the Sixth Amendment is also categorical: "In all criminal prosecutions, the accused shall enjoy the right to a speedy and public trial, by an impartial jury." Military tribunals are secret and the defendant is not judged by a jury of his or her peers, but instead by a commission of military judges appointed by the Deputy Secretary of Defense.

The media and public have been excluded from immigration court hearings of those jailed after September 11. Even the location of the hearings has been kept secret. These policies seems to violate the aforementioned constitutional guarantee of a public trial.

The executive branch is now monitoring attorney-client communications without the judicial branch overseeing such snooping. Previously, surveillance of this kind was permitted only with the approval of a court. This new intrusion threatens to undermine the confidentiality between a lawyer and client, thus jeopardizing the right to have effective counsel. That right is a bulwark of defendant rights in the U.S. judicial system.

But those many encroachments on civil liberties are not all that the Bush administration has planned.

More Police Power Is in the Pipeline

Bush administration officials have predicted that it's a matter of "when, and not if" another major terrorist attack will occur in the United States. And they are ready and waiting. They are already drafting new proposed legislation that promises even greater powers for law enforcement and even fewer civil liberties for Americans. The draft legislation—informally dubbed PATRIOT Act II—was leaked to the public.[82] The following summarizes the provisions of the proposed legislation and comments on them.

The legislative proposal removes the right of legal immigrants to get a fair deportation hearing and ends the authority of federal courts to review immigration rulings. Once again, the executive branch becomes more powerful at the expense of other branches in the all-important checks-and-balances system enshrined in the Constitution.

The proposed legislation ends court-approved restrictions on spying by local police on political and religious activities. This further erodes independent judicial review of government surveillance.

The proposal allows government wiretaps without a warrant for fifteen days after a terrorist attack. That provision is seemingly unconstitutional, given that the Fourth Amendment guarantees against general search warrants. It states that warrants shall not be issued unless "particularly describing the place to be searched, and the persons or things to be seized." Also, there is a lack of clarity about what triggers the provision. One could expect that a major terrorist attack, such as the September 11 incident, would do so, but what about less drastic incidents?[83]

Under the proposal, the government is permitted to seize credit and library records without a warrant. Again, the Fourth Amendment seems to guarantee that no searches will be conducted without a warrant based on "probable cause."

The proposed legislation authorizes the government to make secret arrests in terrorism cases. Surely, secret proceedings belong in the Stalinist Soviet Union, not the "home of the free and the brave," especially given the lower-threat environment now that the Soviet Union is in the dustbin of history. In addition, incommunicado detentions also seem to violate the International Covenant on Civil and Political Rights, to which the United States has subscribed.[84]

The legislative proposal further widens an overly broad definition of terrorism so that those merely practicing civil disobedience could be wiretapped, have their assets seized, or even lose their citizenship. The most audacious proposal in this area allows the government to strip Americans of their citizenship even if they are only engaging in the lawful activities of a group designated by the Attorney General as a "terrorist organization."[85] Indirectly, this augmented police power could chill free speech by making individuals or groups fearful that they could be arrested on the severe charges of being terrorists. In addition, the proposal sets the dangerous precedent of allowing the government to strip citizenship from persons it deems undesirable.

The proposal creates a DNA database in the Justice Department for those the authorities suspect of association with terrorism. Mere suspicion by law enforcement would force people to contribute the samples, and failure to produce samples would be a criminal offense.[86] As repeated on so many of the government's proposals or actual restrictions on civil liberties, the Fourth Amendment seems to prevent such activities without a warrant based on "probable cause."

Why Augmented Government Powers Undermine the Fight Against Terrorism

Some conservatives criticize civil libertarians for being more concerned about defending the rights of terrorists than about the security of the American public. Yet civil libertarians have no problem with severely punishing convicted terrorists, as long as the suspect receives due process according to the Constitution. Such due process includes searches with court-approved warrants based on probable cause, effective counsel, and open, public, and fair jury trials with acceptable standards of evidence. In a free society, even those accused of heinous crimes should be given adequate due process—after all, they might turn out to be innocent.

The problem is that when suspected terrorists are not provided with such safeguards, the rights of everyone are endangered. The best example of such danger can be found in the Justice Department's own Inspector General's report. After the September 11 attacks, more than one thousand people were detained secretively and indefinitely without charges, a trial, or access to counsel, and some of them were physically and mentally abused while in custody. Only a very few of those detained were ultimately suspected of being linked to terrorism. If immigrants can be treated in a way that violates the liberties enshrined in the U.S. Constitution by the founders, U.S. citizens are next. Civil libertarians are sticking up for everyone's rights, not just those of potential terrorists.

Think of Terrorism as a Crime, Not a War

A basic problem is that since September 11, the country is moving from regarding terrorism as a crime to regarding it as a war. There have always been both views in the U.S. fight against terrorism. But President Bush's broad and dramatically announced "war against terror" and his use of military power in Afghanistan and Iraq have put the nation on a permanent war footing. Although military action in Afghanistan was justified to weaken al Qaeda, the broad and hyped general war on terror has been used to claim that draconian domestic measures are needed to effectively fight terrorism. Nothing could be further from the truth.

The Bush II administration used the September 11 attacks to expand U.S. influence overseas (for example, U.S. military involvement in central Asia, Georgia, and the Philippines) and to carry out a vendetta against Iraq. Had the administration instead carried out a quieter campaign against only al Qaeda, using *mainly* the "terrorism as a crime" model, its efforts would have been much more successful. Conducting an excessively broad, high-profile war against terror merely generates more anti-U.S. terrorist attacks via the blowback (or "lightning rod") effect and makes it more difficult for the intelligence services of other nations (especially those of Arab and Islamic countries) to cooperate with U.S. intelligence in tracking down al Qaeda. More important, a nation on a war footing is more likely to take unneeded, draconian actions at home to spy on its own people in the name of fighting terrorism. But even before the PATRIOT Act, the intelligence and law enforcement communities had more than adequate tools to track down al Qaeda members. If the Bush II administration had adopted the quieter "terrorism is a crime" approach and attempted to lessen the public's thirst for revenge after September 11, rather than whipping it into a frenzy in order to create an opportunity to destroy other enemies (for example, Iraq), much less pressure to implement new strictures on civil liberties would have been generated. Those restrictions actually impede the fight against al Qaeda.

The Government Frequently Shoots Itself in the Foot

Fighting terrorism by increasing the already-intrusive police powers of the U.S. government is counterproductive for several reasons. As horrific as the September 11 terrorist attacks were for the thousands of people involved and their loved ones, the chances of any individual American becoming the victim of such an attack are miniscule. And the September 11 attacks were much more catastrophic than the vast majority of terrorist incidents, which usually only kill a few people. Although terrorists could get chemical, biological, or nuclear weapons, there are still barriers for their effective use. For example, nuclear weapons would be hard for terrorists to obtain or build, and chemical and biological weapons require technical expertise and ideal weather conditions to have maximum effect.

Terrorism is primarily designed to produce fear in the population, and the September 11 attacks were successful in doing so. Inducing that effect is especially easy among humans, who have survived and prospered over the millennia because the fear instinct has made them conservative about confronting dangers. But humans are also thinking creatures and should not be convinced to abandon what is truly unique about America—its liberty—based on irrational fear. In fact, the U.S. government is actually helping the terrorists generate terror. To show the public that something was being done about terrorism, it created a highly visible, color-coded terror alert system. But when the alert level is elevated, based on vague government justifications, only greater fear is generated among the public because people have not been told what actions to take to mitigate the risk. The terrorists, with the help of free publicity from the target government, can get much mileage out of a few scattered attacks or even mere threats.

Even before the implementation of the PATRIOT Act and the added executive branch actions that undermined liberty, the government had plenty of investigative and law enforcement power to combat this manageable threat. The law enforcement community already had potent surveillance powers. Also, although special new antiterrorism legislation was alluring to politicians in the wake of a major terrorist incident, the most heinous acts usually committed by terrorists—that is, murder, bodily injury, and destruction of property—were already illegal and could be punished severely.[87] Thus, the need for new government powers to fight terrorism was questionable.

Before enacting new antiterrorism legislation that curbs civil liberties, politicians rarely analyze whether previous restrictions on such liberties (for example, the Antiterrorism and Effective Death Penalty Act, signed into law in 1996 after the first World Trade Center bombing of 1993 and the Oklahoma City bombing of 1995) have been ineffective or whether intelligence and law enforcement officials were negligent or incompetent in preventing the catastrophe. Tim Lynch of the Cato Institute perceptively asks, "If the government cannot discipline itself for dereliction, negligence, incompetence, poor performance, and corruption, why in the world should it be rewarded with additional funds and additional powers?"[88]

After September 11, Congress never paused to consider that the increased law enforcement powers in the 1996 law failed to prevent the attacks on the Pentagon and the World Trade Center. In addition, Congress passed the PATRIOT Act—giving the intelligence community and law enforcement even more power domestically—before investigations showed that incompetence at the FBI, its failure to adequately coordinate with the intelligence community, and intelligence failures impaired the government's ability to prevent the attack. If we continue to reward failure with higher budgets and more powers, we are in for more of the same.

After September 11, funding for homeland security was vastly increased and a whole new bureaucracy, the Department of Homeland Security, was created. The department was proposed by the Bush II administration largely as a "bait and switch" tactic to shift media attention away from new embarrassing revelations about government intelligence and security failures before September 11. Previously, the administration had opposed creating a new agency.

In addition to adding a new layer of bureaucracy over combined existing agencies, the new department did not address the original bureaucratic problem that caused the government failure. Subsequent information has indicated that the government had information that could have been useful in meeting the September 11 threat. The CIA and the FBI, however, failed to coordinate adequately. Yet curiously, those agencies were left out of the new department. More important, the department has a new intelligence office that will exacerbate the coordination difficulties among the multitude of existing U.S. intelligence agencies, which was the original problem. To fight small, mobile, and agile terrorist groups, the already bloated security bureaucracies—normally oriented to counter sluggish nation-states—need to be streamlined, not expanded.

Also, the fight against al Qaeda critically depends on the cooperation of foreign intelligence, law enforcement, and judicial organizations. In many countries, the United States just does not have the information needed to locate, apprehend, and extradite al Qaeda suspects. When the United States erodes the due process rights of both citizens and noncitizens, other nations are reluctant to hand over suspected terrorists (particularly their own nationals). For example, the Europeans have expressed a reluctance to turn suspects over to U.S. military tribunals because those bodies lack due process safeguards. The American Bar Association alluded to such possible negative reactions from foreign governments in recommending that Congress and the executive branch consider how U.S. policies adopted toward "enemy combatants" may affect the response of other countries to future terrorist attacks.[89]

Ethnic communities within the United States can also have an adverse reaction to the U.S. government's intrusive antiterrorist tactics. Interrogating and intimidating thousands of Arab and South Asian immigrants simply because of their ethnicity or country of origin is not the way to get cooperation from groups that might otherwise be naturally disposed to help track terrorists. Only a miniscule minority of those immigrants are terrorists and, in fact, many have come to the United States to flee oppression or strictly Islamic societies. Thus, many immigrants and refugees are naturally suspicious of agents of any government. Instead of using such heavy-handed tactics or racial or ethnic profiling, the U.S. law enforcement community should make every effort to cultivate the support of such communities and act in ways that do not resemble the authoritarian governments of their countries of origin. The U.S. authorities will get much more cooperation using a softer approach than they will using "gangbuster" tactics that are likely to cause those communities to "circle the wagons."

Apparently, racial and ethnic profiling and the use of intrusive investigative tactics that violate civil liberties—favored by Congress and high-level intelligence and law enforcement political appointees, such as Attorney General Ashcroft—are not even that popular with law enforcement professionals. Senior intelligence specialists noted that the use of racial profiling and other investigative tactics that contravene civil liberties could actually reduce security by displacing more effective techniques for identifying suspicious individuals.[90] Similarly, at least eight former high-ranking FBI officials, many from the Reagan and Bush I administrations, attacked antiterrorism proposals that compromised civil liberties on the grounds that they are ineffectual and displace more effective investigative methods.[91]

Just as unconstitutional investigative tactics are no more effective than constitutional ones, neither are military tribunals more effective than public jury trials. The government's claim that military tribunals provide more security for terrorism-related cases is highly questionable. In espionage and Mafia trials, civilian court proceedings have been successfully shrouded to protect government secrets and witnesses, respectively (although in a free society, such secrecy should be kept to a minimum). There is no reason to believe that civilian courts could not handle any terrorism case imaginable. The only advantage of military tribunals for the government is that they can act as "kangaroo courts," which can more easily win convictions and death sentences against suspected terrorists. The tribunals have lower standards of evidence and a panel of executive branch–appointed military judges acting as jurors. But even persons suspected of vile acts of terrorism deserve a fair trial. As noted previously, when the government detained large numbers of immigrants without charges and counsel, the vast majority of those caught up in the sweep had nothing to do with terrorism. Once again, if we fail to defend against government encroachment on the standards of due process for suspected terrorists, we undermine such rights for all Americans.

Similar to the opportunity costs experienced by intelligence and law enforcement officers on any terrorism investigation (see above), those costs also arise on the societal level. Unconstitutional and intrusive law enforcement tactics and military tribunals give the American public a false sense of security and divert attention from measures that would be more likely to enhance the security of Americans from terrorist attacks. Improved homeland security measures that do not result in a wholesale assault on civil liberties (for example, real enhancements to airport security) and a toned-down foreign policy would make successful anti-U.S. terrorist attacks less likely in the first place.

The adoption by the United States of a foreign policy of fewer military interventions cannot be emphasized enough. There is no one perfect solution to terrorism, but this proposed policy change would go a long way toward reducing anti-American attacks. Improvements in intelligence and homeland security can only go so far.[92] The United States is the largest truly open society in the world and has many lucrative targets for terrorists to attack—for example, there are hundreds of skyscrapers and thousands of shopping malls and sports stadiums. Without a change in U.S. foreign policy, effectively safeguarding such a massive landmass, with thousands of miles of borders, against all terrorist attacks would effectively require a police state. Unfortunately, the Bush administration is currently headed in that direction. Long ago, former Supreme Court Justice Louis Brandeis best summed up the state of American liberty in which we find ourselves today: "The greatest dangers to liberty lurk in insidious encroachment by men of zeal, well-meaning but without understanding."[93]

And domestic liberty is not the only thing sacrificed on the altar of empire. Fiscal prudence is also undermined through vested interests taking advantage of war and empire to feed at the public trough.

IMPERIAL WARS SPIKE CORPORATE WELFARE

In the nation's capital, vested interests, such as the law enforcement bureaucracies cited above, routinely take advantage of "crises" to satisfy parochial desires. Similarly, many corporations use crises to get pet projects—a.k.a. pork—funded by the government. And national security crises, because of peoples' fears, are especially ripe opportunities to grab largesse. The public rarely has enough detailed knowledge to distinguish legitimate security expenditures from pork spending for projects that are just riding the wave of support for enhanced security.

Sometimes the "getting while the getting's good" mentality can be taken to ridiculous lengths. In the wake of September 11, President Bush declared that beef subsidies to ranchers and farmers were in the interest of national security because "after all, people have to eat." That may be true, but why beef? Why not pork, chicken, lamb, turnips, or mushrooms? Even if beef producers were so spooked by the September 11 attacks that they all quit raising cattle, al Qaeda could in no way stop the imports of beef from other countries, such as Canada or Argentina. In fact, what was happening here was that the president was using the horrible tragedy of September 11 to hand out a form of welfare to one of the core constituencies of the Republican Party. If the president is presenting beef subsidies as critical to the nation's security, perhaps other increases in spending justified in a similar manner should be examined closely.

In a more mundane example, after September 11, President Bush asked for a whopping $48 billion in added defense spending. Yet only about $20 billion of that was used to fight the war on terror. The requested 2005 budget, to take effect three years after the September 11 attacks, contained a 7 percent increase in defense spending—even excluding the exorbitant sums being spent on the continuing wars in Afghanistan and Iraq. But the defense budget contains weapon systems that are simply unneeded (for example, the Virginia-class submarines), too costly (new aircraft carriers), designed for the cold war (F-22 fighters), or troubled (V-22 Osprey tilt-rotor transport aircraft). The American empire, militarily more dominant than any empire in world history, can fight brushfire wars against terrorists and their "rogue" state sponsors without those gold-plated white elephants. Those weapons programs should be cancelled, but they continue to be produced. The military services, defense industries, and members of Congress, who are worried about employment in their states and districts, all have a vested interest in their continuation. And this is the tip of the iceberg. There are many other systems and programs in the defense budget that could be cut back or terminated. Instead, in the name of fighting the "war on terror," the taxpayer is being bilked for tens of billions of dollars for weapons that make little or no contribution to that war.

The U.S. national security establishment gets an annual budget of over $400 billion. Yet if there is a war—considered the establishment's primary mission—supplemental funds are provided. In fiscal years 2003 and 2004, the Pentagon got $166 billion above its annual allocation to invade and occupy Iraq and conduct an occupation of Afghanistan[94] (DoD will probably get at least another $50 billion for fiscal year 2005). That supplemental request was supposed to be for expenses related only to the military operation and reconstruction of the two countries. But $339 million was included for secret research and development on weapons that are usually part of the regular budget. This strategy took advantage of the crisis to free up more money in the regular budget to research, develop, or acquire larger numbers of other weapons, many of which are unneeded. The Pentagon has used this supplemental funding strategy in previous wars, funding the Joint Stars ground-surveillance aircraft in the Persian Gulf War in 1991 and the Global Hawk remotely piloted reconnaissance plane in the recent wars in Afghanistan and Iraq.[95]

During the Korean War, the same "bait and switch" was used. Only a fraction of the increased defense spending went to munitions for the conflict. Most went to stock the new imperial bases in Britain, Italy, Germany, Japan, and South Korea.

Similarly, during the Kosovo campaign, a spike in defense spending occurred that was greater than the needs for war. This phenomenon happens every time a war is in the offing. Kosovo is an example of liberals falling victim to a friendly president's questionable "humanitarian" justification for a war really fought for reasons of realpolitik. Such humanitarian wars spike an already bloated defense budget (the $400 billion budget for national defense already represents half of federal discretionary spending) and take resources away from other societal needs.

Some liberals promote fighting humanitarian wars but also take the contradictory position of advocating substantial cuts in the defense budget. Crusading advocates of a U.S. empire that brings democracy to developing countries at gunpoint need to face the fact that such a policy costs big money and sucks resources from alternative uses. Liberals must face up to what their nemesis, the conservative then–Speaker of the House Newt Gingrich, was forced to admit: "You do not need today's defense budget to defend the United States. You need today's defense budget to lead the world. If you are prepared to give up leading the world, you can have a much smaller defense budget."[96]

The weapons manufacturers are not the only vested interests benefiting from the American empire. As Chalmers Johnson notes, the empire also supports the military and their families, U.S. diplomats and their families, and the university and federal research community. Also, the empire provides hidden subsidies to the oil industry, other transnational corporations, and banks.[97]

It would be nice to think that vested interests would refrain from taking advantage of horrendous human tragedies, such as September 11. But Washington is a cynical town and vested interests know how the system works. Any crisis permits increased government spending, and plenty of vested interests are lining up to milk the crisis for their own parochial gains. Maintaining the empire and retaliating for the blowback from that empire keeps what President Eisenhower called the military-industrial complex fat and happy.

5 Why All Americans Should Be Against Empire

The previous two chapters have made the case against an American empire to conservatives and liberals, respectively. Each of those chapters included arguments that were directed toward the particular camp concerned. Pacifists, moderates, libertarians, independents, and others will hopefully be convinced by arguments in each or both of those chapters. As a supplement, however, this chapter aims to raise issues that all Americans, regardless of their ideology, should be concerned about.

According to Edward Olsen, a scholar at the Naval Postgraduate School, a diverse grass roots coalition will be needed to get rid of imperial U.S. foreign policy:

> In order for the "Yankee come home" theme to catch on among the masses in the United States, it would be necessary for Americans of very different political persuasions to foster a lasting common front on the issue of non-interventionism. This could yield strange bedfellows indeed, encompassing the McGovernite left, the Buchanan right, alienated new Democrats, Taft Republicans of the paleoconservative stripe, libertarians, pacifists, Perotistas and what is sometimes labeled the "radical middle" whose often inchoate frustrations are rooted in populist desires for a greater domestic focus.[1]

The main purpose of this volume is to bring together the diverse groups that Olsen names by offering debating points that a wide variety of political persuasions can use to argue for dismantling the U.S. empire and restoring the republic. This chapter provides arguments that do not fit neatly into the chapters for liberals or conservatives.

IMPERIAL FOREIGN POLICY LEADS TO AN IMPERIAL PRESIDENCY

In 1787, the framers of the U.S. Constitution envisioned that the most powerful branches of the federal form of government would be Congress and the states. In the Constitution, Article 1 concerns the Congress and gives that body many more powers than the executive branch. The Tenth Amendment in the Constitution's Bill of Rights indicates that unless a particular power is specifically delegated to the U.S. government, it is reserved to the states or people.

Despite sporadic spikes in executive branch power during wars—for example, in the Polk administration during the Mexican War and in the Lincoln administration during the Civil War—the system enshrined in the Constitution worked as it was supposed to until very late in the nineteenth century. The Congress was clearly the strongest branch of government during the last part of the nineteenth century. That period was distinguished largely by congressional restraint of U.S. expansion overseas.

The rise of the executive branch as the nineteenth century closed, however, went hand in hand with the first imperial war, the Spanish-American conflict. The rise in executive power and expansion of the federal bureaucracy culminated in the election of William McKinley in 1896. The rise of executive power also led to the U.S. naval buildup that permitted the United States to grab Spanish lands in the 1898 war.[2] During the twentieth century, a more interventionist foreign policy, and concomitant wars, in turn eventually caused even more power to migrate to the more hierarchical executive branch. Both an expansive foreign policy and wars are difficult for Congress to run because of its many chiefs. In contrast, the president is the lone head of the executive branch. A more assertive foreign policy, after the precedent of the Spanish-American War, led to even bolder executive actions by Teddy Roosevelt, McKinley's successor. As technology marched on, wars got larger and bloodier. World War I was the first war to require the entire mobilization of American society. The only entity capable of orchestrating that feat was the president and the much larger executive branch under his control. The Great War set a precedent for government intrusion into the private economy and society that was theretofore unheard of.

World War II was on a grander scale yet. The conflict required an even larger mobilization of civilian resources to fight a truly global war. Government intrusion into the private sector increased, as did executive power.

The cold war was a different kind of conflict than the hot wars of World Wars I and II. Ostensibly at peace, the United States faced off worldwide with a nuclear-armed Soviet Union. Theoretically at least, nuclear war could happen within minutes. Presidents used the perceived need for fast decision making to accrue even more power vis-à-vis the other branches of government. In the later part of the cold war, the president had so much relative power that scholars and other observers invented the catchphrase "imperial presidency" to describe it.

After the attacks of September 11, 2001, President George W. Bush has used the perceived need for extensive government action to prevent future attacks to extend the accrual of executive power into the twenty-first century. As noted earlier, using executive action and the expanded powers given it by Congress in the PATRIOT Act, the Bush II administration augmented its surveillance and police powers significantly.

But the September 11 attacks were generated in the first place by U.S. government actions overseas. The American empire and its concomitant policies stir up hatred overseas that manifests itself in blowback terrorist attacks against U.S. targets.

This episode is not the first in which U.S. government actions have led to a crisis that then generates increased pressure for more government action to fix the problem. The cycle has repeated itself many times in American history. For example, the roots of World War II and the cold war, with their concomitant growth of executive power, lie in the ill-advised U.S. entry into World War I. According to many historians, World War I—not World War II or the cold war—was the seminal event of the twentieth century. U.S. entry into the Great War tipped the balance in favor of the allies and delayed the exit of the Soviet Union. U.S. allies demanded severe reparations from Germany, and Woodrow Wilson himself insisted on the removal of Kaiser Wilhelm from power. Both of those factors, when combined with World War I's irreparable tearing of Germany's social fabric, led to the rise of the Nazis and to World War II. In Russia, after the fall of Czar Nicholas, the Provisional Government of Aleksandr Kerenski wanted to pull out of the bloody and unpopular World War I. But the U.S. entry into that war delayed the withdrawal of Russian forces. Vladimir Lenin rode the unpopularity of the war into power and created the Soviet Union, which was destined eventually to be a totalitarian superpower.

Given that history, it is clear that even today, the far-reaching American empire leads to the unhealthy accrual of executive power at home. Nowhere has that development been less noticed and more dangerous than in the transfer of the war powers from Congress to the president.

U.S. EMPIRE HAS ERODED THE CONGRESSIONAL WAR POWERS

The most solemn and consequential decision a nation can make is whether or not to go to war. War incurs great costs, both economic and human. The nation's founders, unlike today's leaders, had a greater grasp of those facts. The founders were also appalled by the actions of European monarchs. Those monarchs would regularly launch wars of self-aggrandizement and oppress their subjects by letting the financial and human costs fall on them. The people would be required to supply the personnel for armies and navies and the taxes to pay for them.

The founders wanted to escape the militarism of Europe. To guard against what could have been the death knell of the new republic, the founders, in the Constitution, gave most of the war powers to Congress rather than to the executive branch. James Madison, the principal author of the document, noted, "In no part of the Constitution is more wisdom to be found than in the clause which confides the question of war and peace to the legislature, and not the executive department. . . . The trust and temptation would be too great for any one man."[3] Although the president was the commander in chief of the armed forces after a conflict began, the powers to declare war, raise armies, maintain the navy, and fund and regulate them fell to the branch of government closest to the people—the Congress.

Madison was very right about the executive temptation for war. U.S. presidents, much like the European monarchs of old, have a rich history of finding excuses—or manufacturing them—to go to war. Some examples should illustrate the point. In 1898, an explosion on the U.S. warship *Maine* in Havana harbor was used to stoke war fervor toward the Spanish. That jingoism led to the Spanish-American War and the acquisition of Spanish possessions in the Caribbean and the Pacific. In 1846, the United States provoked a Mexican attack by sending troops into a disputed region on the Texas-Mexican border. The United States wanted to start a conflict with the much weaker foe to grab huge tracts of Mexican land in what is now the American West. In 1964, the Johnson administration either fabricated or exaggerated a North Vietnamese attack on a U.S. ship in the Gulf of Tonkin to escalate U.S. involvement in the Vietnam War. The Reagan administration deliberately provoked conflict with Libyan leader Moammar Qaddafi in the Gulf of Sidra in the 1980s and used the excuse of rescuing medical students to invade Grenada in 1983. In 1989, the Bush I administration labeled Manuel Noriega a drug-running thug and invaded Panama to oust him. The Bush II administration dubiously asserted that Saddam Hussein's "weapons of mass destruction" were an imminent threat, implied a false link between Saddam and the September 11 attacks, and launched an invasion to remove him from power.

Unfortunately, with the post–World War II advent of the American empire, the vital congressional war powers as a check on presidents have eroded considerably. Repudiating the Constitution and an American tradition up until that point, beginning during the long cold war with the Korean conflict, presidents no longer felt the need to ask Congress for a declaration of war. Since 1945, more than one hundred thousand U.S. service men and women have died and another four hundred thousand have been injured in wars that were never declared as such.[4] In 1950 at the outset of the Korean War, for the first time in history, a president failed to get a declaration of war from Congress for a major conflict. Unfortunately, that pattern has continued down to the present day.

Now, presidents curiously claim—in direct contravention of the written Constitution, the intent of the founders as recorded in the debates at the Constitutional Convention, and more than one hundred and sixty years of precedent—that they can take the country to war without a congressional declaration. For example, Presidents Truman and Johnson claimed, respectively, that the Korean War and Vietnam War were "police actions" and therefore did not require Congress to declare war. In Vietnam, the congressional Gulf of Tonkin Resolution had to suffice. President Bush I went to Congress to get support for the first Gulf War but maintained that he had the authority to take the country to war with or without congressional approval. After the Dayton agreements, President Clinton, without congressional approval, deployed twenty-thousand U.S. forces in Bosnia to join a multilateral peacekeeping force.[5] Even worse, Clinton did not get congressional approval to bomb Kosovo or threaten Haiti with invasion.

Truman, Johnson, Bush I, and other presidents essentially claimed that their authority as commanders in chief of U.S. forces allowed them to take the country to war. Unfortunately, the Constitution, on its face, separates the president's role as commander in chief of the military from the Congress's power to declare war. According to the debate on the war powers in the Constitutional Convention, the only exception was that of responding to an imminent attack in which the president had no time to ask Congress for such a declaration. Even then, at the earliest practicable moment, the president was supposed to ask Congress for a declaration. After the end of the cold war, it is unlikely that this situation will occur any time soon. Any nation that attacked the territory of the United States—a country with the most powerful nuclear arsenal on the planet and two great oceans as moats—would be committing suicide.

Of course, as September 11 showed, groups without a home address can attack the United States. In that case, the president, at the earliest possible time, should have asked Congress for a declaration of war against al Qaeda and its sponsor Afghanistan. That request was never made.

For military actions short of major war, such as reprisal raids or punitive launches of cruise missiles, the Constitution gave Congress the power to grant letters of marque and reprisal. That provision has a lot of cobwebs on it. For example, in 1998, Bill Clinton gave Congress no substantive role when he decided to launch cruise missiles at a pharmaceutical factory in Sudan and terrorist training camps in Afghanistan in retaliation for al Qaeda bombings of two U.S. embassies in East Africa.

Disgust with the Vietnam War temporarily roused the Congress from its constitutional slumber to cut off funding and pass the War Powers Resolution in 1973. Unfortunately, the funding termination occurred very late in the game—only as the war was already winding down. Presidents have always regarded the War Powers Resolution as an unconstitutional restriction on their powers as commanders in chief to commit U.S. forces to war. In fact, the resolution is unconstitutional because it allows the president a free pass to employ troops for ninety days without a prior congressional declaration of war before a congressional vote is required to keep those troops in the field. In practice, once American troops are on the ground in a foreign land, Congress politically has little choice but to approve their continued presence on the battlefield or face charges from the president that it is being unpatriotic by endangering American forces. It is a curious form of patriotism and "support for the troops" to approve getting them killed in a military action overseas that has nothing to do with U.S. security. But such are the political pressures if Congress waits to approve the military action after the president has created a fait accompli. Thus, the War Powers Resolution undermines the constitutional requirement for the Congress to declare war, and so approve of a conflict before it starts.

In short, during the cold war with the rise of the global American empire and an environment of perpetual conflict, Congress abdicated one of its most potent powers under the Constitution. That shirking of responsibility continued during the initial post–cold war years and the state of perpetual "war against terror" after September 11. Such lack of congressional courage in keeping the president out of foreign wars would make the founders roll over in their graves. The signers of the Constitution recognized the intrinsic geographical advantages of the United States in the security realm and thus believed it was unnecessary to get embroiled in foreign intrigues and conflicts. They also realized that Britain's isolation from the conflict-ridden European continent had fostered individual freedoms there. There was less need for a large standing army for defense, which also could be used to oppress people domestically. Those British freedoms were in turn transmitted to English colonies in the new world. In other words, the founders realized that war eroded the freedoms of a republic. Yet modern U.S. presidents are allowed by Congress to lead the country into wars of empire on a whim. When blowback occurs—as dramatically illustrated by the terrorist attacks on September 11—and civil liberties are curtailed, the founders' worst fears have come to pass. The American empire is undermining the American republic.

THE EMPIRE DENUDES U.S. SECURITY

When people feel threatened, they seem to look to the government for protection (even though the government, in defending them, may encroach on their liberty). After all, nation-states were created in the first place as attempts to defend societies. Yet few people ever ask whether the government may have helped create the security threat in the first place. That question is especially important in the case of the United States, which should not be inherently prone to external threats. America's geographically isolated position (making foreign conflicts much less threatening to its security), weak and friendly neighbors, and a globally dominant arsenal of thousands of nuclear weapons should make the nation relatively invulnerable to conventional attack. Similarly, all other things being equal, the United States intrinsically should not be a prime target for terrorists. Civil wars—ethnic or otherwise—sometimes spawn terrorism, but the United States has none. Strong, unfriendly neighbors can sometimes attempt to destabilize nearby countries, but the only unfriendly countries in the Western Hemisphere are the very weak Cuba and Venezuela.

Nonetheless, according to the U.S. State Department, anti-U.S. terrorism regularly accounts for between 40 and 60 percent of all international terrorist incidents.[6] For a country that should be inherently unsusceptible to attacks from terrorists, that figure is astounding. Some other factor must be causing the United States to be attacked so frequently. Terrorists do not give up their lives and fortunes and travel halfway around the world to launch suicide attacks unless they have some compelling reasons to do so (regardless of whether or not Americans agree with those reasons or the terrorists' heinous practices).

Terrorists Do Not Attack American Freedoms or Culture

The reasons terrorists disproportionately attack the United States have nothing to do with jealousy of American freedoms, as President George W. Bush declared. In fact, repeated polls of Arabic and Islamic nations indicate that American political and economic freedoms are admired in those countries.[7] Andrew Bacevich, a well-respected scholar at Boston University, perceptively noted: "In offering his own explanation for the attack on the World Trade

Center and the Pentagon, George W. Bush refused to countenance even the possibility that an assault on symbols of American economic and military power might have anything to do with how the United States employed its power. He chose instead to frame the issue at hand in terms of freedom. Why do they hate us? 'They hate our freedoms,' Bush explained. Thus did the president skillfully deflect attention from the consequences of empire."[8]

Also belying the president's view is the fact that other Western nations have free societies—both politically and economically—but are much less threatened by terrorist attacks than is the United States. In one of those aforementioned polls, Canada, France, and Germany—unlike the United States (despite the admiration of its freedoms)—received overall favorable ratings.[9]

And the United States is not attacked disproportionately because American culture is hated. Those same polls indicate that American culture is admired worldwide.[10] In fact, the most telling statistic in this respect may be the astoundingly high approval rating of American movies and TV in even ultraconservative Islamic nations: 54 percent in Saudi Arabia and 75 percent in Iran.[11] Besides, in the Middle East, Indian movies are more watched than U.S. films, and Algerian and Egyptian music are more listened to than U.S. songs. So if there are cries of cultural imperialism in that region, they are directed at those nations.[12]

Contrary to popular belief, Osama bin Laden, in his writings and speeches, does not focus his ire on a decadent U.S. culture. Peter Bergen, a former terrorism expert for CNN, who has been one of the few Western journalists to interview Osama bin Laden, notes:

> In all of the tens of thousands of words that bin Laden has uttered on the public record there are some significant omissions: he does not rail against the pernicious effects of Hollywood movies, or against Madonna's midriff, or against the pornography protected by the U.S. Constitution. Nor does he inveigh against the drug and alcohol culture of the West, or its tolerance for homosexuals.

He leaves that kind of material to the Chrisitian fundamentalist Jerry Falwell, who opined that the September 11 attacks were God's vengeance on Americans for condoning feminism and homosexuality. If we may judge by his silence, bin Laden cares little about such cultural issues.[13]

Blowback Terrorism Is Caused by U.S. Interventionism

So what is the missing factor explaining why the United States is disproportionately attacked by terrorists? Although in America the president, other high-level policymakers, the foreign policy elite, the media, and even large segments of the public are in a state of denial, that factor is obvious to the rest of the world: the interventionist U.S. foreign policy in support of the informal American global empire. The polls cited above noted that the United States received unfavorable ratings from people in both Moslem and non-Moslem countries around the world, not because of its political and economic freedoms, or its culture, but because of its policies—particularly toward the Middle East.[14] In one worldwide poll of foreign political, government, business, media, and cultural elites, non-U.S. opinion leaders concluded that "U.S. policies and actions in the world" were a major reason for the attacks of September 11. In contrast, only a small portion of U.S. elites held that view.[15]

Of course, the state of denial by U.S. elites is predictable. According to Peter Bergen, after September 11, "the airwaves quickly filled with blathering bloviators, who called this an attack on 'the American way of life,' on the very idea of the United States and its culture. While such statements may provide psychological satisfaction to those who make them, they shed more heat than light on the motivations of bin Laden and his followers."[16] But more than psychological satisfaction is behind such statements. Many of those "blathering bloviators"—including President George W. Bush—are the ones who conduct the interventionist, neoimperial U.S. foreign policy and who want to avoid, at all costs, the damning link between that policy and the attacks on September 11.

Of course, the polling results in foreign nations, particularly Arab and Moslem countries, severely undermine the self-serving, baseless arguments of U.S. interventionists and empire-builders, who assert that the United States is attacked for "who it is, not what it does." To attempt to discredit the damning polling data, the interventionists have argued that the results reflect only the thoughts of the general populations of those nations, not the terrorists. Since terrorists do not regularly identify themselves to those taking polls, pollsters must sample the universe of people from which the much smaller number of terrorists arise. If the general populations of Arab and Moslem nations hate the United States for its foreign policy, it is not a stretch to conclude that the most violent elements of those populations hate the United States even more fervently for the same reason.

But there is no need to rely merely on general polling data. If we want to know why terrorists do what they do, we can just ask them. Occasionally, terrorists or terror groups agree to talk to reporters. They also issue manifestos and record audio or video statements. For example, Peter Bergen, who has been "up close and personal" with Osama bin Laden and has studied his writings and statements, notes that bin Laden has been "incredibly consistent" about why he's at war with America: "It's about basically four strands of American foreign policy. One, the continued U.S. military presence in Saudi Arabia. Two, the continued support of Israel. Three, the continued campaign against Iraq. Four, American support for regimes like Egypt and Saudi Arabia that he regards as apostates."[17]

Although Bin Laden's war against the United States has religious aspects, Bergen correctly identifies it as a "political war, justified by his own understanding of Islam, directed at the symbols and institutions of American political power." Bergen adds that the September 11 attack "fits the pattern of previous al Qaeda attacks on U.S. embassies, military installations, and warships."[18]

Even Amy Chua, who minimizes U.S. foreign policy in favor of economic causes as a source of anti-American terrorism, provides quotes from bin Laden and his associates that cast doubt on her view. Chua quotes bin Laden as saying in 1993: "The United States has been occupying the lands of Islam in the holiest of its territories, Arabia, plundering its riches, overwhelming its rulers, humiliating its people, threatening its neighbors, and using its peninsula as a spearhead to fight neighboring Islamic peoples."[19]

Even the plundering of riches implies an absence of mutually beneficial commerce and probably refers to the U.S. use of military power and support for corrupt, despotic Arab governments—both to ensure the flow of Persian Gulf oil. Chua then quotes Abdul-Bari Atwan, an associate of bin Laden, as saying after the al Qaeda bombings of American embassies in Kenya and Tanzania, "America's insistence on imposing its own puppets on the Muslim world in order to expedite exploitation of oil and other riches—and not U.S.-Israeli relations—was at the core of the Islamist eruption."[20]

But how did the United States generate so much hatred in bin Laden and his followers? The interventionists would have us believe that bin Laden would have begun attacking the United States no matter what polices the U.S. government adopted. They imply that bin Laden attacks the United States because of its wealth or success—that is, the "who we are" argument. But up until recently, when bin Laden began exploiting the widening fissures between the United States and its allies, he focused his attacks on the United States rather than on those rich, successful nations. Such wealthy allies have far less of a problem with terrorism than does the United States, and wealthy neutral countries, such as Sweden and Switzerland, have almost no problem with it at all. Moreover, it stretches believability to argue that a group of people could become so enraged at the United States—spending years and large sums of money plotting, acquiring skills, and gathering materiel to give up their lives to kill thousands of American innocents—simply because of U.S. wealth, culture, or freedom.

In other words, it is hard to accept intuitively that the terrorists can whip themselves into such a feverish hatred of America just because they dislike Starbucks franchises or the spread of the English language in their homeland. A few examples illustrate the dichotomy between foreign affinity for America and its culture and products and hate for its foreign policy. The same Chinese students who stoned the American embassy in Beijing after the U.S. military bombed the Chinese embassy in Belgrade during the 1999 war for Kosovo returned a few weeks later to apply for U.S. visas. Also, Palestinians shown on TV celebrating the September 11 attacks were wearing American T-shirts, sneakers, and baseball caps. In fact, many U.S. companies—for example, McDonald's—have so successfully adapted to local markets that many foreign customers think the firms are domestic ones.[21] (Even most consumers in sophisticated Western markets do not know a company's country of origin—for example, not many Americans realize that Benetton is an Italian company.)

And Americans quietly enjoying their wealth, culture, or economic and political freedoms half a world away—like the citizens of other advanced, industrialized nations—would not seem to be that provocative. The United States is much less globally dominant economically than it is militarily (America accounts for 30 percent of the world's GDP and almost 40 percent of its military spending), and other wealthy, politically free nations export their culture and products. America now accounts for the same percentage of the world's economy as it did before World War I. But at that time, America was following its traditional noninterventionist foreign policy and was not nearly so hated.

The U.S. interventionist foreign policy that is designed to maintain the informal American empire is the main reason the United States has a much greater problem with terrorism than other industrialized nations. The United States is the only country in the world that regularly intervenes militarily outside its own region, and it does so in almost every region of the world.

The United States is the focus of bin Laden's attacks primarily because it has inserted itself into someone else's—read Islam's—civil war. Of the four issues mentioned above that enrage bin Laden, the two involving U.S. support for despotic and corrupt regimes in the Middle East—and especially the Saudi regime—are the oldest and most inflammatory. In the early 1990s, after he returned from the Islamic fight against the Soviets in Afghanistan, Bin Laden became incensed by the presence of "infidel" U.S. military forces in his homeland of Saudi Arabia, the site of Islam's most holy shrines. Bin Laden's objections to American support for Israel and the U.S. "in-your-face-policy" against Saddam Hussein's Iraq came later and seemed designed only to pick up added support in the Islamic world for his war against the United States and its client states in the Middle East. Bin Laden, following a recurring tradition in the history of Islam, features himself as the outsider coming in to cleanse the faith of the corrupt power structure—that is, the Saudi government and other corrupt U.S.-backed regimes. Because the United States erroneously regards oil as a strategic commodity (see Chapter 6) and because two-thirds of the world's known oil reserves sit under Saudi Arabia, the United States supports that authoritarian regime by remaining its ally, selling it billions of dollars' worth of arms, and guaranteeing the security of its oil.

Bergen alludes perceptively to such U.S. interference in what amounts to a Saudi and Islamic civil war: "Superficially, bin Laden seems to fit into the 'clash of civilizations' thesis. After all, he revels in attacks on American targets. But a closer look shows that his rage is as much directed against one of the most conservative Muslim states in the world, Saudi Arabia—as against the United States."[22] Because the Saudi government feared that the U.S. military presence was destabilizing the kingdom by inflaming radical Islamic terrorists, the United States is withdrawing its forces from Saudi soil. Comments by Paul Wolfowitz, the U.S. Deputy Secretary of Defense, implicitly acknowledged that Islamist terrorists were attacking the United States because of that presence (see below).[23] Secretly perceiving that a U.S. withdrawal would lessen such anti-American attacks, U.S. officials may have been pleased to have been asked to leave the Saudi peninsula. (They may have planned to recoup the lost Saudi installations on the Persian Gulf with Iraqi bases after a successful invasion there.) At this late date, however, and because the United States will continue to support the Saudi regime in other ways, the troop withdrawal will probably not cause bin Laden to end his holy war against the United States.

al Qaeda Terrorists Are Not the Only Ones Who Hate U.S. Foreign Policy

And bin Laden is not the only terrorist to attack the United States because of its foreign policy. Long before the September 11 attacks, the author did a historical study that linked more than sixty terrorist incidents against U.S. targets to the activist American foreign policy.[24] The specific listing of incidents is by no means comprehensive; many more existed then and have occurred since the study was done in 1998. A couple of examples should suffice.

In the early 1980s, U.S. Marines entered the Lebanese civil war as ostensibly neutral peacekeepers. In reality, as noted earlier, those forces began aiding the minority Christian-controlled government against the majority Moslem forces. The Iranian-sponsored Lebanese Shiite Moslem group Hezbollah began attacking U.S. forces in Lebanon. The most spectacular attacks, which killed several hundred people, were against the U.S. embassy and annex and the Marine Corps barracks. Hezbollah attacks against U.S. targets dissipated rapidly after U.S. forces left Lebanon.[25]

Moammar Qaddafi had focused his terrorism against European targets before President Ronald Reagan, who believed the Libyan leader was a Soviet pawn, decided to militarily harass him. The U.S. pressure led Qaddafi to begin targeting Americans with terror strikes. In early April 1986, the Libyan ruler sponsored the bombing of the La Belle nightclub in West Berlin, which was frequented by U.S. military personnel. In mid-April 1986, the United States launched air strikes from Navy carriers and bases in the United Kingdom in an attempt to kill Qaddafi. Conventional wisdom is that Reagan's military strikes cowed Qaddafi into ending support for terrorists. Both the Defense Science Board and the historical record indicate just the opposite. Qaddafi merely went underground and was more secretive about sponsoring his attacks—this time principally against U.S. targets. In fact, beginning in April 1986, analysts from the U.S. State Department linked Libyan agents to an attack per month. The worst of those attacks was the bombing and destruction of U.S.-bound Pan Am Flight 103 over Lockerbie, Scotland, in 1988.[26] Even neoconservative and Reaganophile Max Boot questions the successes of the Reagan air strikes.[27] After Reagan left office, Quaddafi's terrorism dissipated.

U.S. Government May Have Little Interest in Protecting Its Citizens

The first responsibility of any government is to protect its citizens, their property, and the homeland territory from attack. But unfortunately, as public choice theory argues, the government itself can develop interests separate from its citizens. The government reflects the interests of powerful pressure groups and the interests of the bureaucracies and the bureaucrats in them. Although this problem occurs in both foreign and domestic policy, it may be more severe in foreign policy because citizens pay less attention to policies that affect them less directly. For that reason, the president often has more flexibility in foreign than domestic policy.

Despite the risks of blowback attacks on Americans at home and abroad, the interests of the government, the foreign policy elite, and other pressure groups are furthered by an interventionist foreign policy to maintain the American empire. To put it bluntly, the Pan Am 103 bombing and the spectacularly horrific attacks on September 11 are two examples (among many) of U.S. citizens suffering dire consequences from the interventionist foreign policy formulated by their own government to satisfy vested interests. This situation resembles the European monarchs of old launching wars of self-aggrandizement at the expense, in blood and treasure, of their people—the very outcome that the framers of the Constitution explicitly wanted to avoid by establishing a system of checks and balances against executive power.

It should not be unpatriotic to publicly remind the nation of this stark reality. Quite the contrary, it should be patriotic to recall the founders' preference for a policy of military restraint overseas and the concomitant constraints on the president's war-making power that they inserted into the Constitution. Instead, the United States has become an empire—both driven by and fueling excessive executive power—that has fewer constraints than ever before. War and empire undermined Athenian democracy and ruined the Roman republic. Similarly, the American empire and the wars needed for its maintenance are slowly destroying the American republic.

But it is politically incorrect to point out such uncomfortable facts, especially in the wake of a major terrorist strike. The president, the government, and the vested interests can usually manipulate for their own ends the nationalistic impulses of an understandably enraged citizenry. Instead of following where the evidence leads—to the fact that the U.S. government's foreign policy might have had a primary role in motivating the terrorists to do their evil deed in the first place—citizens usually close ranks behind their president and government. The citizenry is thus persuaded to support even more aggressive policies that merely exacerbate the threat to U.S. security from terrorists. As alleged causes for disproportionate terrorist attacks on U.S. targets, the vested interests and the foreign policy establishment focus on American wealth, culture, or freedoms, which cannot be changed easily, to divert attention from interventionist U.S. foreign policy, which is the principal cause of the terrorism and could be rolled back rapidly. In fact, the policymakers in Washington usually manipulate fear and feelings of "patriotism" caused by terrorist incidents to garner support for further empire-building.

"War on Terror" Used to Cloak Imperial Actions

Instead of fighting only al Qaeda, the attackers on September 11, in Afghanistan and elsewhere, the Bush administration used the public fear and outrage after the September 11 attacks to obtain support for an expansive, "preemptive" global war on terror and "rogue" states. One reason for this may be that the September 11 terrorists were too hard to find and neutralize, and the administration hoped to perform a "bait and switch.[28]

But imperial designs more likely drove the wider war. Donald Rumsfeld candidly admitted that "maybe out of this [September 11] tragedy comes opportunity . . . the kind of opportunities that World War II offered, to refashion much of the world."[29] In the name of eradicating support for terrorism or eliminating weapons of mass destruction that could fall into the hands of terrorists, the war on terror has provided a cover to launch offensive warfare against any country the United States does not like. The U.S. National Security Strategy indicates the administration believes that the "best defense is a good offense,"[30] which Jack Snyder, an eminent academic researcher on foreign policy and empires, has called one of several imperial myths.[31] The administration has put in U.S. crosshairs groups and nations that had nothing to do with the September 11 attacks, for example, Iraq and the other countries of the "axis of evil."

The comments of Paul O'Neill, formerly Bush II's Secretary of the Treasury, indicated that Bush II administration officials were preoccupied by Iraq even in the early days after taking office and months before the terrorist attacks of September 11, 2001. (That revelation shows that the administration never really meant its campaign pledge to conduct a "more humble foreign policy.") The administration then took advantage of increased public support and fear after September 11 and fabricated a false link between those attacks and Saddam Hussein.

Invading and occupying Iraq, the country with the world's second largest oil reserves, also gave the United States a new military outpost to guard Persian Gulf oil just in the nick of time. The Saudi government had indicated that the U.S. military presence in Saudi Arabia had to end soon because of the instability it caused in the desert kingdom—read agitation by radical Islamists of the bin Laden variety. In addition, in the name of fighting terrorism, the United States also established new bases in Central Asia and sent troops to the Philippines, moves that were really designed to tighten the containment ring around China.

President George W. Bush managed to convince many Americans that his offensive, "preemptive" strategy was the correct one, but it has been wildly unpopular with almost everyone else in the world. The strategy is better designed to expand and maintain an empire than to reduce the number of Americans killed by terrorism. In fact, attacking groups and countries—particularly Islamic ones—that have no connection to the September 11 attacks is a sure way to paint an even bigger bull's-eye on Americans, both at home and abroad. In addition to invading Iraq, the Bush II administration has been unnecessarily stirring the hornet's nest by conducting covert operations against groups that do not, or no longer, focus their attacks on U.S. targets—for example, Hamas and Hezbollah, respectively. Invading Iraq and battling other terrorist groups after being attacked by al Qaeda on September 11 is analogous to attacking the Russians in 1941 after the Japanese strike on Pearl Harbor and the Nazi declaration of war on the United States.

Similarly, the Clinton administration concentrated on attacking Serbia in 1999 over developments in Kosovo instead of focusing its actions against al Qaeda after the group's bombing of two U.S. embassies in Africa in 1998. But the Bush II administration's distraction with Iraq is less forgivable than Clinton's with Kosovo, because the September 11 attacks had demonstrated that al Qaeda was so severe a threat that it could inflict catastrophic mayhem on the U.S. homeland. Both administrations are guilty of wasting government attention and resources on the U.S. empire when American security was truly threatened.

By widening the war against al Qaeda into a war against Iraq, the axis of evil, and other terrorist groups, the Bush II administration fell into bin Laden's trap. A common tactic of weaker terrorists and guerrilla groups is to attack the stronger party and hope for an overreaction. The overreaction helps to generate recruits, money, and/or outside assistance for the cause. For example, the Kosovo Liberation Army (KLA) used this tactic in the late 1990s. The KLA attacked Serbs in Kosovo and hoped that President Milosevic of Serbia would overreact. When he did, the KLA was able to radicalize Kosovar Albanians, rally them to its cause, and internationalize the conflict by getting the U.S.-led NATO alliance to attack Serbia. The KLA's tactics paid off. Kosovo gained autonomy from Serbia and is trying to move toward independence, its real goal.

Similarly, bin Laden has benefited greatly from the U.S. military excursion into Iraq. After the U.S. victory in Afghanistan, al Qaeda's organization was crippled, but not by any means destroyed. By diverting attention and resources to Iraq, the United States allowed al Qaeda time to recover during a critical period. Also, by invading another Moslem country without provocation, the United States has provided bin Laden with a global recruiting poster for jihadists and financial donations.

The Quran mandates that Muslims defend, even ruthlessly, the *dar al Islam*—homeland of Muslim nations. Traditional Jewish teachings obligate Jews also to use ruthless tactics to reconquer traditional biblical Jewish lands from non-Jews. But the mainstreams of both faiths now reject such notions.[32] Unfortunately, militants in both faiths prefer more traditional interpretations.

Money and new terrorists are undoubtedly flowing to the Islamist cause from around the world. Evidence of that phenomenon can be seen in Iraq, as foreign terrorists from all over now appear to be fighting U.S. forces the way Islamic jihadists in the 1980s flocked to fight the "infidel" Soviet Union, which was also occupying a Moslem nation. The situation ultimately might prove to be even worse for the United States in Iraq, because that land contains Moslem holy sites, which Soviet-occupied Afghanistan did not.

Already, in the wake of the U.S. invasion of Iraq, there has been a spate of Islamic terrorist attacks against U.S. forces in Iraq and against targets in countries around the world. According to Richard Clarke, the former chief counterterrorism adviser to both the Clinton and Bush II administrations, the Bush II administration fought "an unnecessary and costly war in Iraq that strengthened the fundamentalist radical Islamic terrorist movement worldwide."[33] He also stated that "there have been more major terrorist attacks by al Qaeda–related organizations since 9/11 than there were before 9/11."[34] According to the U.S. State Department, terrorist attacks have increased worldwide. In addition, radical Islamists have gained politically in Kuwait and in the volatile, nuclear-armed Pakistan, possibly the most dangerous country on the planet. Assassination attempts have recently been made on Pakistan's president. If radical Islamists took over that nation, they would be in charge of Pakistan's nuclear arsenal.

The invasion of Iraq also made it more difficult for friendly governments, both democratic and authoritarian, to help the United States neutralize al Qaeda. Among the publics of many countries worldwide, support for the American war on terror has declined after the U.S. invasion of Iraq.[35] Public opposition to the Iraq war in those countries has put pressure on their governments to cooperate less with the United States against terrorism or be seen as U.S. lackeys. Thus, the invasion of Iraq was an imperial distraction that has undermined the war against al Qaeda at a time when the U.S. homeland is in peril. The situation is reminiscent of the 1930s, when France and Britain wasted resources protecting their worldwide empires as the rise of Nazi Germany threatened their home territories.

In short, history shows that empires usually overstretch and get themselves into trouble. After September 11, the American empire has shown itself to be as vulnerable to that danger as were the empires of old.

EMPIRE-BUILDING IS OUTDATED AND DANGEROUS

Empires have always been hated. This was as true of the Spaniards in the sixteenth and seventeenth centuries as it was of the Americans and Soviets in the twentieth century.[36] Also, empires throughout history have always faced some opposition in peripheral areas. But with modern technology, resistance that originates on the periphery can now create a cataclysmic threat to the central power. Prior to September 11, 2001, terrorism was regarded as only a nuisance by the superpower and the other great powers. But on September 11, terrorism became a strategic threat.

Several factors contributed to that drastic change. In the 1980s, suicide truck bombing originated in Lebanon's civil war—yet another indirect consequence of U.S. imperial policies. On September 11, suicide attacks were taken to a new level. The attacks in Lebanon and on September 11 demonstrated that if terrorists are willing to commit suicide, they can achieve mass slaughter. On September 11, a small group of foreign men caused more destruction to the continental United States than during either of the world wars or the cold war. Such damage to the continental homeland at the hands of foreigners has not been experienced in the United States since the War of 1812. And if terrorists are able to obtain chemical, biological, or nuclear weapons and the expertise to use them, the threat could be much greater. Indications are that al Qaeda, and perhaps other groups, would like to get such weapons. Al Qaeda has so far been incompetent in its attempts to develop chemical weapons, but could try to buy them or other "superweapons."

Even without those "superweapons," terrorists—through the potential for perpetrating more catastrophic attacks using conventional means—have caused widespread fear, economic dislocations (for example, in the airline and travel industries), the spending of billions on extra security, and the aforementioned U.S. government crackdown on civil liberties. Bin Laden, a shrewd operator, had planned on those economic and political effects, as well as on the mass loss of innocent life.

Curiously, as the threat to the homeland from global thermonuclear war between the superpowers faded, this new threat arose. But the two threats are dissimilar. The Soviet nuclear threat was one of mass annihilation from a nation-state with a home address, which meant that it could be deterred with the U.S. nuclear arsenal. The threat of superpower nuclear war was unlikely and well-managed because of the cataclysmic destruction the two superpowers could inflict on each other. Each superpower refrained from direct military intervention in the other's sphere of influence—the Western Hemisphere for the United States and Eastern Europe for the Soviet Union. Brushfire or proxy wars there or elsewhere were managed so as not to escalate to general nuclear war between the two behemoths.

Offensive Strategy Will Be Ineffective in Today's World

An argument could be and was made during the cold war for the "best defense is a good offense" strategy. The U.S. military has always been a proponent of this strategy, because going on the offensive is designed to hold the enemy as far away from the homeland as possible. During the cold war, with the shadow of nuclear destruction looming, the United States had to adopt a more restrained version of the strategy—aggressive containment of the Soviet Union. The American empire either fought in faraway places (in Vietnam and Korea) or recruited proxies to do so (for example, in El Salvador, Afghanistan, and Angola) to prevent inroads on its periphery by the Soviet empire. The idea was that running a "forward defense" (or "offensive defense") strategy was the most cost-effective way of preventing falling dominoes.[37] But expensive U.S. wars in unimportant backwater regions were hardly cost-effective.

Even during the cold war, some analysts in the United States convincingly quarreled with the strategy of wasting U.S. lives and money in nonstrategic backwater areas, but at least a plausible argument could be made that the strategy would be effective against a rival nation-state.

But this military model, which has been adopted by the Bush II administration in its "war on terror", is a more questionable one to use against al Qaeda and other mobile, shadowy groups that can penetrate all of the layers of the American defense perimeter and strike at the homeland. The war against such groups has no front line and the groups have no home address to hold hostage—making deterrence of their attacks extremely difficult. They merely attack and then melt back into the woodwork.

Offensive Strategy at a Time of Defensive Advantage

The Bush administration is adopting an offensive strategy at a time in the international system when the advantage to the defense is growing. In President Bush's so-called "preemptive" war doctrine, he asserts that "America will act against emerging threats before they are fully formed." He further notes: "The United States can no longer solely rely on a reactive posture as we have in the past. The inability to deter a potential attacker, the immediacy of today's threats, and the magnitude of potential harm that could be caused by our adversaries' choice of weapons, do not permit this option. We cannot let our enemies strike first." Finally, he declares: "To forestall or prevent such attacks by our adversaries, the United States will, if necessary, act preemptively." But the best summary of his new doctrine is his assertion that "the best defense is a good offense."[38]

Throughout history, there have been periods of offensive or defensive ascendancy. For example, during the imperial consolidation by the Ch'ing Dynasty in China, the Napoleonic wars, and most of World War II, the offense had the advantage. In contrast, during the European feudal period, the Byzantine empire, the American Civil War, and World War I, the defense had the advantage. However, military historian Bevin Alexander reports that over most of history, defensive weapons have been more potent than offensive arms.[39] Jack Snyder, a researcher on empires, agrees that military advantage to the offense is rare and therefore cannot account for the repeated attempts at empire-building throughout the centuries. In land warfare, throughout history, the defense has had the advantage in most cases because of geography or technology. Even the advent of long-range bombers and intercontinental missiles has not led to many knockouts by surprise attacks.[40]

Ironically, most experts agree that the advent of "offensive" nuclear weapons and their delivery systems dramatically increased the power of the defense during the cold war and post–cold war eras.[41] Nuclear weapons have had only limited power to coerce the compliance of other nations. But even a country with just a few nuclear weapons can deter a nuclear superpower from attacking.[42] For example, the Bush II administration has treated destitute North Korea, which is reputed to have a few nuclear weapons, much more respectfully than it did Iraq, which had none.

Bush II's offensive doctrine, designed to intimidate countries from getting nuclear (and chemical and biological) weapons, may have the opposite effect. That is, the doctrine may encourage nations to launch secret programs to acquire deterrents against U.S. invasions or to accelerate existing superweapons programs. For example, prior to the invasion of Iraq, North Korea had offered to get rid of its nuclear weapons program (going beyond offering again to implement a freeze, as it promised to do in 1994 but later cheated on) and allow international arms inspectors to return in exchange for a nonaggression treaty with the United States. In the wake of the invasion of Iraq, the North Koreans rescinded that offer, suggested that any nonaggression pact would not avert a war, and insisted that only a military deterrent could ensure that North Korea was secure.[43]

Libya's renunciation of unconventional weapons programs has been attributed to the "demonstration effects" of Bush II's hardline policy toward Iraq's superweapons programs. But Moammar Qaddafi had been trying to mend fences with the West for more than a decade. He only gave up such programs after the Bush administration allowed the United Nations to rescind crippling economic sanctions against Libya and after a shipment of illicit nuclear technology to the North African nation was intercepted in transit. The ending of sanctions was a carrot, which showed that the Bush policy toward Qaddafi was not all "stick." And the chaotic quagmire after the U.S. invasion of Iraq probably mitigated any fear by Qaddafi that Libya also might face the same fate if he did not give up his weapons programs.

But even if Bush does have an occasional success with intimidation, questions arise about whether the preventative policy can be sustained, given the high cost in money and lives likely to be required. According to the U.S. DoD, prior to the invasion of Iraq, some thirteen "threat" countries had biological weapons, sixteen had chemical weapons, twenty-eight had ballistic missiles, and twelve had nuclear weapons programs.[44] Invading and occupying even one country with purported weapons of mass destruction programs, namely Iraq, has proved difficult and costly, let alone doing so to all such "threat" countries. In the wake of the loud domestic and international protests against Iraq War II, the American and international publics likely would not stand for many more preventative wars, especially after no "superweapons" were found.

Also, preventative attacks need to rest on good intelligence about the kinds of superweapons an adversary has and where they are located. As Clinton's bombing of Iraq in the 1998 Desert Fox campaign and Bush's invasion of that nation in 2003 show, intelligence is not good enough for such an offensive, preventative doctrine to be practical.[45]

In fact, one indicator of defensive ascendancy is that cross-border aggression has dropped in the last few decades. In the post–cold war world, intrastate conflicts now account for almost 95 percent of the wars.[46] Nuclear weapons are partly responsible for that development.

The advent of nuclear weapons as the ultimate defense-by-deterrence during and after the cold war should have raised questions about the need for globe-spanning alliances and the forward basing of U.S. military forces overseas to ensure security for the U.S. homeland from attack. But those issues have never been raised.

There have been other factors inhibiting offensive military action against other countries, including the rise of international law and norms against cross-border aggression and an upsurge in nationalism. So although the United States is the greatest military power in world history, both absolutely and relative to other powers, it is likely to be constrained in using military power effectively. As noted earlier, there has been no internationally recognized large-scale annexation of territory via war since the 1945 Soviet acquisition of territories formerly belonging to Poland, Germany, Czechoslovakia, and Japan. Since then, international borders have been largely stationary.[47] (Even the Israeli occupation of the West Bank and Gaza may eventually be rescinded under international pressure.)

Unlike the days of old, when empires could expand into areas outside of the nation-state system, now most of the territory in the developing world, which had been colonized by European empires, has been decolonized into independent states under pressure of fierce nationalistic feelings. Urbanization and rising incomes and education levels spur such nationalism.[48] The nationalism has made great powers wary of trying to subdue native populations by force. When great powers have disregarded modern nationalism and invaded foreign lands, they have run into trouble—for example, the Soviets in Afghanistan and the United States in Vietnam and in its current troubled invasion and occupation of Iraq.

All of those conflicts are guerrilla wars. Throughout history, guerrilla warfare has been the most effective form of warfare.[49] Guerrilla tactics are powerful defensive techniques that the weak can use against the strong. The United States currently cannot be defeated on a conventional battlefield by any nation or nations on earth but has difficulty occupying poor countries (for example, Iraq and Afghanistan) when even a small portion of the population is unhappy with the occupation and is willing to use guerrilla tactics. In Vietnam, the weaker side took advantage of jungle as sanctuary after using hit-and-run tactics; in Afghanistan, the Mujahadeen used the mountains to hide out against the Soviets; in Iraq, the opposition is using urban areas to melt away from U.S. forces. In all cases, guerrillas use the support of the local population for refuge after surprise attacks on isolated elements of the stronger side.

Today, guerrilla tactics, when combined with nationalism, tribalism or religious fervor, may increasingly dissuade large powers from engaging in cross-border interventions. Thus, overseas empires may be harder to subdue these days, even with the strength of a superpower. "Demonstration" wars by the empire to intimidate other problem countries may only demonstrate the vulnerabilities and weaknesses of the great power—as have U.S. difficulties in postwar Iraq and Afghanistan.

Ever since the Vietnam War, analysts have been pushing the U.S. Army to get better at fighting guerrilla warfare. But during the cold war, the Army concentrated on midintensity war and large conventional battles against the Soviet Union, which would have been fought with heavy weapons (for example, armored vehicles). Even after the cold war ended, progress in changing Army doctrine was slow. Only after September 11 did the Army realize that a new kind of war was at hand and that a substantial change in approach was needed.[50] Unfortunately, change takes time, and the Army is still too heavy to get anywhere fast and not well-trained or equipped to fight counterinsurgency warfare. For example, lumbering armored and mechanized forces are not always that effective in fighting against hit-and-run guerrilla strikes in Iraq.

Strategically, Terrorism Is an Effective Defensive Technique

In formulating its offensive doctrine, the Bush II administration ignored the aforementioned trends that have been obvious since the beginning of the cold war. But the attacks of September 11 illustrate that yet another arrow—low-cost, catastrophic terrorism—has been added to the quiver of groups and small states deterring or defending against U.S. attack.

Terrorism is simply guerrilla warfare that does not attempt to hold ground. And like conventional guerrilla methods, terrorism is tactically on the offense, but strategically plays defense. Even Paul Wolfowitz, Bush II's Deputy Secretary of Defense, indirectly acknowledged the power of this retaliatory weapon and the role of assertive U.S. foreign policy in causing it to be used—a stunning admission from an official in an interventionist administration operating under an offensive doctrine. Wolfowitz implicitly advocated invading Iraq so that the United States could reduce its target profile vis-à-vis al Qaeda by withdrawing American troops from Saudi Arabia.[51] Of course, Wolfowitz's implication was that U.S. troops would no longer be needed in Saudi Arabia because they could guard Persian Gulf oil from newly occupied Iraq. But how he thought invading another Islamic country would lower the U.S. target profile from retaliatory terrorism is a mystery.

Wolfowitz also directly admitted that the invasion of Iraq, ostensibly undertaken to fight terrorism and the proliferation of WMD, was prosecuted primarily for the imperial objective of securing Persian Gulf oil. When asked why nuclear-armed North Korea was being treated less severely than nonnuclear Iraq, Wolfowitz answered, "The most important difference between North Korea and Iraq is that economically, we just had no choice in Iraq. The country swims on a sea of oil."[52] Wolfowitz had previously admitted that the WMD issue was the one justification for war with Iraq that all of the U.S. security bureaucracies could agree on. This shocking statement implies a U.S. government on autopilot to war and in search of a justification that all the bureaucracies could get behind.

The Bush II administration's promulgation of an offensive doctrine at a time of defensive supremacy is also a mystery. The administration apparently has not learned much from Israel's use of the offensive military model. Israel has launched repeated offensives into Palestinian-held areas to root out Palestinian suicide bombers. The offensives have had the short-term effect of lessening the number of suicide bombings by disrupting terrorists. But in the long term, those offensives merely inflame the Palestinian community and act as a recruiting poster for even more suicide bombers.[53] Even the top military official in Israel has denounced Prime Minister Ariel Sharon's hard-line policies toward the Palestinians. Lt. Gen. Moshe Yaalon, Israel's military chief of staff, said that such policies increase "hatred for Israel and strengthen the terror organizations."[54] Several former chiefs of Shin Bet, Israel's internal security organization, have also criticized Sharon's hawkish policy.[55]

Similarly, a spate of terrorist incidents has arisen after the start of the aggressive and general U.S. "war on terror"—for example, one in Saudi Arabia, two in Indonesia, and multiple incidents in U.S.-occupied Iraq, including the bombing of the UN headquarters, an important mosque, and the Jordanian embassy. For years to come, like the Israeli offensives, the egregious and unnecessary U.S. invasion and occupation of Iraq will likely turn many radical Islamists worldwide into terrorists. Already, foreign Islamic fighters have migrated to Iraq to fight U.S. forces, much as they did during the 1980s when another "infidel" nation, the Soviet Union, invaded the Islamic nation of Afghanistan. In occupied Iraq, the U.S. Army's imitation of aggressive Israeli tactics—bulldozing buildings, detaining the relatives of guerrillas, quarantining villages with razor wire, and firing artillery in urban areas—may reap short-term gains against the insurgency. But those tactics will also likely turn Iraqi public opinion against the United States in the long term and make the U.S. occupation difficult. In both the Israeli and U.S. cases, the terrorist attacks will continue until the underlying issue driving the terrorism is resolved.

Attacks by terrorist groups are hard to deter because terrorists are zealous, often willing to die for their cause, and have no territory that can be held at risk. Terrorists are also hard to stop, catch, or kill. The U.S. intelligence community admits that it cannot be perfect all of the time. Some potential terrorist attacks have been foiled, but the intelligence community admits that it is only a matter of time before another significant attack succeeds. And despite the creation of the new Department of Homeland Security and the implementation of other domestic security-enhancing measures, the United States remains very vulnerable to future terrorist attacks due to its size and openness—it is the largest truly open society in the world. Furthermore, the country has more than seven thousand miles of borders, five hundred skyscrapers, three hundred nuclear power plants, thousands of sports stadiums, etc. In short, America is a rich country with many targets to hit.

Yet closing U.S. society and curtailing civil liberties—as the Bush II administration has already begun to do with the PATRIOT Act, executive actions, and proposals for successor legislation—gives the terrorists of September 11 a second victory, destroys what is unique about America, and provides little benefit in the fight against terrorism. One of bin Laden's stated goals in attacking the United States is to change the character of U.S. society (implying a destruction of U.S. freedoms). As noted in Chapter 4, even senior law enforcement officers argue that instead of curtailing peoples' liberties, the focus should be on more effective law enforcement techniques. After using intelligence and law enforcement techniques to locate terrorists, the United States and other countries can cooperate to bring them to justice. For example, negotiations with Sudan led to the handover of the terrorist "Carlos the Jackal" to the French government. Negotiations with Libya eventually led to the trial in the Netherlands of two Libyan intelligence agents for the bombing of Flight 103.[56] Using intelligence, law enforcement, and extradition (that is, the very effective law enforcement model) to fight terrorism and minimizing the use of inflammatory imperial armed intervention (the military model) will result in fewer terrorists to battle over the long term.

Interventionist Policy: Costs Increase Benefits Decline

All this leads to the conclusion that the post–World War II interventionist U.S. foreign policy designed to maintain, police, and expand the American empire is unnecessary, outdated, expensive, and even dangerous. During the cold war, a better—although disputed—case could be made that the benefits of an interventionist U.S. foreign policy outweighed the costs, which were manageable. But the demise of the rival Soviet empire means that far fewer places on the planet are strategic to the United States. And the few that remain are not in danger of falling to a rival hegemonic power or empire. Thus, the benefits of profligate U.S. intervention abroad have declined. Providing security for rich U.S. allies is now merely an expensive anachronism. As noted earlier, the United States spends on defense what the next thirteen highest countries do and fails to get even trade concessions from its best allies.

The United States continues to accept that unfair situation in order to prevent its allies from bolting the empire and becoming independent. The U.S. government and supporting vested interests gain from having a worldwide empire that the globally dominant American military polices. The U.S. president is always in the center of the summit photo. Members of Congress and high-level presidential appointees are treated like royalty overseas. U.S. academics are keynote speakers at foreign conferences, because it is assumed that they have their finger on the pulse of what is happening in the imperial capital. Those elites frequently speak of the need for U.S. interventions to show American leadership, retain U.S. prestige, and gain unspecified American "influence" in foreign nations. What they are really talking about is retaining their own leadership, prestige, and influence overseas.

And if the benefits of empire for the American people have declined since the end of the cold war, the costs they bear have skyrocketed. They continue to pay excessive taxes to defend countries that are rich enough to defend themselves or to occupy conquered countries in the world's backwaters (for example, Iraq and Afghanistan). Their sons and daughters are killed on remote foreign battlefields for reasons even more remote from U.S. vital interests. So although the benefits and costs of empire haven't changed much for the elite after the cold war ended, they have changed for the average American. In a post–cold war world, taking into account only the security of American citizens, their property, and U.S. territory, the benefits of an interventionist foreign policy have declined and the costs have escalated dramatically. Americans are being put at risk from catastrophic terrorism, perhaps even from an attack with chemical, biological, or nuclear weapons, just so the American government can conduct imperial wars in remote regions of the world that have little to do with U.S. security—except to undermine it.

Rather than conduct an offensive general campaign against terrorism and rogue states, dramatically increase spending on defense and homeland security, and clamp down on civil liberties, the United States should give up its forward-based overseas empire and adopt a more restrained foreign policy. It should intervene overseas only in the rare cases where its vital interests are really at stake or when the balance of power breaks down in any one of a small number of key regions. That change in policy will save money, improve the economy, and dramatically lessen the motivation of terrorists to attack U.S. targets, while at the same time obviating the need to destroy U.S. society by protecting it with draconian security measures. A detailed proposal for a more restrained U.S. role as an "offshore balancer" is the subject of the next chapter.

6

An Appropriate U.S. Foreign Policy for the Modern Age

No empire has been retrospectively deemed as successful. In the long term, the U.S. empire, in contrast to the American republic, is unlikely to have any better luck. In previous chapters, evidence was presented and arguments were made that the overextended American empire is eroding the status of the United States as a great power and actually undermining the security of its citizens. It was also noted that the country's founders realized that the geographic remoteness of the United States from the world's zones of conflict provided unparalleled intrinsic security. In fact, buffered by two great oceans, the United States is probably the most intrinsically secure great power in world history.[1] Therefore, they believed that unnecessary U.S. meddling in conflicts overseas would merely bring unwanted retaliatory interventions by European powers into the Western Hemisphere. Than "live and let live" foreign policy has never been more relevant that it is today.

THE FOUNDERS' FOREIGN POLICY IS MORE RELEVANT THAN EVER

The American public, reflecting that earlier tradition, usually tends to be much less interventionist than the foreign policy elite in Washington and New York. The elite has been captured by vested interests that benefit or are subsidized by the exercise of American military power overseas. The *public choice* school of economics notes that when benefits are concentrated among certain influential or well-organized groups and costs are diffused among the entire

American public, the vested interests will dictate policy. This maxim is even truer in foreign policy than in domestic affairs because the public is less attentive to such issues. In elections, most people vote on domestic issues rather than foreign policy, and the elite know it. This reality allows the politicians and bureaucrats to intervene overseas willy-nilly. And after September 11, it has become even easier for them to get public acquiescence or even active support for imperial military actions disguised as a "war on terror."

In any debate, the interventionists and empire-builders first try to smear anyone who advocates returning to a more restrained foreign policy as an "isolationist." In doing so, the interventionists usually use the example of former presidential candidate Pat Buchanan to portray conservative proponents of "military restraint" as protectionist, anti-immigrant reactionaries. Alternatively, they portray liberal proponents as naïve pacifists divorced from the real world. But many advocates of the United States as an "offshore balancer" are quite concerned about real U.S. security requirements and advocate free commerce, liberal immigration, and diplomatic and cultural exchange among nations. In fact, they object to the recent militarization of U.S. foreign policy and would like to return to traditional U.S. foreign policy, which emphasized international commerce and severely limited U.S. military interventions worldwide. They realize that all other elements of national power and security derive from a strong economy.

Why Did the Founders Adopt a Policy of Military Restraint?

If labeling their opponents as isolationists fails to stick, the interventionists then have to resort to substantive arguments. They try to argue that the proponents of the founders' original foreign policy of nonintervention overseas are advocates of a nostalgic return to an idyllic bygone era that is naive, and even dangerous, in an age of globalization and increased interdependence. The interventionists often maintain that the founders adopted a policy of military restraint only because the young country was a weak player in the international system. One interventionist, Max Boot, even tries to argue that the United States never really followed the founders' policy, pointing to interventions throughout U.S. history even before the cold war. For example, Boot mentions Thomas Jefferson's use of the U.S. Navy against the Barbary pirates and U.S. interventions in the Caribbean shortly before World War I and during the interwar period.[2] Certainly, although the last quarter of the eighteenth and almost all of the nineteenth centuries were not perfectly devoid of exceptions to the founders' policy of limited overseas interventions, the United States remarkably did follow a policy of military restraint. As for Jefferson's action in the Mediterranean against the Barbary pirates, it was clearly self-defense against countries that had initially attacked U.S. ships. Few proponents of nonintervention would begrudge such military actions in self-defense.

Even Boot, however, seems to admit that most of the significant small overseas interventions he cites happened after the precedent-setting Spanish-American War in 1898.[3] Even during the years after that war and after World War I, those small U.S. interventions mainly occurred in the traditional American sphere of influence in Latin America. Since 1823, using the Monroe Doctrine, the United States has taken a special interest in keeping other great powers out of its Latin American sphere of influence—the region of the world in closest proximity and the one most vital to U.S. security. But less well-known is that the Monroe Doctrine also pledged the United States to stay out of other great powers' business elsewhere. With the exception of the War of 1812, the United States wisely avoided wars with those distant great powers until World War I.

Even if Boot's proposition that the United States has never lived up to the founders' ideal of nonintervention is true, it does not follow that the United States should conduct profligate military interventions overseas today merely because it has intervened at times before or now has the wherewithal to do so. Boot's argument is essentially that since the United States has conducted some such interventions in the past, it should do so in the future. It does not seem to matter to Boot whether such interventions are needed or successful. He even admits that nation-building in the developing world has been less than successful.[4] The question should be, "Does the United States need to intervene to safeguard its security?" not, "Does the United States have the power to intervene?"

The founders' noninterventionist policies were not based solely on weakness. Rapid industrialization made the United States a world class economy by 1830 and allowed it to surpass Britain as the world's largest economy by the 1880s. Yet the peacetime U.S. military remained small until the Civil War and demobilized after both world wars. The United States did not retain a large peacetime military until the cold war.

More important than doing so out of weakness, the founders adopted an anti-interventionist foreign policy for geopolitical and philosophical reasons. As noted above, the founders astutely realized that the geographical advantages of the United States made it intrinsically very secure and so gave it the luxury of avoiding getting dragged into irrelevant conflicts in faraway lands. As Thomas Jefferson noted, the United States was "separated by nature and a wide ocean from the exterminating havoc of one-quarter of the globe," thus greatly enhancing U.S. security.[5] The country had and continues to have two great oceans as moats and no great powers in its traditionally peaceful neighborhood. Furthermore, the United States today—as at the time of its founding—is so remote and huge that any foreign invader would be likely to fail in invading, conquering, or ruling it. In other words, most foreign conflicts do not affect the vital interests of the United States.

Realizing this fact, the founders astutely eschewed foreign entanglements. In his farewell address, President George Washington noted that "our detached and distant situation" allowed the nation, compared to other countries, the advantage to take "a different course" and "steer clear of permanent alliances with any portion of the foreign world."[6] The United States avoided joining long-lived alliances until the cold war. Similarly, Thomas Jefferson explicated

America's traditional foreign policy as "peace, commerce and honest friendship, with all nations—entangling alliances with none."[7]

Also, the founders realized that their liberties, imported from Britain, were a byproduct of that island nation's intrinsic geographical security from the conflicts of continental Europe. Therefore, Britain had the luxury of keeping only a small land army, which in turn was less useful in trampling on the liberties of British citizens. With a much wider moat than the British, the Americans were in an even more advantageous position to preserve their inherited liberties. The founders were suspicious of large militaries, because they were often used by European monarchies to oppress their subjects at home and drag them into costly wars abroad. The founders realized from the continental European experience that average citizens lose the most from wars—paying with their lives and, through exorbitant taxation, their wealth—while politicians, bureaucrats in power, and large businesses providing arms and supplies to the military reap the largest gains. In short, they concluded that enmeshing the country in foreign wars would doom the experiment with limited government—as it had in continental Europe.

Today in the United States, there is not as much of a threat that the large (by historical standards) peacetime U.S. Army or Army National Guard, expanded during the cold war to maintain the empire, will be turned inward and used against U.S. citizens. That threat, however, cannot be entirely ruled out. Examples include the killing of Vietnam War protestors by National Guardsmen in the 1970s at Kent State University and the recent encroachment of the military into law enforcement. The use of the military in the war on drugs marks the erosion of Posse Comitatus law, which was supposed to keep the military out of law enforcement. But today, the main threat to liberty at home caused by overseas wars comes from pressure to increase the powers of civilian law enforcement agencies.

Modern America, unlike sixteenth- and seventeenth-century Britain, has a vast array of local, state, and federal law enforcement agencies to keep its citizens in line and needs to rely on the Army and Army National Guard only in extreme circumstances (for example, if riots break out). As noted in the last chapter, when the United States enmeshes itself in imperial (read unnecessary) conflicts overseas, particularly ethnic or religious civil wars, blowback terrorism—for example, the September 11 attacks—can occur. In the climate of pervasive fear that follows such attacks, the powers of law enforcement agencies are augmented generally—not just for antiterrorism investigations—at the expense of the citizenry.

In addition, the cold war and post–cold war periods have shown that imperial wars overseas break down the checks-and-balances in the Constitution and result in an imperial presidency at home. So the founders' fears have proven justified—the wars of empire have undermined the American republic. Similarly, as noted earlier, wars undermined democracy in ancient Athens and ended the Roman Republic. The erosion of the Constitution's liberties and checks-and-balances is the most pernicious effect of the American empire and the best reason for abandoning it in favor of a return to the more restrained and enlightened foreign policy of the founders.

In Some Key Respects, the World Has Become Less Interdependent

What of the platitude that in a more interdependent and "globalized" world, the U.S. government cannot ignore turmoil in remote corners of the globe lest it snowballs into a real threat—either through terrorism or armed attack—to the United States? President Clinton, in a 2000 speech at the Coast Guard Academy commencement, argued that "the central reality of our time is that the advent of globalization and the revolution in information technology have magnified both the creative and the destructive potential of every individual, tribe and nation on our planet." Clinton concluded that the destructive potential was "making us more vulnerable to problems that arise a half a world away; to terror, to ethnic, racial, and religious conflicts; to weapons of mass destruction, drug trafficking, and other organized crime."[8]

But upon closer inspection, such reasoning is suspect. First, that fear merely repackages the discredited domino theory of communism's advance during the cold war. In other words, according to this line of reasoning, instability in remote and insignificant countries could fester and multiply into eventual threats to the United States. Yet instability is a constant in the international system and does not threaten U.S. vital interests per se. Second, there is no longer a rival superpower to exploit such minor conflicts. Third, during the cold war period, the United States became directly or indirectly embroiled in brushfire wars in nonstrategic countries—for example, Korea, Vietnam, Laos, Cambodia, Angola, Nicaragua, El Salvador, and Afghanistan—trying to prevent communist takeovers that would have mattered little even if successful. After all, for example, the roof did not cave in on the American republic when the communists finally took control over Vietnam, Laos, and Cambodia.

If catastrophe failed to befall the United States from instability and conflict in backwater areas during the much more threatening cold war period, it is certainly less likely to do so now. In fact, conflicts in any one country are less likely than ever to spill over into other countries. Data show that cross-border aggression has been declining for decades. Now, about 95 percent of the world's conflicts are civil wars. Yet if any overseas wars are threats to U.S. security, they are interstate, not intrastate, conflicts. And not even most of the interstate wars—many of which are in remote, nonstrategic areas—are threats to the relatively secure and removed United States.

But the interventionists magnify the threat to the United States of even intrastate wars, so that ever more public money will be pumped into unneeded spending on military forces and foreign aid. After the demise of the Soviet Union, interventionists scrambled to create new threats to justify overseas military action, bases, alliances, and continued exorbitant defense spending. Just when the outlook was bleak for them, the September 11 attacks provided a winning horse on which their imperial policy goals could ride.

The modern-day version of the cold war domino theory is the "failed state" thesis. Failed states are usually poor states with fragile or nonexistent governments and civil wars raging within their borders. The thesis, which is very self-serving for the interventionists, is that in such states, the United States must intervene militarily, provide boatloads of foreign aid, and restructure their societies to bring free markets and democracy. Otherwise, the argument goes, such conflicts could spawn terrorists.

Civil wars in remote places can spawn terrorism. And modern technology in communications, transportation, and even weapons of mass destruction (if the terrorists can buy or build them and effectively use them) today make the United States more vulnerable to terrorist attacks.

That said, the cliché that the world is becoming more interdependent and globalized should be examined. No one can deny that technology has fostered increased trade, financial flows, communication, and transportation among nations and peoples. And terrorists can make use of all of those modes of interdependence when attacking U.S. targets.

But in other parts of the security realm, the world has become less interdependent. Despite the advance of technology, the United States is arguably even less vulnerable to conventional attacks from other nation-states than it was at the founding. First, the United States' arch superpower rival, the Soviet Union, is in the dustbin of history, and for thirty years no other great power will likely replace it. Second, although long-range bombers and missiles have been developed (but only a few countries have them), as noted above, cross-border aggression has been declining for years. Part of the reason for that trend is increased nationalism (making subduing foreign populations more difficult), but the biggest factor is undoubtedly the spread of nuclear weapons.

Nation-states—even quirky "rogue" states, such as Iran or North Korea—have a home address and can be deterred from attacking the United States by the threat of retaliatory annihilation at the hands of the world's most potent nuclear arsenal. After the advent of nuclear weapons as the ultimate form of defense by deterrence, questions should have arisen about the need for worldwide, U.S.-led permanent alliances and far-flung American overseas military deployments to deter surprise conventional attacks on U.S. territory. But no debate on those issues has ever been conducted. In fact, the United States never had such alliances or deployments until the nuclear age. In sum, in terms of conventional military action, the world has become less interdependent.

The demise of the archrival Soviet Union and the increased security of the homeland from conventional military threats provided by nuclear weapons have dramatically reduced the need for the United States to take military action overseas. Happily, that fortunate state of affairs, if acted upon, can help reduce a less deterrable threat to the United States—that is, terrorism—which has increased because the "world has become a smaller place." The bad news is that terrorists are less deterrable than nation-states because they do not always have a home address that can be reached with nuclear weapons.

The good news, however, is that there is no cause for such terrorists to target the distant United States unless it intervenes in brushfire conflicts overseas. For example, if the United States had not inserted itself into the Islamic civil war by supporting the Saudi government and stationing U.S. forces on Saudi soil, bin Laden and al Qaeda would have had no reason to travel to the other side of the globe and attack the Pentagon and World Trade Center on September 11. Similarly, if the United States had stayed out of Somalia's civil war, the warlord Mohammed Aideed would have had no reason to target American soldiers there. Finally, if the United States had refrained from aiding the governing Christian minority in Lebanon at the expense of the Moslem majority, the Moslem factions would have had no reason to kill U.S. Marines en masse. In fact, after the United States withdrew the Marines from Lebanon, Hezbollah attacks against U.S. targets dissipated.

Thus, the bottom line is that the otherwise favorable post–cold war security situation should allow the United States to stay out of most virulent civil wars in remote lands. Those conflicts have nothing to do with U.S. vital interests but could generate significant amounts of anti-U.S. terrorism, catastrophic or otherwise. Since intelligence is not perfect and homeland security is a tall order in the largest truly open society in the world, a policy of military restraint overseas may be the only way to inhibit terrorists from attacking the United States—by removing their very obvious (to everyone else but Americans) motivation for doing so.

But what does adopting a policy of military restraint or acting as an offshore balancer really mean? The following section gives the details of what that policy should entail.

RETURNING TO AN OFFSHORE BALANCING STRATEGY

For almost 175 years of its more than 225-year history, the United States, with a few lapses, pursued an offshore balancing strategy, staying out of major foreign wars except when the perceived balance of power in a key region or regions was threatened by a potential hegemon. By keeping military spending (and general government expenditures that often spike when security spending increases) low, the country grew into the world's largest economy and individual liberties generally flourished. Even after World War II, the United States quickly demobilized the vast bulk of its temporarily vast military. But in late 1949 and in 1950, the policy of military restraint overseas and concomitant small peacetime military changed. Most historians place the start of the cold war in 1947 when President Truman began aiding the governments of Greece and Turkey against communist insurgencies. But the real change in U.S. strategy came in late 1949 and early 1950, when the United States shifted from political and economic to military containment of the Soviet Union. Between 1945 and 1949, the United States avoided policies in Europe that would aggravate Soviet insecurities and limited U.S. military commitments in peripheral areas. In 1949 and

1950, the United States dramatically increased U.S. military commitments by creating many alliances—commonly called Pax Americana—that spanned the globe. Those commitments would embroil the United States in many brushfire wars in the developing world, either directly or by proxy.[9] That policy shift marked the beginning of the global American empire.

Abandon Outdated Alliances

Many analysts would say that the worldwide formal and informal alliances were created to fight communism. (As noted earlier, no one ever asked whether nuclear weapons might obviate the need for permanent alliances and far-flung U.S. military bases overseas to deter future conventional attacks on the homeland.) But this argument is severely undermined by their continuation, and even expansion, after the cold war ended. The United States expanded NATO—both in territory and mission—enhanced East Asian alliances, became mired in the previously nonstrategic Balkans, erected quasi-permanent bases in the Central Asian nations of the former Soviet Union, reinvigorated the U.S. alliance with the Philippines, tightened the informal alliances with Israel and Taiwan, and invaded and occupied Iraq and Afghanistan in the name of fighting terrorism.

Even during the cold war, continued containment of the Soviet Union by political and economic means—which the policy's architect George Kennan had originally envisioned—would have been better than creating entangling military alliances that dragged the United States, either directly or indirectly, into wars in backwater regions of the globe unimportant to U.S. vital interests. Examples of such wars were the conflicts in Korea, Vietnam, Cambodia, Laos, Angola, Congo Nicaragua, Cuba, Chile, Dominican Republic, Grenada, and El Salvador. Later, Kennan said he had regretted not specifying which regions of the world were strategic to the United States.[10] Even in Europe, if the Soviet Union had not invaded the Western European nations after the end of World War II when they were prostrate and weak, it probably was not going to do so. Even if one believes that the Soviet threat was more severe, as the allies recovered economically from World War II, they should have, over time, assumed the bulk of the burden for defending their regions, instead of leaving it to the United States.

Early in the cold war, Kennan criticized the militarization of U.S. foreign policy by an inordinate emphasis on such alliances. Perhaps some of those alliances were mainly designed to prevent countries from going communist and entering the rival Soviet empire's sphere of influence. Alternatively, perhaps the United States wanted to prevent France, Britain, Germany, and Japan from again becoming rivals to the American empire.[11]

It is high time the U.S. government reassessed those cold war–era alliances and its vital interests. President Truman deceived Congress in 1949 by saying that ratification of the NATO treaty would not lead to the stationing of U.S. forces in Europe. Even during the height of the cold war, President Eisenhower wanted to bring U.S. forces home in order to compel West European nations to defend themselves against the Soviet threat. From the 1960s through the 1980s, significant sentiment in Congress existed for doing just that.[12] Strangely, a total withdrawal of U.S. forces from Europe never happened during the cold war, even as U.S. allies got back on their feet and became rich. Eisenhower once said that the NATO alliance would have failed if the U.S. military presence remained permanent. Yet even after the Soviet threat has long gone, the U.S. troop presence remains. In fact, the NATO alliance, which is used to justify the U.S. military presence, is expanding in territory and missions.

Cold war alliances have become ends in themselves, and, today, the phrase "protecting U.S. vital interests" is promiscuously applied to any dubious military intervention that the president or any other U.S. politician wants to sell to the public.

A return to the founders' policy of avoiding "permanent" (George Washington) or "entangling" (Thomas Jefferson) alliances is needed. All of those cold war–era alliances are from a bygone epoch and impede U.S. flexibility in a drastically changed post–cold war world. Alliances are not ends in themselves but are supposed to be a means to an end—that is, increased security for the United States. But alliances can also reduce a nation's security, especially when U.S. partners in all the alliances are weaker than the United States. Those "mutual" defense alliances—formal or informal—around the world represent a promise for a superpower to defend its allies, rather than vice versa. So the word *allies* is really a euphemism for *supplicants.*

As stretched as American forces are in conducting the military campaign in one nation, Iraq, the U.S. military would probably have trouble fulfilling more than one of those many alliance commitments simultaneously, should they come due. That problem is reflected in George Kennan's comments about the enlargement of NATO: "This expansion would make the founding fathers of this country turn over in their graves. We have signed up to protect a whole series of countries even though we have neither the resources nor the intention to do so in any serious way."[13]

Why Is the U.S. Defending Rich Allies?

Most U.S. friends and allies are rich and can defend themselves adequately without U.S. help. Japan, South Korea, Israel, Saudi Arabia, the Gulf states, and the NATO allies are all considered relatively wealthy by world standards. And those rich allies have relatively poor potential opponents: the South Korean economy is almost twenty-four times larger than North Korea's, Japan's economy is about three times China's, and four of the NATO allies (Germany, the United Kingdom, France, and Italy) each have economies that are larger than Russia's. Similarly, Israel's economy is five-and-a-half times that of Syria, and the Gulf Cooperation Council states (Saudi Arabia, Kuwait, Oman, Qatar, Bahrain, and the United Arab Emirates) have combined economies more than three times that of Iran.[14]

Yet some U.S. allies actually keep defense spending low to ensure that the United States will have to come to their aid in any conflict. So unless the United States removes these security guarantees, those nations will never do more for their own defense. Allied nations realize that even though the United States is half a world away from most regions of conflict, in all foreign theaters America has been and will continue to be more worried about the allies' neighbors than they are. Several examples should suffice. After Iraq's invasion of Kuwait in 1990, the United States practically had to beg Saudi Arabia to let the United States deploy troops on its soil. And according to the late international relations specialist Eric Nordlinger, the faraway United States worries more than its allies about threats to them in their own neighborhoods.

> The country's inordinate anxieties are clearly highlighted in a comparative perspective, in contrasting America's reactions with those of its allies to the same security threats. Although they were much more closely exposed and vulnerable to communist expansionism, we have regularly been more concerned about its likely emergence and the power behind it. The "devil theory" of China was widespread in America during the 1950s and early 1960s, although barely known in Japan, South Korea, Pakistan and Southeast Asia. It took years for Washington to pressure and cajole the Organization of American States into "recognizing" the Cuban threat under Castro. During the Vietnam War the nearby SEATO [Southeast Asian Treaty Organization] countries were less nervous about the threat to their security than was Washington for theirs and ours. Marxist Nicaragua and the radical insurgents in El Salvador prompted considerably more anxiety in America than among bordering and nearby Mexico, Costa Rica, Panama, Colombia, and Venezuela. Though the massive Warsaw Pact tank forces were positioned almost right up against Western Europe, in every disagreement about the danger of an invasion the NATO allies regarded it with greater equanimity. And we were consistently more anxious

than the Europeans about the spread of neutralism, Soviet advances in the Third World, and the risks to the Middle Eastern oil supplies.[15]

Alliances: Costs Outweigh Benefits

Although the cold war is over, the U.S. still worries more about "instability" in those faraway regions than the countries in them. But given that the United States is relatively secure geographically and is the most dominant military power in world history, both absolutely and relatively, those cold war era alliances do not contribute to U.S. security. In fact, they threaten to drag the United States into unnecessary, and perhaps catastrophic, wars. Inflexible alliances unwillingly dragged major European powers into World War I. Similarly, in ancient Greece, Athens and Sparta were dragged into the Peloponnesian War by their smaller Greek allies (Corinth, Corcyra, Megara, and Potidaea).[16]

In the future, the repeated expansion of NATO into the territory of the former Soviet Union could risk eventual war with an alarmed Russia, and the tightening informal alliance with non-strategic Taiwan could embroil the United States in a war with a nuclear-armed China. Since the advent of democracy in Taiwan, many Taiwanese no longer think of themselves as Chinese and may be emboldened by the enhanced, informal American security guarantees to take the provocative action of declaring independence from China. That step would risk war between a nuclear China and Taiwan's superpower benefactor. One Chinese official wondered out loud whether the United States would be willing to give up Los Angeles to save Taipei. Hopefully, U.S. policy would not be so rash, but those could be the stark, unintended implications of the Bush II administration's closer military ties with Taiwan.

Similarly, the American alliance with Israel is costly, because Israel is the largest recipient of U.S. aid and could embroil the United States in unneeded wars and quagmires in the Middle East—and may have already done so. Many analysts speculate that the neoconservatives in the Bush II administration took advantage of the September 11 attacks to invade Iraq and eliminate one of Israel's few remaining enemies. Also, although U.S. support for Israel is not bin Laden's number one gripe against the United States, the informal U.S. alliance with Israel most certainly spawns anti-U.S. terrorism by some Arab and Islamic groups. The alliance may make domestic political groups happy for American elections, but it has a negative effect on U.S. security.

Thus, the United States does not get very much except the bill in return for its "leadership" in such alliances. During the cold war and thereafter, the United States could have used its protection of Western Europe to negotiate an opening of European markets to U.S. products and services. But in return for U.S. security guarantees, rich American allies have failed to open their markets or end subsidies on competing products. In fact, the United States makes the foolish trade of U.S. foreign aid or allied access to U.S. markets without adequate reciprocity in return for usage of overseas military bases to protect those allies! In other words, maintaining the U.S. empire of military alliances to serve vested interests is more important than the prosperity of the American people.

Given those facts, the term *ally* is an Orwellian misnomer designed to convince the American people that those cold war alliances are needed to defend U.S. interests. Instead, even during the cold war, the alliances were one-sided—with the United States spending vast sums of money for allies' security and fighting wars on their behalf, both of which had nothing to do with defending U.S. territory.[17] The same is true today, but such one-way alliances are even harder to justify after the demise of the Soviet threat.

The United States keeps exhorting its allies to spend more on their own defense so that it can redirect spending toward expanding its empire, while retaining American control over the existing alliances. But why should the allies do so when they have an American protective umbrella and can spend the money saved on other things, perhaps even subsidizing their companies to compete with U.S. businesses?

Given that the cold war is over, allied nations are now rich, and few benefits are derived for all the costs of U.S. "leadership," why does the United States continue to spend billions defending other countries that are rich enough to defend themselves? The answer is short: to maintain the American empire. If the United States would terminate existing alliances and withdraw its troops from foreign soil, allied nations would be forced to develop more competent defense capabilities. The United States then fears that those nations would become power centers independent of American "influence." But, of course, given the vast amounts the U.S. government dumps into defending those nations, it is debatable what concrete benefits accrue to the U.S. taxpayer from vague American influence over them.

Furthermore, the current crushing dominance of the United States in the military sphere is unique in world history, unnatural, and unlikely to last. Normally, there is more than one great military power in the world. Even during the British empire and (at times) during the Roman empire, there were other military powers. So the unnatural situation of U.S. military dominance will probably erode over time, especially since wealth among the great powers is more diffuse than military power. India and China already have the highest economic growth rates on the planet, and the size of the combined economies of the European Union already exceeds that of the U.S. economy. Japan and Russia also have relatively large economies and could develop as independent power centers.

So competing power centers have been natural throughout world history and their rise now should not necessarily threaten the United States. In fact, the United States will remain a great power longer if it abandons the overseas empire, reduces defense spending, and funnels those savings into the private sector to increase the American economic growth rate. The United States should not make the same mistake that Britain and France made before World War II when they used their limited resources to maintain vast worldwide empires at the expense of safeguarding their homelands against a rising threat. The United States should not continue to retain an overextended empire, spending exorbitant amounts on defending and subsidizing allies and thus weakening itself, in case China, India, or a resurgent Russia eventually becomes a peer competitor. In fact, the United States may be currently subsidizing a future peer competitor in the form of the European Union or Japan.

Given the intrinsic security of the United States, it can afford to abandon the global empire and safeguard only its vital interests. But what are those vital interests?

U.S. Vital Interests

Contrary to common red herrings served up by the interventionists, being an offshore balancer does not mean being weak or appeasing threatening enemies. Truly vital interests need to be declared and vigorously defended. Other countries must be clear that America will take action to safeguard critical interests in a limited number of cases. Instead of profligate and often vague "security" commitments spanning the globe (for example, America's nebulous commitment to Taiwan if attacked by China), the United States needs a narrow, clearly defined set of paramount interests that will be staunchly defended. General Anthony Zinni, the former tough Marine commander in charge of the U.S. military forces in the Middle East, summed it up best when he advised that the United States should make few enemies but refrain from treating gently those it does make.

Withdrawing from unnecessary and entangling alliances overseas is not appeasement. First, there is no hegemonic great power rival, such as the Soviet Union, left to appease. Thus, bringing U.S. forces back to the United States merely indicates that the United States will no longer be suckered into paying the bill for the defense of other rich nations.

Focus on Three Key Regions

The offshore balancing strategy focuses only on regions critical to U.S. security—that is, North America, Europe, and East Asia.

Those three regions contain the bulk of the world's economic and technological power. Obviously, North America is critical to the United States because of its proximity to U.S. territory. The economic power of South America is not sufficient to make it a key region for U.S. security. It is also important to the United States that no potential hegemonic agressor takes over either Europe or East Asia. The aggressor could then use the immense economic and technological power in either region to threaten the United States.

But giving credence to the post–cold war version of the interventionists' erroneous domino theory—that any aggression or instability anywhere in the world needs to be stopped or it will snowball into a threat to America—should be avoided. U.S. foreign policy is still based on the fear, generated by the British and French appeasement of Adolf Hitler at Munich in 1938, that any negotiation with a potential adversary can be perceived as a sign of weakness and lead that nation to take advantage of the situation. The vast majority of scenarios are not comparable to that rare attempt by a reckless, rich aggressor to take over one of the wealthiest continents on the planet.

Several mitigating factors should allay fears about a future European or Asian hegemonic power threatening U.S. security, thereby requiring U.S. micromanagement of even those regions. The first is that a modern-day Nazi Germany, Imperial Japan, or Soviet Union does not threaten to overrun either region. Even if China, India or a resurgent Russia eventually became a potential hegemonic power, it would not happen for decades. Those countries are all so far behind the United States in commercial and military technology that it would take twenty to thirty years for them to catch up.

Dealing With Rising Powers

Of the three potential rising powers, China is regarded by the U.S. security establishment as the most likely to be a future threat. The Pentagon knows that a new nation-state competitor is needed to justify the purchase of new generations of aircraft, ships, tanks, and artillery.

Fighting small brushfire wars in the developing world, either within or outside the nebulous "war on terror,"just does not provide adequate justification for those expensive state-of-the-art weapons systems. So in the Department of Defense's mind, China needs to replace the Soviet Union as the major threat. Ironically, the United States supported a more radical communist China against a more moderate communist Soviet Union during some of the cold war (1971–1978 and 1985–1991). Yet now, when China is freer—both economically and politically—than ever before, the United States has suddenly grown suspicious of Chinese intentions. The United States has begun an unstated policy of encircling and containing China by keeping and enhancing all cold war alliances in East Asia, building up its military in the region, improving relations with Russia and India (China's great power neighbors and potential rivals) and creating "temporary" military bases in Central Asia, to China's west.

China has conducted extensive market reforms, held semifree local elections, adopted mandatory retirement rules for officials (including the top leadership posts), and strengthened the Chinese legislature. Many of the American suspicions about China have to do with the U.S. security establishment's need to find a new foe worthy of justifying astronomically high defense budgets and the continued production of cold war–era weapons, which are designed primarily to fight another great power (for example, F-22 fighters and Virginia-class submarines).

China, India, or Russia may never become a hegemonic rival to the United States. The rapid growth rates of China and India will probably slow as their economies mature and as they reach their ideological limits to market liberalization. Russia's successful transition to capitalism is still in doubt. But undoubtedly, all three nations will become—and already are, to some extent—regional powers that legitimately want spheres of influence (as most great powers have had throughout history).

The realist school of foreign policy believes that the uneven growth of power leads to wars. In other words, when rising powers expand and bump against the spheres of influence of stagnant or declining powers, conflict is more likely. Therefore, within reason, the United States could easily accommodate rising powers without compromising its security—for example, the way Great Britain accommodated a rising United States in the late 1800s.

Although the rise of a geographically-removed United States in the nineteenth century was probably less threatening to other great powers, including Great Britain, than the rise of powers nearer to them,[18] that unique geosecurity also gives the United States the opportunity to be less threatened by a future rising great power. At the same time, the U.S. geographical separation, when combined with the adoption of an American offshore balancing strategy, should make a rising power—for example, China—less fearful of the United States.

The United States should and does have the geographic luxury of avoiding what Britain did in the 1930s. Englishman E.H. Carr criticized his own country for not meeting the just demands of a rising Weimar Germany, thus accelerating its demise, and then being unwilling to stop a Hitler springing out of its ashes[19] (presumably because vast British imperial commitments took resources away from meeting the more urgent threat). But unlike Weimar Germany, China has little recent history of major war with its great-power neighbors. Nevertheless, the current de facto U.S. policy of containing China and constraining it from having a legitimate sphere of influence (a policy that China notices[20]) could needlessly create a future enemy. According to Professor David Calleo, the international system breaks down not only because new powers rise, but also because established powers, instead of adjusting to them, convert eroding dominance into aggressive behavior.[21] If it fails to withdraw its forward deployed defense perimeter and end the alliances that support it, the United States might run into needless conflict with China or any other rising nation.

In the worst case, even if one of those three nations—India, China, or Russia—begins to be more aggressive in either of the

Asian or European regions, the United States could rely on balancers in the region to be the first line of defense instead of taking on that role. In Europe, the United States could rely on a regional organization, the European Union, to balance against a resurgent Russia. Against a rising China, regional powers such as Japan, Taiwan, and South Korea could combine to balance against the rising power. Despite spending only 1 percent of its massive economy on defense, Japan already has the most capable military forces of any East Asian nation. In Asia, regional security organizations would probably become much more fashionable if the U.S. withdrew its protective umbrella. If China becomes an aggressive power, India might form either an informal or formal security relationship with Russia or the three aforementioned nations. If India becomes a potential aggressor, China might do the same.

Because the United States galloped to the rescue of Europe in World War I and Europe and East Asia during World War II and the cold war, a culture of security dependency has arisen. Thus, the foreign policy elites in the United States and even in Europe and East Asia have come to believe that if the United States reverts to its historical role as an offshore balancer, both regions will explode in internecine conflict. But World War II and the cold war were fairly unique periods. Prior to World War II, in the Asia-Pacific theater, there were no great powers, except the United States, that could have balanced against Imperial Japan. The British and Dutch had colonies in East Asia, but they were too overextended to put up much of a fight against the Japanese. China and India were both poor, underdeveloped nations. Russia was busy in the west with Hitler's Germany. Similarly, in Europe, Britain and France could have balanced against Hitler's Germany, but they were spending too many resources defending their overseas empires.[22] The historical case is a lesson for the United States to worry less about maintaining an overseas empire and more about a rising China or defending the U.S. homeland against catastrophic terrorism. In the couple of decades after World War II, the United States was the only great power available to balance against the Soviet Union in Europe and East Asia, because all of the other powers were recovering from the war.

As noted above, the situation is much different today—greater and lesser powers galore are available in both regions to balance against contingent threats that are probably decades away from fruition. Even the fear of a resurgent Germany and Japan does not have the potency that it once did. Germany is fully embedded in the European Union, which could provide security for the entire continent. Japan, like Germany, has been a model citizen now for more than half a century and has pacifistic tendencies as a result of the devastation of World War II. Besides, even though many countries in Asia regard Japan warily, based on its history, they also know in their hearts that China, with an economy growing by leaps and bounds, is potentially much more dangerous down the road (although even that adverse development is uncertain). Japan's economy has been stagnant for more than a decade. In other words, when push comes to shove, countries look to the future, rather than the past, to determine threat potential.

Some fear that if the United States withdraws American military forces from Germany, Japan, and South Korea and abrogates its security guarantees for those nations, they will build up their militaries and pursue nuclear weapons. But even with a globe-spanning American empire, more volatile countries or nations in much more dangerous neighborhoods—India, Pakistan, Israel, and North Korea—have obtained nuclear arms. For more than half a century, Germany, Japan, and South Korea have proven themselves to be friendly and responsible states. In fact, in the 1950s, President Eisenhower unsuccessfully tried to end the U.S. obligation to defend Western Europe against the Soviet Union and give West Germany nuclear weapons to fend for itself.[23] Eisenhower was inclined to turn over Germany's security to Germans, including trusting Germany with nuclear weapons, during the early years of the cold war when the world was much more tense and Germany's new government was untested. So why can't Germany be trusted in the more benign European threat environment of today? The proliferation of these weapons in such status quo and technologically capable states is probably inevitable and may actually reduce the chances of war in the European and East Asian regions. In Europe, a nuclear Germany could be deterred by a nuclear Russia, France and United Kingdom. A nuclear Japan and South Korea could deter each other and be deterred by a nuclear Russia and China.

Thus, the United States can rely on current and possibly future regional organizations or balances among the great powers in Europe and East Asia to be the first line of defense. The United States can then be the second line of defense—in other words, an offshore balancer—active only if an aggressive hegemonic power attempts to take over either one or both of those two key regions. But formal and informal alliances left over from a prior era can impede needed U.S. flexibility in the future the way Germany's alliance with the declining Austro-Hungarian empire dragged it needlessly into the disastrous World War I. Thus, the United States needs to abrogate all formal and informal alliances, withdraw all armed forces based overseas, convert to a military that can project power from the United States, and cut the massive U.S. annual defense budget of more than $400 billion[24] by a little more than half, to $184 billion.[25]

The existence of a U.S. empire calls for many wars to maintain and police it—more after the cold war than during that more threatening period. Wars lead to increased defense spending and more capable armed forces. High-level officials are then pressured to, or sometimes willingly (for example, Secretary of State Madeleine Albright), employ such "marvelous" forces ever more often to ostensibly right the wrongs of the world or protect U.S. "vital interests" (fig leaves for maintaining the empire). And thus the cycle repeats itself.

Currently, the United States alone accounts for about 40 percent of the world's military spending.[26] Even a reduced U.S. military budget ($184 billion) would still be more than three and a half times what China and Russia, the world's next highest spending countries, each expend annually on defense ($51 billion and $50.8 billion, respectively).[27] (And unlike the United States, those nations have to spend much of their defense budgets operating, maintaining, and repairing excessively large, aging forces.) Even with such healthy cuts in the U.S. military budget, America would remain very secure; in fact, with its superior geographical position, the United States could actually spend less on security than most countries. So spending $184 billion on national defense per year would give America an ample hedge against uncertain future security problems.

Even as an offshore balancer, however, the United States should be leery of jumping into wars. American policymakers should be very sure that the balance of power in a region has been irreparably harmed by the hegemonic power and that no other great power or regional organization can deter or stop the aggressor from further expansion. For example, both Britain and the United States—successful users of the offshore balancing strategy—were seduced into World War I. If they had stayed out of the Great War, the world would have been better off. Germany would have probably won and the boundaries of Europe would have adjusted, much as they had after all of the other European wars that the United States had avoided. The Kaiser's Germany did not have dreams of conquering all of Europe. Instead, as noted before, U.S. entry into the war led to Germany's defeat—sowing the seeds for the subsequent rise of Hitler—and indirectly to Russia's Bolshevik revolution.

Define Protection of Trade Narrowly

Another vital interest that the United States needs to secure is its international trade. Trade to and from the United States, regardless of the nationality of the ship carrying it, should be safe. If modern-day pirates (yes, there still are some) or a foreign navy regularly tries to intercept or destroy U.S. trade on the high seas, the U.S. Navy should be there to protect it. This function, however, should be construed narrowly. One of the U.S. Navy's major arguments for more ships is that globalization has brought about more international commerce, which needs to be protected.

Of course, the Navy is talking about protecting "freedom of navigation" around the globe. That broad interpretation of the "protection of trade" mission requires a forward-deployed Navy that protects the trade of all nations. Often the U.S. Navy uses the façade of enforcing freedom of navigation on the high seas as a way to engage in provocative naval actions against countries out of favor with the United States. In order to provoke a reaction, the Untied States sometimes conducts "in-your-face" shows of force in international waters near "rogue" nations. For example, President Ronald Reagan did this on several occasions to Moammar Qaddafi of Libya, the Saddam-Husseinesque punching bag of the 1980s. Such provocations are unnecessary and have to stop. Freedom of navigation should be narrowly construed.

And other nations should pay to protect their own trade. The United States can protect trade routes to and from the United States. But this protection should not require U.S. ships to be deployed permanently at overseas bases. If the U.S. Army is superior to any foreign army and the U.S. Air Force is dominant over any foreign air force, the U.S. Navy has bone-crushing dominance over any foreign navy. Navies are the most expensive of military services to build and maintain, and most nations cannot afford to compete with the United States. The United States currently has twelve large and twelve medium aircraft carriers; no other country has a fully functioning large carrier and only a few countries have one or two small ones. The mere threat of even a reduced U.S.-based naval juggernaut steaming to combat any pirates or foreign nations intercepting U.S. trade should dissuade such behavior against U.S. commercial interests. If such deterrence fails, the Navy can steam from U.S. ports to the problem region, resupplying and refueling at friendly overseas ports along the way or in the region. If an extended time is required on-station to deal with the problem, the

United States can reach an agreement with a friendly nation for temporary access to bases in the region.

In short, the United States should bring home and reduce its navy. Shows of force overseas may still be needed, but they should be rare if the United States begins to define its vital interests more narrowly. Even if they prove necessary on occasion, ships often have a greater political impact if they steam from the United States rather than from U.S. bases overseas. For example, in the crisis with China in the Taiwan Strait during 1995 and 1996, the first U.S. carrier steaming from its base in Japan had less political impact than the second one arriving from the United States.

Because the United States is fundamentally a maritime nation—trading by sea with nations all over the world—it should retain a capable navy. But after the cold war ended with the Russian Navy rusting in port, no other country for decades to come will even come close to threatening the United States at sea. Thus, the United States could reduce its navy by more than a third and still remain far more capable than the other navies of the world.

Reduce the U.S. Nuclear Arsenal

Finally, the United States must maintain a viable nuclear arsenal as the ultimate deterrent against attack. Nuclear weapons are the most destructive weapons ever invented. They are the ultimate deterrent to enemy attack, albeit a dangerous one.[28] Even in the unlikely event that all nations would agree to give up those terrible weapons, there is no guarantee that one or more countries would not cheat and retain some. This situation would allow that nation to blackmail or coerce other nations. Thus, the United States is faced with the need to maintain a nuclear arsenal. But even with the latest agreement between Russia and the United States to reduce their arsenals further, the U.S. arsenal is still too large. The United States could reduce its arsenal to 1,000–1,500 strategic warheads, and maybe go even lower.[29] (Russia's long-range strategic arsenal is decaying and China's is expected to grow to about 100 warheads from the 20 on hand now.) Most or all of the remaining American warheads should be at sea in invulnerable strategic ballistic missile submarines. If the United States wanted to retain a dyad, some of these warheads could be reserved for use by land-based Air Force bombers.

Nonvital Interests

More significant may be what is not included in a narrow list of vital interests. From a security standpoint, conflict in most regions of the globe is irrelevant to U.S. vital interests. Surprisingly, that assessment includes the Persian Gulf. In Washington, the national-security policy-making apparatus—usually lacking economists—has declared oil a strategic commodity and the Persian Gulf a region that needs about half of U.S. military capabilities for its defense. But strangely, the Pentagon got really interested in the Persian Gulf only after the sole threat to the region's oil (albeit a remote one, even during the cold war)—a feared Soviet attack through Iran—went away. (The fear was that a rival superpower would control key oil reserves needed by the West.) That is, the U.S. did not have a permanent military presence on land in the Persian Gulf region until after the 1991 Gulf War.

So suspicions might arise that after the cold war ended, the defense establishment, lacking its traditional Soviet enemy, had to find other threats to defend against to prevent drastic cuts in forces. After the first Persian Gulf War, the Pentagon came up with the idea of requiring enough forces to fight two medium regional wars "nearly simultaneously" (this phrase should have been a warning sign of the artificial nature of the planning process). One of those regional wars was a North Korean invasion of South Korea. Korea is strategic for Japan but not for the United States. And South Korea—with almost twenty-four times the GDP of North Korea—should be able to defend itself without U.S. assistance. The other was an Iraqi invasion of Saudi Arabia and the other Gulf oil states. That Saddam Hussein had only one-half to one-third of his military capability remaining intact after the drubbing he took during the first Gulf War did not deter the U.S. military from planning for the last war. Because a big chunk of the U.S. defense budget is justified by the need to safeguard oil, the Pentagon will continue to ignore what prominent economists say about the need to defend oil.

After Saddam Hussein's invasion of Kuwait, but before the first Gulf War, David R. Henderson, formerly a senior economist for energy on President Reagan's Council of Economic Advisers and currently a professor of economics at the Naval Postgraduate School, calculated the maximum economic damage to the United States from oil-price spikes arising from an unfriendly takeover of Persian Gulf oil fields.[30] In Henderson's worst-case scenario, he assumed that Saddam had invaded Kuwait, Saudi Arabia, and the United Arab Emirates. (According to General Norman Schwarzkopf, during the first three weeks of the crisis, Saddam had the opportunity to take Saudi Arabia without opposition. Historians Stephen Ambrose and Douglas Brinkley note that Saddam did not and that this restraint may have indicated that perhaps he never intended to do so.[31]) Saddam would have conquered the oil fields to get the oil, so he probably would not have refused to sell it. After Saddam's hypothetical invasion, his control over a greater market share of worldwide oil production and reserves would have allowed him to drive oil prices higher by cutting production somewhat. Yet, according to Henderson, those price increases would have amounted to less than one-half of 1 percent of U.S. Gross National Product.

At the time, prominent economists from across the political spectrum agreed with Henderson's analysis. On the left, James Tobin, a Nobel Laureate, stated, "There are other ways of coping with \$30- or \$40-a-barrel oil [in 1991 dollars] than going to war. The ultimate loss to a \$5,500 billion economy [in 1991 dollars] is less than 1 percent. It's hard to say we should go to war to save 1 percent of GNP." On the right, Milton Friedman, also a Nobel Laureate, agreed with Tobin: "Henderson's analysis is correct. There is no justification for intervention on grounds of oil." Friedman added that an oil price that optimized Saddam's revenues "would be higher than a competitive price, but not that much higher, and certainly not enough to justify what we are doing in the Middle East."[32] Another prominent economist, William A. Niskanen, former Acting Chairman of President Reagan's Council of Economic Advisers, also concurred: "If we consider only the economics of oil, the costs of the U.S. response to the Iraqi invasion are higher than any potential benefits from deterring any further Iraqi aggression. Oil is clearly not worth a war."[33] Eric Nordlinger, an international-relations specialist, agreed with the economists and pointed out that if Saddam had gained control of all Gulf oil, that amount would have been about 20 percent of world production. He also pointed out that each year the U.S. Justice Department regularly approves mergers of that magnitude.[34]

Donald Losman, a professor of economics at the Department of Defense's National Defense University, thinks that using the military to pursue economic goals—such as safeguarding cheap oil—"diverts a significant portion of military resources away from more appropriate, core national security ends." In an excellent analysis, Losman points out that cheap oil is not needed for economic prosperity. For example, from the fourth quarter of 1998 to the third quarter of 2000, the German economy saw a 211 percent increase in the price of crude oil but continued growing, while experiencing a reduction in inflation and unemployment.[35]

Much of the myth that cheap oil is vital to the U.S. economy is residue from the "oil crisis" of 1973. In the public mind, high oil prices are associated with the inflation, high interest rates, and economic turmoil of the 1970s. In fact, the oil crisis was really a governmental crisis. Instead of allowing oil prices to rise and demand to decline, the U.S. government relied on price controls, rationing, and expansionary monetary and fiscal policies to offset the oil shock. Had the price been allowed to rise to market levels, the market would have automatically cut back usage and given priority to critical users willing to pay the higher prices. The below-market price ensured that demand would exceed supplies. The trauma of gas lines in 1973 still haunts public discussion of the energy security issue. During the 1970s, Japan let the price of oil rise naturally and experienced no gas lines. Furthermore, the inflation, high interest rates, and economic dislocations were caused more by expansionary monetary policy and budget deficits than by high oil prices. According to economist Douglas Bohi, in reality, oil shortages in the 1970s reduced U.S. gross domestic product by only .35 percent.[36]So the good news is that even when the variable global oil price spikes, modern industrial economies can prosper, provided that market forces are allowed to operate. Even better news is that over the long term, the inflation-adjusted cost of energy, including oil, has declined. In contrast, according to Losman, the cost of a college education or a meal at a good restaurant has increased. An even better measure of the cost of gasoline to consumers is how much time a worker has to work, at the average manufacturing wage, to afford to buy a gallon. That statistic has been declining since the 1920s. Better news yet is that after the oil crisis of 1973, the U.S. economy became much more oil-efficient. Losman notes that in the twenty years after the crisis, the oil consumed per billion dollars in real U.S. GDP declined almost 37 percent.[37]

The U.S. economy depends on many imports to make it function, and the national obsession with the fear-mongering phrase "dependency on foreign oil" is misplaced. In fact, Persian Gulf countries are more dependent than the West on oil. Oil makes up a greater share of the exports of Persian Gulf nations than it does the imports of Western nations. Also, in 2001, about 21 percent of the world's oil production originated in the Persian Gulf.[38] The United States gets only 23.5 percent of its oil imports from the Gulf.[39] (Although Middle Eastern oil accounts for a lower percentage of U.S. petroleum consumption than it does of Japanese or European oil consumption, those nations provide few forces to defend the supplies.) But semiconductors are also important for the economy and the Pentagon's weapon systems, and around 80 percent of U.S. imports of circuits come from East Asia.[40] Thus, the United States is much more dependent on a specific region of the world for semiconductors than it is for oil. Yet the military does not spend billions defending semiconductors from East Asia the way it does securing oil from the Persian Gulf. According to Losman, the Pentagon spent an estimated $30 billion to $60 billion per year to defend oil imports from the Persian Gulf that were worth, on average, only about $10 billion annually during most of the 1990s.[41] Chalmers Johnson cites similar figures: $50 billion in U.S. defense costs and $11 billion for the value of the oil.[42]

Losman also makes moral arguments against using military force to ensure access to cheap oil. He points out that Imperial Japan was driven to conquer East Asia because of fears of losing raw materials for its industries. He notes that such motivations have been morally unacceptable to Americans yet have made it into the American national security strategy without a whimper of protest.[43] The Japanese empire's quest for autarky by military means is eerily similar to the American empire's use of its military to ensure supplies of cheap oil. In sum, the United States should not get involved in the Persian Gulf or any other nonstrategic area of the world.

EMPIRE OR ROLE MODEL?

America's geographic advantages should allow it the luxury of narrowing its list of vital interests and safeguarding them, while adopting a policy of military restraint overseas. The United States needs to monitor the balance of power in two key regions—Europe and East Asia—and take action only if regional powers or organizations fail to maintain that balance of power. The policy of military restraint should allow the United States to cut its military budget by more than half, but would still require America to have a capable Navy to protect U.S. trade and a minimum strategic nuclear force to act as the ultimate deterrent to an attack on the United States. Using a policy of military restraint to defend a narrower set of vital interests will lower the cost to the taxpayer and actually increase the security of Americans by lowering the motivation of outside parties to attack them.

The United States should go back to the traditional U.S. foreign policy so eloquently described by Senator Henry Clay in 1852:

> By following the policy we have adhered to since the days of Washington we have prospered beyond precedent; we have done more for the cause of liberty in the world than arms could effect, we have shown to other nations the way to greatness and happiness.
>
> But if we should involve ourselves in the web of European politics, in a war which could effect nothing . . . where, then, would be the last hope of the friends of freedom throughout the world? Far better it is . . . that, adhering to our wise pacific system, and avoiding the distant wars of Europe, we should keep our own lamp burning brightly on this western shore, as a light to all nations, than to hazard its utter extinction amidst the ruins of fallen or falling republics in Europe.[44]

Such a more humble U.S. foreign policy is not dependent on other nations reciprocating Jefferson's principle of "peace, commerce and honest friendship with all nations—entangling alliances with none" or George Washington's rule of conduct for U.S. relations with foreign nations, "in extending our commercial relations—to have with them as little political connection possible." But perhaps U.S. behavior will be a beacon for other nations to follow. Citing evidence from the historical record, Richard Rosecrance noted the following: "When successful nations created a paradigm that included territorial expansion as one of its central tenets, others were willing to follow their lead, at least for a time. When successful nations favored territorial abstention and policies of peaceful trade, they again gained adherents. Countries with novel and efficient practices gained many followers and continue to do so today. Imperialism went in-and-out of fashion not simply because of power balances or imbalances, vulnerability or invulnerability, but because of reigning foreign policy paradigms."[45] Of course, Rosecrance is talking about the old-style imperialism here. The informal American empire still lives. But if America renounced its empire in favor of a more efficient, prosperous, secure, morally uplifting, and constitution- and power-preserving policy of military restraint and peaceful commerce, many nations in the world just might follow.

Historically, many proponents of democracy in foreign lands have used the United States as a model, citing its founding documents. For example, as the cold war ended, the democratic movements in Eastern Europe and the Soviet Union did so. America can be a positive force in the world without being an empire.

7

Conclusion

Although imperial stirrings began with a colonial foray in the Spanish-American War of 1898 and U.S. dabbling in the Caribbean and Central America in the early 1900s, a global American empire did not explode onto the world scene until 1950. Only during the cold war did America finally abandon its traditional foreign policy of acting as an offshore balancer in favor of Pax Americana—a worldwide network of alliances, forward-deployed military forces at bases scattered around the globe, and a policy of direct and indirect intervention in the affairs of many other nations. Ostensibly, Pax Americana was created to fight communism, but U.S. policymakers have admitted that they hyped the threat. The Soviet Union had a large military but an economic underpinning of quicksand—a veritable Upper Volta with missiles. Even more convincing was the failure of Pax Americana to dissolve when its major rival did; in fact, the American empire grew larger after the cold war ended.

Unlike the Roman and British empires, the American empire, for the most part, is not one of territorial conquest—though the cases of Bosnia, Kosovo, Afghanistan, and Iraq indicate that occupation of foreign territories is now occurring more frequently. America's empire is a subtler, more informal version, along the lines of Ancient Sparta. The United States has more control over the foreign policy of its allies than over their domestic affairs, though ultimately America likely would not allow its major allies to revert to authoritarian or totalitarian states. Another difference is that the empires of old gained resources and plunder, captive markets for their exports, and a flow of taxes from their peripheral areas. The United States gets none of those things from its allies and client states (U.S. allies even refuse to fully open their markets to U.S. exports and investment); instead, it gets a bill—in blood and treasure—for the defense of nations that are now rich enough to defend themselves.

Conservatives should be against an American empire, because war is the primary cause of big government, including government encroachment in non-security-related areas. Of course, bloated government requires increased taxes to support it. Hostile relations with other nations also bring protectionism and controls on trade and financial flows, thus undermining the principles of free trade. Bloated government, high taxes, and restricted foreign commerce lead to lower economic growth. In short, the U.S. empire undermines the prosperity and well-being of American society—two goals that should be paramount to the U.S. or any other government.

Over time, lower U.S. economic growth rates, compared to those of rising powers that have smaller security burdens, could cause the U.S. empire to go into relative decline and perhaps even cause America to lose its status as a great power. Britain was at the height of its power at the turn of the last century but is now barely a great power. The United States is already overextended, accounting for almost 40 percent of the world's military spending but possessing only a little more than 30 percent of global GDP. It may meet the same fate as Britain if it fails to retrench. Conservatives worry about the nation's security, but the United States does not need an empire to ensure it. America has distance between it and most of the world's zones of conflict, two great oceans as moats, weak and friendly neighbors, and the most potent nuclear arsenal on the planet.

Liberals should be against empire because many of the United States' so-called humanitarian military interventions are really done for reasons of realpolitik. And the abysmal U.S. track record of trying to bring democracy and free markets to countries at gunpoint shows that most such interventions fail in the difficult task of restructuring fractured and violent societies. In fact, in the long term, violations of nations' sovereignties—even for "humanitarian" ends—undermine international norms against cross-border aggression and encourage separatist groups to revolt and then try to win the support of the United States and its Western allies. If that happens, over time, more people are likely to be killed than saved by U.S. interventions into failed states. Instead, the international community should concentrate on helping nations in which all parties to a conflict are exhausted by war and ready to stop fighting—instead of expecting the United States to risk the lives of its soldiers trying to intercede between two sides that are not yet ready to make peace. Also, if a military intervention is unnecessary, then even killing innocent civilians accidentally is immoral. Furthermore, foreign wars lead to the erosion of civil liberties at home. Finally, many vested interests—including the arms industry—turn war fervor into corporate welfare.

All Americans should be against a U.S. empire, because it destroys the republic. This is probably the most important argument against empire. Repeated wars undermined democracy in Ancient Greece and doomed the Roman Republic. In the United States, an imperial foreign policy has lead to an imperial presidency that is much more powerful than the founders intended. In short, war distorts the Constitution and the liberties therein.

As much as some would like to use American military power to restructure failed states, this is likely to be an unsuccessful and dangerous undertaking. Bitter civil wars—ethnic and otherwise—breed terrorism. The United States is hated worldwide for its interference in the affairs of other nations and peoples, and the attacks on September 11 were blowback from American foreign policy. Because intelligence is imperfect, and America—the largest truly open society in the world—is very vulnerable to terrorism, improved homeland security measures can only go so far in protecting Americans from future catastrophic terrorist attacks. A better solution is to white out the bull's-eye painted on America by getting rid of both its empire and concomitant interventionist foreign policy.

With the demise of America's chief rival, the Soviet Union, the benefits of Pax Americana and profligate military interventions worldwide have declined dramatically. With the advent of catastrophic terrorism, the costs of such an activist foreign policy have increased precipitously. Thus, the quest for empire is a foreign policy, but not a security policy.

The founders of the republic realized that America's geographical remoteness vis-à-vis other nation-states allowed the luxury of distancing itself from entangling alliances and foreign quarrels, defining its vital interests narrowly, and adopting a policy of military restraint. In an age of catastrophic terrorism, the founders' original foreign policy is more relevant than ever. Profligate intervention overseas is not needed for security against other nation-states and only leads to blowback from the one threat that is difficult to deter—terrorism.

In short, the U.S. empire lessens American prosperity, power, security and moral standing. It also erodes the founding principles of the American Constitution.

Notes

CHAPTER ONE

1. Quoted in Warren Zimmerman, *First Great Triumph: How Five Americans Made Their Country a World Power* (New York: Farrar, Straus and Giroux, 2002), 327.
2. George W. Bush, "A Distinctly American Internationalism," speech, Simi Valley, Calif., November 19, 1999.
3. Ibid., remarks to U.S. troops in Doha, Qatar, June 5, 2003, the White House, Office of the Press Secretary.
4. Ibid., "State of the Union Address," U.S. Capitol, January 20, 2004.
5. The results of the debate and poll were reported in Dan Morgan, "A Debate Over U.S. 'Empire' Builds in Unexpected Circles," *Washington Post,* August 10, 2003, A3.
6. Quoted in Andrew Bacevich, *American Empire: The Realities and Consequences of U.S. Diplomacy* (Cambridge, Mass.: Harvard University Press, 2002), 219.
7. Niall Ferguson, "The 'E' Word," *Wall Street Journal,* June 6, 2003, A10.
8. Quoted in Niall Ferguson, *Empire: The Rise and Demise of the British World Order and the Lessons for Global Power* (New York: Basic Books, 2003), 345.
9. Alexander J. Moytl, *Revolutions, Nations, Empires* (New York: Columbia University Press, 1999), 138.
10. Zimmerman, *First Great Triumph,* 33.
11. Ibid., 37–39, 242.
12. Doyle, *Empires,* 153–54.
13. Zimmerman, *First Great Triumph,* 6–8, 13, 444.
14. Ibid., 5–6, 8, 11, 13, 429–36, 443–44; Gore Vidal, "The Day the American Empire Ran Out of Gas," in *The Decline and Fall of the American Empire* (Tucson: Odonian Press, 1986–1992), 11, 14–17.
15. Jacob Hornberger, "Dismantling America's Military Empire," in *The Failure of America's Foreign Wars,* ed. Richard M. Ebeling and Jacob Hornberger (Fairfax, Va.: The Future of Freedom Foundation, 1996), 2.
16. Bacevich, *American Empire,* 70; Chalmers Johnson, *The Sorrows of Empire: Militarism, Secrecy, and the End of the Republic* (New York: Metropolitan Books, 2004), 192.

17. J. David Singer and Melvin Small, *National Material Capabilities Data: 1816–1985* (Ann Arbor, Mich.: Inter-University Consortium for Political and Social Research, 1993).
18. Edward A. Olsen, *U.S. National Defense for the Twenty-First Century* (London: Frank Cass, 2002), 42.
19. Ralph Raico, "Rethinking Churchill," in *The Costs of War: America's Pyrrhic Victories,* ed. John V. Denson (New Brunswick: Transaction Books, 1997), 270.
20. John Mearsheimer, *The Tragedy of Great Power Politics* (New York: W.W. Norton and Company, 2001), 216.
21. Author's conclusions from *National Material Capabilities Data,* published by Singer and Small.
22. Ambrose and Brinkley, *Rise to Globalism,* 83.
23. Nordlinger, *Isolationism Reconfigured,* 115.
24. Chalmers Johnson, *Sorrows of Empire,* 154–160, 288.
25. Robert Kaplan, "Supremacy by Stealth," *Atlantic Monthly* 292, no. 1 (2003), 66. Using 1997 data, John Rudy and the author estimated the total at 143 countries. See John Rudy and Ivan Eland, "Special Operations Military Training Abroad and Its Dangers," *Cato Institute Foreign Policy Briefing* no. 53 (Washington, D.C.: Cato Institute, 1999), 2. Similarly, in 2004, Chalmers Johnson says the total is 150 nations. See Chalmers Johnson, *Sorrows of Empire,* 124, 132–33. In any case, the number of countries in which those secretive U.S. Special Forces operate is great. Among other missions, they essentially train foreign militaries to keep order in their own countries (critics call this internal repression), conduct diplomacy, and gain political influence for the United States. The State Department has its own military training program for foreign militaries.
26. Kerry Dumbaugh, "China-U.S. Relations," *Congressional Research Service Issue Brief for Congress,* January 31, 2003, CRS-8.
27. Bacevich, *American Empire,* 151.
28. Chalmers Johnson, *The Sorrows of Empire,* 137.
29. U.S. Commission on National Security/21st Century, *New World Coming: The United States Commission on National Security/21st Century* (Washington, D.C.: Government Printing Office, 1999), 128.
30. Lawrence J. Korb, "Overpaying the Pentagon: How We Can Meet Our Security Needs for Less than $500 billion," *American Prospect,* September 2003, 17.
31. Bacevich, *American Empire,* 228.
32. Harold Laski, "America-1947," *Nation,* December 13, 1947, 641.
33. Olsen, *U.S. National Defense,* 23. For the American empire, keeping the wealthy allies from developing military power independent of the

United States may be more important than deterring the generally much poorer U.S. rivals from competition. The Department of Defense's 2001 Quadrennial Defense Review lists four guiding principles for developing U.S. military forces: (1) assuring allies and friends that the United States will fulfill its security commitments; (2) dissuading adversaries from undertaking programs or operations that would threaten U.S., allied, or friendly interests; (3) deterring aggression by threatening an adversary's military; and (4) defeating aggression if deterrence fails. Note that assuring allies and friends that their security will be guaranteed is priority one and that even dissuading adversaries (priority two) is couched partly in terms of looking out for allied or friendly interests. Both were provisions included presumably so that those rich democratic nations will not build independent military forces that could challenge U.S. power. Furthermore, in justifying the forward deployment of U.S. military forces all over the world, the document also mentions assuring allies and friends before countering coercion and aggression from adversaries. See forward to Department of Defense, Quadrennial Defense Review 2001, http://www.defenselink.mil/pubs/qdr2001.pdf. Given the current military weakness of poorer potential adversaries, keeping down rich allies may be more important to the American empire.

34. Bacevich, *American Empire,* 98–99.

CHAPTER TWO

1. Robert Kaplan, "Supremacy by Stealth," 66.
2. Robert Gilpin, *War and Change in World Politics* (Cambridge: Cambridge University Press, 1981), 170–72.
3. Quoted in Zimmerman, *First Great Triumph,* 13.
4. David Lake, "The Rise, Fall, and Future of the Russian Empire," in *The End of Empire? The Transformation of the USSR in Comparative Perspective,* ed. Karen Sawisha and Bruce Parrott (Armonk, New York: Sharpe, 1997), 34.
5. George Lichtheim, *Imperialism* (New York: Praeger, 1971), 5.
6. Motyl, *Revolutions, Nations, Empires,* 118.
7. Geir Lundestad, *The American "Empire"* (Oslo: Norwegian University Press, 1990), 37.
8. Motyl, *Revolutions, Nations, Empires,* 128.
9. Doyle, *Empires,* 12, 40, 130.
10. Real spending on U.S. security is in fact much higher than the table or figure indicates. Robert Higgs notes that the stated budget for the Department of Defense should be doubled to get the actual U.S. expenditures for U.S. security. That enlarged total includes spending on nuclear weapons (in the Department of Energy budget), homeland security, for-

eign aid, veterans benefits, and interest on the national debt attributable to defense spending. Robert Higgs, "The Defense Budget Is Bigger than You Think It Is," *San Francisco Chronicle,* January 18, 2004.

11. Table 1 actually understates the disparity between the United States and its allies in spending on national defense. The last year in which all nations reported was 2002. In 2003, the United States substantially increased spending again. It now spends more than $400 billion annually on national defense and another $100 billion per year in supplemental funds to fight in Iraq and Afghanistan. As Lawrence J. Korb, Director of Security Studies at the Council on Foreign Relations in New York, puts it, "We essentially give the military a $400 billion budget, but we have to pay extra to use it." Lawrence J. Korb, "Overpaying the Pentagon," 17.
12. Peter Bender, "The New Rome," in *The Imperial Tense: Prospects and Problems of American Empire,* ed. Andrew Bacevich (Chicago: Ivan R. Dee, 2003), 85.
13. International Institute for Strategic Studies, *The Military Balance: 2003–2004,* (London: Oxford University Press, 2003), 235, 248–250, 269, 276, 279, 288, 298, 299, 313.
14. Stockholm International Peace Research Institute figures cited by Chalmers Johnson in *Blowback: The Costs and Consequences of American Empire* (New York: Henry Holt and Company, 2000), 86. G. John Ikenberry argues that U.S. spending for military research and development as a portion of the world's total is even higher—80 percent. G. John Ikenberry, "American Power and the Empire of Capitalist Democracy," in *Empires, Systems and States: Great Transformations in International Politics,* ed. Michael Cox, Tim Dunne, and Ken Booth (Cambridge: Cambridge University Press, 2001), 191.
15. Robert Payne, *Ancient Rome* (New York: Ibooks, 2001), viii.
16. Ibid., 68.
17. Paul Johnson, "From the Evil Empire to the Empire for Liberty," *The New Criterion,* June 2003, http://www.newcriterion.com/archive/21/jun03/johnson.htm.
18. Zimmerman, *First Great Triumph,* 11–12.
19. Ferguson, *Empire,* xii, 330.
20. Paul Cartledge, *The Spartans: The World of the Warrior-Heroes of Ancient Greece, form Utopia to Crisis and Collapse* (Woodstock, New York: Overlook Press, 2003), 144, 153.
21. Doyle, *Empires,* 58–60; Peter J. Fliess, *Thucydides and the Politics of Bipolarity* (Baton Rouge, La.: Louisiana State University Press, 1966), 91.
22. Ibid., 58–60.
23. For more on the harsh domination of democratic Athens over its Greek allies, see Thomas R. Martin's *Ancient Greece: From Prehistoric to Hellenistic Times* (New Haven: Yale University, 1996), 105–108.

24. Doyle, *Empires,* 30, 68.
25. Anatol Lieven, "A Trap of Their Own Making," *London Review of Books* 25, no. 9 (2003), http://www.lrb.co.uk/v25/n09/liev01_.html.
26. Paul Kennedy, *The Rise and Fall of Great Powers* (New York: Vintage Books, 1987), 519.
27. Andrew Bacevich quotes outspoken Marine General Anthony Zinni, former CINC of the U.S. Central Command in the Middle East, as comparing the CINC's role with that of a Roman military proconsul. Andrew Bacevich, *American Empire,* 175, 178, 180.
28. Cartledge, *The Spartans,* 190.
29. Doyle, *Empires,* 71, 98.
30. Ibid., 54–58.
31. Bender, "The New Rome," 82.
32. Jack Snyder, *Myths of Empire: Domestic Politics of International Ambition* (Ithaca and London: Cornell University Press, 1991), 1, 3.
33. Doyle, *Empires,* 108–9, 146, 340.
34. Mearsheimer, *Great Power Politics,* 380–92.
35. Robert Eldridge, "U.S. Security Strategy and U.S.-Japan-China Relations: Stabilizer and Engager," in *An Alliance for Engagement: Building Cooperation in Security Relations with China* (Washington, D.C.: The Henry L. Stimson Center, September 2000), 120–21.
36. Snyder, *Myths of Empire,* 8.
37. Ibid., 11.
38. Gilpin, *War and Change,* 51, 95.
39. Thucydides, *History of the Peloponnesian Wars,* trans. Rex Warner (Harmondsworth: Viking Press, 1954), 1, 76.
40. As characterized by Richard Rosecrance in "Overextension, Vulnerability and Conflict: The Goldilocks Problem in International Security (A Review Essay)," *International Security* 19, no. 4 (1995): 162.
41. Charles Kupchan, *The Vulnerability of Empire* (Ithaca, New York: Cornell University Press, 1994), 18.
42. Snyder, *Myths of Empire,* 17–18, 20, 31, 32, 38–39, 256, 306.
43. Wolfowitz is cited in Karen DeYoung and Walter Pincus's article, "Despite Obstacles to War, White House Forges Ahead: Administration Unfazed by Iraq's Pledges to Destroy Missiles, Turkish Parliament's Rejection of Use of Bases," *Washington Post,* March 2, 2003, A18.
44. The exception is a unitary oligarchy such as the Soviet Union in which the oligarchy—in the Soviet case, the Politburo—is a counterweight to parochial military and imperialist interests. Snyder, *Myths of Empire,* 18.
45. Christopher Layne, "Kant or Cant: The Myth of the Democratic Peace," in *Debating the Democratic Peace,* ed. Michael E. Brown, Sean M. Lynn-Jones, and Steven E. Miller (Cambridge: MIT Press, 1996), 160, 161, 164.

46. Snyder, *Myths of Empire,* 53.
47. Motyl, *Revolutions, Nations, Empires,* 148.
48. Zimmerman, *First Great Triumph,* 405–9.
49. Mearsheimer, *Great Power Politics,* 210.
50. Martin, *Ancient Greece,* 160–61.
51. Peter S. Temes, *The Just War: An American Reflection on the Morality of War in Our Time* (Chicago: Ivan R. Dee, 2003), 57–58.
52. Layne, "Kant or Cant," 159, 191.
53. For the Athens-Syracuse case, see Cartledge, *The Spartans,* 195; Doyle, *Empires,* 78.
54. An example of redefining "democracy" so that the democratic peace theory works is found in Spencer Weart's *Never at War: Why Democracies Will Not Fight One Another* (New Haven: Yale University Press, 1998), 1–23, 297–318.
55. Mearsheimer, *Great Power Politics,* 26.
56. That sentiment is not only voiced by revisionist historians, such as Harry Barnes, who argued that Russian and French official documents about the secret Franco-Russian agreements from 1892–1914 proved that France, Russia, and Serbia were mainly responsible for the outbreak of World War I. See Harry Elmer Barnes, *Revisionism: A Key to Peace and Other Essays* (San Francisco: Cato Institute, 1980), 15. For example, Bevin Alexander, a mainstream historian, implies that the balance of power in Europe was sent askew by the secret Anglo-French military alliance in response to German economic growth—not by the German naval buildup, which the British had more than outpaced by 1909. Bevin Alexander, *How Wars are Won: The 13 Rules of War—From Ancient Greece to the War on Terror* (New York: Crown Publishers, 2003), 277.
57. Kupchan, *Vulnerability of Empire,* 488.
58. Layne, "Kant or Cant," 192–93.
59. Weart, *Never at War,* 23, 279–81.
60. Research by Edward Mansfield and Jack Snyder establishes a correlation between war and states in transition, whether toward democracy or authoritarianism. Edward Mansfield and Jack Snyder, "Democratization and the Danger of War," *International Security* 20 (1995), 5–38.
61. Snyder, *Myths of Empire,* 17.
62. Nordlinger, *Isolationism Reconfigured,* 100.
63. Layne, "Kant or Cant," 164.
64. Cited in John V. Denson's introduction to *The Costs of War: America's Pyrrhic Victories,* ed. John V. Denson (New Brunswick: Transaction Books, 1997), xii–xiii.
65. Henry Kamen, *How Spain Became a World Power: 1492–1763* (New York: Harper Collins, 2003), 96, 107-110, 117–18, 492–93, 501, 504.

66. Doyle, *Empires,* 63.
67. Robert Gilpin, "Economic Interdependence and National Security in Historical Perspective," in *Economic Issues and National Security,* ed. Klaus Knorr and Frank Trager (Lawrence, Kans.: Regents Press of Kansas, 1977), 19–66.
68. Victor Davis Hanson, "What Empire?" in *The Imperial Tense: Prospects and Problems of American Empire,* ed. Andrew Bacevich (Chicago: Ivan R. Dee, 2003), 146–48, 152.
69. Ronald Steel, *Pax Americana* (New York: Viking, 1967), 13.
70. Ikenberry, "American Power," 200–1, 202–3.
71. Ferguson, *Empire,* xx–xxii.
72. Ibid., 313, 346.
73. Ibid., 346.
74. Robert Kaplan, "Supremacy by Stealth," 68–69.

CHAPTER THREE

1. Warren Zimmerman, *First Great Triumph,* 330–31.
2. Bruce Porter, *War and the Rise of the State: The Military Foundations of Modern Politics* (New York: The Free Press, 1994), 14.
3. Ibid., 244–45.
4. Ibid., 245.
5. Ibid., 269–71.
6. Robert Higgs, "War and Leviathan in Twentieth-Century America: Conscription as a Keystone," in *The Costs of War: America's Pyrrhic Victories,* ed. John V. Denson (New Brunswick: Transaction Books, 1997), 309, 313–15. Higgs's quote on the regulation of farms was from James L. Abrahamson's *The American Homefront* (Washington, D.C.: National Defense University Press, 1983), 103. Higgs's quote of Franklin Roosevelt was from Porter, *War and the Rise of the State,* 277.
7. Raico, "Rethinking Churchill," 292.
8. Higgs, "War and Leviathan," 320.
9. Allan Carlson, "The Military as an Engine of Social Change," in *The Costs of War: America's Pyrrhic Victories,* ed. John V. Denson (New Brunswick: Transaction Books, 1997), 324–25.
10. Robert Higgs, *Crisis and Leviathan: Critical Episodes in the Growth of American Government* (New York: Oxford University Press, 1987), 226–227, 229–230, 237.
11. Porter, *War and the Rise of the State,* 278.
12. Veronique de Rugy, "The Republican Spending Explosion," *Cato Institute Briefing Paper* no. 87, March 3, 2004, 1.
13. Higgs, "War and Leviathan," 310, 313–15.
14. Bill Ahern, "Government Spending = Nearly One-Third U.S. Economy,"

Heartland Institute, January 1, 1999, http://www.heartland.org/PrinterFriendly.cfm?theType=artId&theID=387.

15. Higgs, *Crisis and Leviathan,* 258.
16. Porter, *War and the Rise of the State,* 292.
17. Cited in John V. Denson, introduction to *The Costs of War*, xii–xiii.
18. Randolph S. Bourne, *War and the Intellectual: Collected Essays, 1915–1919,* ed. Carl Resek (New York: Harper and Row, 1964), 71.
19. Porter, *War and the Rise of the State,* xviii.
20. Max Boot, *The Savage Wars of Peace: Small Wars and the Rise of American Power* (New York: Basic Books, 2002), 345, 352.
21. Porter, *War and the Rise of the State,* 105.
22. Charles Tilly, "Reflections on the History of European State-Making," in *The Formation of National States in Western Europe,* ed. Charles Tilly (Princeton: Princeton University Press), 42.
23. Temes, *The Just War,* 55.
24. Otto Hintze, "The Formation of States and Constitutional Development: A Study in History and Politics"; "Military Organization and the Organization of the State"; and "The Origins of the Modern Ministerial System: A Comparative Study," in *The Historical Essays of Otto Hintze,* ed. Felix Gilbert (New York: Oxford University Press, 1975).
25. Layne, "Kant or Cant," 197.
26. Martin van Creveld, *The Rise and Fall of the State* (Cambridge: Cambridge University Press, 1999), 291, 293.
27. Zimmerman, *First Great Triumph,* 37–39.
28. Mearsheimer, *Great Power Politics,* 74.
29. Dean Acheson, *Present at the Creation* (New York, 1969), 374–75.
30. Stephen Kinzer, "Iran and Guatemala 1953–54, Revisiting Coups and Finding Them Costly," *New York Times*, 30 November 30 2003, WK3.
31. White House, *The National Security Strategy of the United States of America* (Washington, D.C.: Government Printing Office, September 2002), 15.
32. Chalmers Johnson, *Sorrows of Empire,* 33–34.
33. Thomas Blanton, "When Did the Cold War End?" *War International History Project Bulletin*, no. 10 (1998), 185–91, cited in Chalmers Johnson, *Sorrows of Empire,* 19–20.
34. Walter McDougal, *Promised Land, Crusader State: The American Encounter with the World Since 1776* (Boston: Houghton Mifflin, 1997), 156.
35. Nordlinger, *Isolationism Reconfigured,* 114–15.
36. John Lewis Gaddis and Terry Diebold, *Containing the Soviet Union: A Critique of U.S. Policy* (Washington, D.C.: Pergamon-Brassey, 1987), 3; John Lewis Gaddis, *Strategies of Containment: A Critical Appraisal of Post-War American National Security Policy* (New York: Oxford University Press, 1982), 212–13.

37. Porter, *War and the Rise of the State,* 18–19.
38. Quoted in Tom Hamburger, "Despite Bush's Credo, Government Grows: As Conservatives Groan, Study Cites Increase of Employees on Federal Contracts, Grants," *Wall Street Journal,* September 4, 2003, A4.
39. Richard W. Stevenson and Edmund L. Andrews, "No Escaping Red Ink As Bush Pens '04 Agenda," *New York Times,* November 29, 2003, A10.
40. Quoted in Hamburger, "Despite Bush's Credo," A4.
41. Ibid.
42. The F-22 and new Virginia-class submarines are only the tip of the iceberg in unneeded weapons systems. For more detailed examination of those and other such systems, see Ivan Eland, *Putting "Defense" Back into U.S. Defense Policy: Rethinking U.S. Security in the Post-Cold War World* (Westport, Conn.: Praeger, 2001), 133–75.
43. For more on this topic, see Ivan Eland, "Reforming a Defense Industry Rife with Socialism, Industrial Policy and Excessive Regulation," *Cato Institute Policy Analysis* no. 421, (Washington, D.C.: Cato Institute, December 20, 2001).
44. Edmund A. Optiz, "Armaments and Our Prosperity," in *Leviathan and War,* ed. Edmund A. Optiz (New York: Foundation for Economic Education, Inc., 1995), 118.
45. Mark Ahlseen, "Do Wars Cure Ailing Economies?" in *Leviathan and War,* ed. Edmund A. Optiz, 122–23.
46. Radley Balko, "Bush Pursues Big-Gov Nanny State," *Fox News,* January 28, 2004, http://www.foxnews.com.
47. Joseph T. Salerno, "War and the Money Machine: Concealing the Costs of War Beneath the Veil of Inflation," in *The Costs of War: America's Pyrrhic Victories,* ed. John V. Denson (New Brusnwick, N.J.: Transaction Publishers, 1997), 368–73, 381.
48. Ibid., 368–73, 384–86.
49. Robert Higgs, *Crisis and Leviathan,* 234–35.
50. Salerno, "War and the Money Machine," 381.
51. Ferguson, *Empire,* 363.
52. Robert Higgs, "World War II and the Triumph of Keynesianism," in *The Failure of America's Foreign Wars,* ed. Richard M. Ebeling and Jacob G. Hornberger (Fairfax, Va: The Future of Freedom Forum, 1996), 271–72.
53. Ferguson, *Empire,* 319.
54. The United States imposes economic sanctions on the following countries: Angola, Burma, Cuba, Iran, Liberia, Libya, North Korea, Russia, Rwanda, Sudan, Syria, and Zimbabwe. *Sanctions Program and County Summaries,* Office of Foreign Assets Control, U.S. Department of the Treasury, http://www.ustreas.gov/offices/eotffc/ofac/sanctions/index.html

(February 25, 2004). See also "Regional Considerations," Bureau of Industry and Security, U.S. Department of Commerce, http://www.bxa.doc.gov/PoliciesAndRegulations/regionalconsiderations.htm.

55. Doyle, *Empires,* 101–2.
56. Martin, *Ancient Greece,* 150–51.
57. Peter Huchthausen, *America's Splendid Little Wars: A Short History of U.S. Military Engagements: 1975–2000* (New York: Viking, 2003), 118.
58. Figures on Iraqi deaths attributed to Saddam Hussein were estimated by the author from data by the U.S. State Department and Human Rights Watch. Moreover, a significant number of those deaths were Kurds and Shiites whose rebellions were encouraged after the first Gulf War by the Bush I administration. When those groups revolted, the United States did not come to their aid.
59. Zimmerman, *First Great Triumph,* 357–58, 360.
60. Adam Smith, *An Inquiry into the Nature and Causes of the Wealth of Nations,* ed. Edwin Cannan (Chicago: University of Chicago Press, 1976), Vol. I, 484–87.
61. Kennedy, *Rise and Fall,* 537.
62. Doyle, *Empires,* 23, 153–54.
63. Deepak Lal, "In Defense of Empire," in *The Imperical Tense: Prospects and Problems of Empire,* ed. Andrew Bacevich, 32. Although a defender of American empire for other reasons, Lal at least gets these points right.
64. Mearsheimer, *Great Power Politics,* 148–50.
65. Patrick O'Brien, "Debate: The Costs and Benefits of British Imperialism: 1846–1914," *Past and Present,* no. 125 (1989): 193.
66. Quoted in David North, "America's Drive for World Domination," in *The Imperial Tense: Prospects and Problems of Empire,* ed. Andrew Bacevich (Chicago: Ivan R. Dee, 2003), 73.
67. Quoted in Bacevich, *American Empire,* 128.
68. Eugene Gholz and Daryl Press, "The Effects of Wars on Neutral Countries: Why It Doesn't Pay to Preserve the Peace," *Security Studies* 10, no. 4 (2001), 1–57.
69. Ibid.
70. Gilpin, *War and Change,*52, 203.
71. Martin, *Ancient Greece,* 174–75.
72. Alexander, *How Wars Are Won,* 167–168, 173.
73. Joseph Stromberg, "The Spanish-American War as a Trial Run," in *The Costs of War,* ed. John V. Denson (New Brunswick: Transaction Books, 1997), 194, 196.
74. Snyder, *Myths of Empire,* 9.
75. Ambrose and Brinkley, *Rise to Globalism,* 381–82.
76. Some analysts argue that the Soviet quagmire in Afghanistan caused the USSR to collapse. Although the Afhgan war cost the Soviets money and

lives, that conflict was only a small contributor to the overextension of the Soviet Empire. The basic reason for the Soviet collapse was its attempt, using massive military spending, to conduct a worldwide cold war against the United States—a country with a large and efficient economy based on the private sector—with a much smaller, creaking communist economy.

77. Robert Kaplan, "Supremacy by Stealth," 68.
78. Polls cited in Edward Alden, "U.S. Stance 'Making Terrorism More Likely,'" *Financial Times,* September 12, 2003.
79. Lal, "In Defense of Empire," 31.
80. Snyder, *Myths of Empire,* 6.
81. Gilpin, *War and Change,* 156–58.
82. Carlo M. Cipolla, introduction to *The Economic Decline of Empires,* ed. Carlo M. Cipolla (London: Methuen and Company, Ltd., 1970), 1, 5–7, 9, 11. Martin van Creveld echoes Cipolla's assessment that enlargement of the Roman army in the late empire led to economic collapse; Van Creveld, *Rise and Fall,* 41.
83. Cited in Gilpin, *War and Change,* 164.
84. Ibid., 175–81.
85. William C. Wohlforth, "The Russian-Soviet Empire: A Test of Neorealism," in *Empires, Systems and States: Great Transformations in International Politics,* ed. Michael Cox, Tim Dunne and Ken Booth (Cambridge: Cambridge University Press, 2001), 213–14, 233.
86. Doyle, *Empires,* 98–101.
87. Kennedy, *Rise and Fall,* xvii.
88. Gilpin, *War and Change,* 175–81.
89. Cipolla, *Economic Decline,* 14.
90. Victor Davis Hanson, "What Empire?" 150–51.
91. Ibid., 151.
92. Robert Kaplan, "Supremacy by Stealth," 69, 83.
93. Jim Garrison, *America as Empire: Global Leader or Rogue Power?* (San Francisco: Berrett-Koehler Publishers, Inc., 2004), 9, 202.
94. Quoted in McCullough, *John Adams* (New York: Simon and Schuster, 2001), 39.
95. Ferguson, *Empire,* 296.
96. Even Britain's alleged low defense spending is controversial. David O'Brien disagrees with Paul Kennedy, a proponent of that view, and argues that Britain had the second highest defense burden in Europe from 1860 to 1914. He also implies that those heavy expenditures ultimately contributed significantly to the decline of the British empire. David O'Brien, "British Imperialism," 196–97; Paul Kennedy in the same publication, 190–91.
97. Gilpin, *War and Change,* 174.
98. Ferguson, *Empire,* 358.

99. Niall Ferguson, *The Pity of War: Explaining World War I* (New York: Basic Books, 1999), 458–62.
100. Kupchan, *Vulnerability of Empire,* 1; Kennedy, "British Imperialism," 125–26; Patrick O'Brien, "British Imperialism," 195.
101. Michael Swaine and Minxin Pei, "Rebalancing United States-China Relations," *Carnegie Endowment for International Peace Policy Brief* no. 13 (Washington, D.C.: Carnegie Endowment for International Peace, February 2002), 1.
102. Greg Jaffe and Christopher Cooper, "Stretched Army Makes Do in Afghanistan," *Wall Street Journal,* August 1, 2003, A4.
103. Snyder, *Myths of Empire,* 2.
104. Gilpin, *War and Change,* 192.
105. Alexander, *How Wars are Won,* 204–5.
106. Rosecrance, "Overextension, Vulnerability and Conflict," 160.
107. Chalmers Johnson, *Sorrows of Empire,* 81.
108. William Graham Sumner, *War and Other Essays* (New Haven: Yale University Press, 1914), 351.
109. Kennedy, *Rise and Fall,* xxiii–xxiv.
110. Gilpin, *War and Change,* 192.
111. Alexander, *How Wars are Won,* 102.
112. Eric J. Labs, "Beyond Victory: Offensive Realism and the Expansion of War Aims," *Security Studies* 6, no. 4, (1997), 2.
113. Mearsheimer, *Great Power Politics,* 57.
114. Ambrose and Brinkley, *Rise to Globalism,* 380.
115. The calculations are based on data from the International Institute for Strategic Studies, *The Military Balance: 2003–2004,* the recognized authoritative source for data on national military budgets, equipment, and personnel.
116. Nicholas Kristof estimates U.S. GDP to be only about 21 percent of the world's total. Nicholas D. Kristof and Sheryl WuDunn, *Thunder from the East: Portrait of a Rising Asia* (New York: Vintage Books, 2000), 41.
117. Cited in Paul Krugman, "Another Bogus Budget," *New York Times,* February 3, 2004, A27.
118. Robert Higgs, "The Defense Budget."
119. International Institute for Strategic Studies, *The Military Balance, 2003–2004,* 235. This figure is for the year 2002. Dramatic defense budget increases since then may very well make it higher.
120. Van Creveld, *Rise and Fall,* 347.
121. The United States Civil War Center, Louisiana State University, Statistical Summary: *America's Major Wars,* http://www.cwc.lsu.edu/cwc/other/stats/warcost.html. Louisiana State's figures were listed in 1990 dollars. The author converted them to 2004 dollars.

122. That comparison is calculated from data in the International Institute for Strategic Studies' *Military Balance.* There is some controversy about the use of that comparison. When the noted historian Paul Kennedy used the same comparison in an op-ed in London's *Financial Times* (Paul Kennedy, "The Eagle Has Landed: The New U.S. Global Military Position," *Financial Times*, February 1, 2002), he was criticized by Peter Robinson, Senior Economist of the Institute for Public Policy Research in London (Peter Robinson, "Tricky Arithmetic of Military Spending," *Financial Times*, February 9–10, 2002). Although Kennedy cites no source for his comparison, the closeness of the fit with data from the *Military Balance* indicates that his data probably came from there. In criticizing Kennedy's comparison, Robinson wrongly asserts that the defense spending of the United States and the other countries is figured in dollar terms at current exchange rates. In fact, the *Military Balance* accounts for the lower costs in the transitional economies of nations like Russia and China by adjusting for purchasing power parity (PPP). Because Robinson has not looked at the fine print in this volume, he erroneously alleges that China is spending 85 percent of what the United States is spending on defense. In fact, China's military spending, even adjusted for PPP and including spending not in the official Chinese defense budget, is a mere fifty-one billion dollars—a small fraction of the U.S. total. Although there is controversy about the level of China's actual defense budget, Robinson's number is much higher than even China hawks allege and wrong because he failed to closely examine the *Military Balance's* methodology. Also, intuitively, Robinson's assertion is incredible. If Robinson's assertion were correct, the Chinese government would need to ask where all the money is going. Even Robinson admits the vast superiority of the U.S. military over the Chinese armed forces but argues that such dominance demonstrates the limited value of budgetary comparisons. But inputs of resources should have some effect on outputs. And given the importance of intangibles—for example, training and command, control, communications, computers, and intelligence (as opposed to troop and equipment counts)—on the modern battlefield, budgetary comparisons may still be the best measure of defense capabilities. If China really spent 85 percent of what the United States did on defense, it presumably would no longer have such a sagging, antiquated force with only pockets of modernization. So Robinson's critique of Kennedy's budget comparison is erroneous. Regardless, what is obvious to virtually all military analysts, including Peter Robinson, is the current crushing dominance of the United States on every measure of military power—equipment, personnel, training, intelligence, and logistics—compared to the militaries of the rest of the world.

123. Paul Kennedy, an historian at Yale University and an observer of imperial overextension and excessive military spending in declining powers, cited U.S. economic growth in the 1990s, but maintains U.S. "imperial over-stretch" is still a problem. Part of that surge in economic growth may be accounted for by a restraint in the growth of federal spending during that decade, much of which was attributable to declines in defense spending after the cold war ended. That restraint in general spending, and the decline in defense spending, have since been reversed; U.S. federal spending, including that for defense, has recently exploded.
124. Kennedy, *Rise and Fall,* 446.
125. Cipolla, *Economic Decline,* 5.
126. G. John Ikenberry, "Illusions of Empire: Defining the New American Order," *Foreign Affairs* 83, no. 2 (2003), 153.
127. Charles Krauthammer, "The Unipolar Era," in *The Imperial Tense: Prospects and Problems of American Empire,* ed. Andrew Bacevich (Chicago: Ivan R. Dee, 2003), 54.
128. *International Herald Tribune*, "Europeans Reach Deal on Defense," *New York Times,* November 30, 2003, 8.
129. Kristof and WuDunn, *Thunder from the East,* 41, 328.
130. Ibid., 329.
131. Ibid., 12.
132. International Institute for Strategic Studies, 298.
133. Kristof and Wudunn, *Thunder from the East,* 41.
134. Amy Waldman, "Sizzling Economy Revitalizes India: Despite Widespread Poverty, a Consumer Class Emerges," *New York Times,* October 20, 2003, A1.
135. Ibid., 12, 16, 29, 30.
136. Snyder, *Myths of Empire,* 5–6.
137. Such is the cogent conclusion of Chalmers Johnson, *Sorrows of Empire,* 310.
138. Kristof and WuDunn, *Thunder from the East,* 346.
139. Payne, *Ancient Rome,* 209–211, 229.
140. George Washington, Farewell Address, September 17, 1796.
141. Quoted in McCullough, *John Adams,* 70.
142. James Madison, "Letters to Helvidius," in *The Writings of James Madison,* ed. Gaillard Hunt (New York: G.P. Putnam, 1900–1910), 171–72.
143. Quoted in Max Farrand, ed., *The Records of the Federal Convention of 1787* (New Haven: Yale University Press, 1911), 465.
144. Ralph Raico, "The Case for an America First Foreign Policy," in *The Failure of America's Foreign Wars,* ed. Richard M. Ebeling and Jacob G. Hornberger (Fairfax, Va.: The Future of Freedom Forum, 1996), 33.
145. Robert Kaplan, "Supremacy by Stealth," 67–83.

CHAPTER FOUR

1. Vidal, "Should Our Intelligence Services Be Abolished?" 71.
2. George W. Bush, *National Security Strategy of the United States.*
3. North, "America's Drive for World Domination," 73.
4. Chalmers Johnson, *Sorrows of Empire,* 51–52.
5. Chalmers Johnson, 15–16, 23, 26; Bacevich, *American Empire,* 122–24, 126.
6. Temes, *The Just War,* 178.
7. Paul Johnson, "From the Evil Empire to the Empire for Liberty."
8. McDougal, *Promised Land,* 119, 174.
9. Cited in Allan Murray, "Manifesto Warns of Dangers Associated with an Empire," *Wall Street Journal,* July 15, 2003.
10. Mearsheimer, *Great Power Politics,* 364.
11. Quoted in Ferguson, *Empire,* xv.
12. Noam Chomsky, *Rogue States: The Rule of Force in World Affairs* (Cambridge, Mass.: South End Press, 2000), 18.
13. For more on the exact chronology of Libya's conflict with the United States during the 1980s, see Ivan Eland, "Does U.S. Intervention, Overseas Breed Terrorism?: The Historical Record," *Cato Institute Foreign Policy Briefing* no. 50 (Washington, D.C.: Cato Institute, 1998), 12–13.
14. Alan Tonelson, "U.N. Military Missions and the Imperial Presidency: Internationalism by the Back Door," in *Delusions of Grandeur: The United Nations and Global Intervention,* ed. Ted Galen Carpenter (Washington, D.C.: Cato Institute, 1997), 102.
15. Robert Kaplan, "Supremacy by Stealth," 83.
16. Quoted in Joseph Stromberg, "Spanish-American War," 190.
17. Bacevich, *American Empire,* 206, 223–24.
18. Chalmers Johnson, *Sorrows of Empire,* 283–84.
19. William Blum, *Rogue State: A Guide to the World's Only Superpower* (Monroe, Maine: Common Courage Press, 2000), 234.
20. Kinzer, "Iran and Guatemala," WK3.
21. Chomsky, *Rogue States,* 8.
22. Chalmers Johnson, *Sorrows of Empire,* 69; Arundhati Roy, "Instant-Mix Imperial Democracy (Buy One, Get One Free)." Remarks given at Riverside Church, New York, May 13, 2003, posted on Center for Economic and Social Rights website at http://www.cesr.org/roy /royspeech.htm#roy.
23. Kevin Gray, "Declassified U.S. Documents Indicate Kissinger Offered Verbal Support to Argentine Junta," *San Francisco Chronicle,* December 9, 2003, http://www.sfgate.com/cgi-bin/article.cgi?f=/news/archive/2003/12 /04/international1948EST0805.DTL.
24. Chalmers Johnson, *Sorrows of Empire,* 25, 72.
25. Mearsheimer, *Great Power Politics,* 47.

26. For more on that episode, see Chomsky, *Rogue States,* 9–10 and Tim Weiner and Lydia Polgreen, "Veterans of Past Murderous Campaigns Are Leading Haiti's New Rebellion," *New York Times,* February 29, 2004, A4.
27. Boot, *Savage Wars of Peace,* 346.
28. Weiner and Polgreen, "Veterans of Past Murderous Campaigns," A4.
29. Bacevich, *American Empire,* 104.
30. Huchthausen, *America's Splendid Little Wars,* 189.
31. For more on this episode, see Chomsky, *Rogue States,* 182.
32. Huchthausen, *America's Splendid Little Wars,* 187.
33. Chomsky, *Rogue States,* 184.
34. Huchthausen, *America's Splendid Little Wars,* 217.
35. Ibid., 217.
36. Bacevich, *American Empire,* 104–5. Bacevich's quote is from Bill Clinton, "Remarks by the President to AFSCME Biennial Convention," Washington, D.C., March 23, 1999.
37. Chalmers Johnson, *Sorrows of Empire,* 214.
38. Chalmers Johnson, *Blowback: The Costs and Consequences of American Empire* (New York: Henry Holt and Company, 2000), 12.
39. David Rieff, "Liberal Imperialism," in *The Imperial Tense: Prospects and Problems of American Empire,* ed. Andrew Bacevich (Chicago: Ivan R. Dee, 2003), 10.
40. Sheldon Richman, "The Roots of World War II," in *The Failure of American's Foreign Wars,* ed. Richard M. Ebeling and Jacob Hornberger (Fairfax, Va.: The Future of Freedom Foundation, 1996), 91.
41. Boot, *Savage Wars of Peace,* 345–346, 352.
42. Walter McDougal, "What the U.S. Needs to Promote in Iraq (Hint: It's Not Democratization Per Se)," *Foreign Policy Research Institute Wire* 11, no. 2 (2003), http://www.fpri.org.
43. Amy Chua, *World on Fire: How Exporting Free Market Democracy Breeds Ethnic Hatred and Global Instability* (New York: Doubleday, 2003), 261, 273. Chua's thesis of the "poor majority oppressing an economically dominant minority" within democratizing developing countries is convincing until she commits a logical fallacy by trying to apply it to America's role in the world. She attempts to argue that terrorism against the United States is a result of its status as an economically dominant minority. The problem with her reasoning will be explored in the next chapter.
44. Huchthausen, *America's Splendid Little Wars,* 174.
45. Ibid., 161, 174–76.
46. Ibid., 60, 63.
47. Garrison, *America as Empire,* 179–180.
48. Rieff, "Liberal Imperialism," 23.
49. Bacevich, *American Empire,* 184.
50. Mearsheimer, *Great Power Politics,* 106–107.

51. Temes, *The Just War,* 67–80.
52. Rieff, "Liberal Imperialism," 22–23.
53. McDougal, *Promised Land,* 180; McDougal, "What the U.S. Needs," http://www.fpri.org.
54. Boot, *Savage Wars of Peace,* 345–46, 352.
55. George Soros, *The Bubble of American Supremacy: Correcting the Misuse of American Power* (New York: Public Affairs, 2004), 187.
56. Gregory Clark, "More Aid, More Regrets Later," *Japan Times,* January 22, 2002.
57. Boot, *Savage Wars of Peace,* 347–48.
58. For a more detailed examination of this issue, see John Rudy and Ivan Eland, *Special Operations.*
59. Olsen, *U.S. National Defense,* 82–84.
60. Jonathan Schell, *The Unconquerable World: Power, Nonviolence and the Will of the People* (New York: Henry Holt and Company, 2003), 6.
61. McDougal, *Promised Land,* 37.
62. John Quincy Adams, *An Address Delivered at the Request of the Citizens of; on the Occasion of Reading the Declaration of Independence, On the Fourth of July, 1821* (Washington, D.C.: Davis and Force, 1821).
63. Martin, *Ancient Greece,* 160–161, 162, 166, 168–169; Michael Doyle, *Empires,* 74.
64. Payne, *Ancient Rome,* 85.
65. Alexis de Tocqueville, *Democracy in America* (New York: Vintage Books, 1990), 269.
66. Madison, "Political Observations," 491–492.
67. Roy, http://www.cesr.org/Roy/royspeech.htm#roy.
68. William J. Watkins, Jr., *Reclaiming the American Revolution: The Kentucky and Virginia Resolutions and Their Legacy* (New York: Palgrave Macmillan for The Independent Institute, 2004), 27–40.
69. Rhodri Jeffreys-Jones, *Cloak and Dollar: A History of American Secret Intelligence* (New Haven: Yale University Press, 2002), 56–57.
70. John V. Denson, "War and American Freedom," in *The Costs of War: American Pyrrhic Victories* ed. by John V. Denson (New Brunswick: Transaction Books, 1997), 39.
71. Raico, "Rethinking Churchill," 274.
72. Chalmers Johnson, *Sorrows of Empire,* 121.
73. The discussion of the erosion of civil liberties in the Bush II administration's "war on terror" that follows is based on Ivan Eland, "Bush's Wars and the State of Civil Liberties," *Mediterranean Quarterly,* vol. 14 no. 4 (Fall 2003), 158–175.
74. Quoted in Mark Helm, "Homeland Agency Leads Crackdown on Child Porn," *San Francisco Chronicle,* July 10, 2003, A4.

75. The provisions of the act were summarized in American Civil Liberties Union, *Insatiable Appetite: The Government's Demand for New and Unnecessary Powers After September 11* (white paper), October 2002, 4. The commentary included after the ACLU's factual description is the author's.
76. Unless otherwise indicated, the factual material in each bullet came from American Civil Liberties Union, *The USA PATRIOT Act and Government Actions that Threaten Our Civil Liberties,* http://www.aclu.org. The commentary following the factual material is the author's.
77. Amnesty International, *USA: One Year in Detention Without Charge,* 2, http://www.amnestyUSA.org/news/2003/usa06092003.html.
78. Seattle Post-Intelligencer Editorial Board, "Defiant Justice Dept. Makes No Apologies," *Seattle Post-Intelligencer,* June 8, 2003, http://www.seattlepi.nwsource.com/opinion/125457_righted8.html.
79. American Bar Association, *Task Force on Treatment of Enemy Combatants, Report to the House of Delegates, Revised Report 109,* February 10, 2003, 1.
80. Amnesty International, *United States of America: Memorandum to the U.S. Government on the Rights of People in U.S. Custody in Afghanistan and Guantanamo Bay,* April 2002, 45.
81. Neil Lewis, "Rules Set Up for Terror Tribunals May Deter Some Defense Lawyers," *New York Times,* July 13, 2003, A1.
82. The provisions of the leaked legislative proposal were summarized in American Civil Liberties Union, *How "Patriot Act 2" Would Further Erode the Basic Checks on Government Power That Keep America Safe and Free,* March 20, 2003, 1–2 and American Civil Liberties Union, *ACLU Fact Sheet on PATRIOT Act II,* March 28, 2003, 1. Unless otherwise noted, the factual statements in each of the bullet points are taken from those documents. The commentary included after the ACLU's factual description is the author's.
83. Tim Lynch, director of the Cato Institute's Project on Criminal Justice, pointed out those items in an e-mail correspondence on July 18, 2003.
84. Amnesty International, *One Year in Detention,* 2.
85. Friends Committee on National Legislation, *Talking Points I: Domestic Security Enhancement Act of 2003* ("Patriot II"), 2, http://www.fcnl.org/issues /immigrant/sup/patriot-2_tlkpts.html.
86. Charles Lewis and Adam Mayle, "Justice Department Drafts Expansion of Anti-Terrorism Act: Center Publishes Secret Draft of 'Patriot II' Legislation," The Center for Public Integrity, February 7, 2003, 2, http://www.publicintegrity.org/dtaweb/report.asp?ReportID=502&L1=10&L2=10&L3=0&L4=0&L5=0 and Friends Committee, 2.
87. Tim Lynch, "Breaking the Vicious Cycle: Preserving Our Liberties While Fighting Terrorism," *Cato Institute Policy Analysis* no. 443 (Washington D.C.: Cato Institute, 2002), 2.

88. Lynch, *Breaking the Vicious Cycle,* 204.
89. American Bar Association, 1.
90. *ACLU Fact Sheet,* 2. That information was originally reported in Bill Dedman, "Memo Warns Against Use of Profiling as Defense," *Boston Globe,* October 12, 2001.
91. *ACLU Fact Sheet,* 2. That information was originally reported in Jim McGee, "Ex-FBI Officials Criticize Tactics on Terrorism; Detention of Suspects Not Effective, They Say," *Washington Post,* November 28, 2001, A1.
92. For more on the likely limited effects of improvements in intelligence and homeland security, see Ivan Eland, "Preserving Civil Liberties in an Age of Terrorism," *Issues in Science and Technology* XV, no. 1 (1998): 23–24.
93. Quoted in Ralph Ness, "After Fifteen Years Absence, the FBI Returns to Your Library," People for the American Way, 2003, 2, http://www.pfaw.org/pfaw/general/default.aspx?oid=10341.
94. Eric Schmidt and Robert Pear, "Plan Omits Mention of Costs of Operations in Iraq and Afghanistan," *New York Times,* February 3, 2004, A15.
95. Thom Shanker and Eric Schmitt, "Pentagon's Request for Iraq Includes Money for Troops, Weapons, Rewards and Allies," *New York Times,* October 5, 2003, 12.
96. Newt Gingrich, "Remarks Delivered at the Center for Strategic and International Studies," quoted in Barbara Conry, "U.S. Global Leadership," *Cato Institute Policy Analysis* no. 267 (Washington, D.C.: Cato Institute, 1997), 13.
97. Chalmers Johnson, *Sorrows of Empire,* 26.

CHAPTER FIVE

1. Olsen, *U.S. National Defense,* 50.
2. Zimmerman, *First Great Triumph,* 4, 37–39.
3. Quoted in Chalmers Johnson, *Sorrows of Empire,* 292.
4. Joseph G. Dawson III, *Commanders-in-Chief: Presidential Leadership in Modern War* (Lawrence, Kansas: University Press of Kansas, 1993), 31.
5. Ambrose and Brinkley, *Rise to Globalism,* 420–21.
6. The author's calculations from U.S. Department of State, *Patterns of Global Terrorism,* 2003, Washington, D.C.: U.S. Department of State, April 2004, http://www.state.gov/s/ct/rls/pgtrpt/2003/31569.htm and the 2002 and 2001 versions of the same report at http://www.state.gov/s/ct/rls/pgtrpt/2002 and http://www.state.gov/s/ct/rls/pgtrpt/2001 respectively. The State Department's later correction to its 2003 report does not appear to affect this calculation.
7. For example, Karen De Young, "Poll Finds Arabs Dislike U.S. Based on Policies It Pursues: American Freedoms, Values Viewed Favorably, Survey Says," *Washington Post,* 7 October 2002, A13; Sue Pleming, "Poll:

Foreigners Like U.S., Movies, Not Mideast Policy," Reuters, 11 April 2002; Keith B. Richburg, "Divergent Views, of U.S. Role In World: 'Elite' Abroad Tie Sept. 11 to Policies," *Washington Post,* 20 December 2001, A34; and Pew Charitable Research Center, 3 June 2003, http://people-press.org/reports/display.php3?ReportID=185.

8. Andrew Bacevich, "New Rome, New Jerusalem," in *The Imperial Tense: Prospects and Problems of American Empire,* ed. Andrew Bacevich (Chicago: Ivan R. Dee, 2003), 96–97.
9. De Young, "Arabs Dislike U.S.," A13.
10. Ibid., Pleming, "Foreigners Like U.S.," and Richburg, "Divergent Views," 34.
11. Pleming, "Foreigners Like U.S.,"
12. Comments by Tyler Cowen, "Globalization and Cultural Diversity: Friends or Foes?" at an Independent Policy Forum held at The Independent Institute, Oakland, California, May 27, 2003.
13. Peter L. Bergen, *Holy War, Inc.: Inside the Secret World of Osama bin Laden* (New York: The Free Press, 2001), 222.
14. De Young, "Arabs Dislike U.S.," A13; Pleming, "Foreigners Like U.S.," and Richburg, "Divergent Views," 34; and Pew Charitable Research Center, http://people-press.org/reports/display.php3?ReportID=185.
15. Richburg, "Divergent Views," A34.
16. Bergen, *Holy War, Inc.,* 222.
17. "The Hill Interview: Peter Bergen: Moral Clarity of Sept. 11 No Longer Prevails, Says CNN's Terrorism Expert," *The Hill,* July 10, 2002, 41.
18. Bergen, *Holy War, Inc.,* 222–23.
19. Chua, *World on Fire,* 255.
20. Ibid., 255–56.
21. Those examples were noted in Chua, *World on Fire,* 230–31, 235, and 240. Chua believes that the United States is so hated because America is the market dominant minority of the world—that is, it has wealth and economic power disproportionate to its tiny (by world standards) population. Yet Chua's own examples provide contrary evidence. Chua is like many other authors who concoct pet theories about why the United States is attacked disproportionately by terrorists without examining what public opinion polls in foreign countries (especially Arab and Moslem nations) and the terrorists themselves say. Such evidence all points to U.S. foreign and military policies as the root of the problem. Also, there are many other wealthy "minorities" in the world besides Americans, and are less hated and to have less of a problem with terrorism.
22. Bergen, *Holy War, Inc.,* 223.
23. Wolfowitz cited in Karen DeYoung and Walter Pincus, "Despite Obstacles to War, White House Forges Ahead: Administration Unfazed by

Iraq's Pledge to Destroy Missiles, Turkish Parliament's Rejection of Use of Bases," *Washington Post,* March 2, 2003, A18.

24. See Ivan Eland, *U.S. Intervention.*
25. Ibid., 11–12.
26. Ibid., 12–13.
27. Boot, *Savage Wars of Peace,* 344.
28. Benajmin J. Barber, *Fear's Empire: War, Terrorism, and Democracy* (NY: W.W. Norton and Co., 2003), 17.
29. U.S. Department of Defense, "Secretary Rumsfeld Interview with the *New York Times*" transcript, October 12, 2001.
30. White House, *The National Security Strategy of the United States of America,* 6.
31. Snyder, *Myths of Empire,* 4.
32. Temes, *The Just War,* 103–105, 113–114.
33. Todd Purdum, "An Accuser's Insider Status Puts the White House on the Defensive," *New York Times,* March 23, 2004, A16.
34. Richard Clarke, "War on Terror: Richard Clarke," *News Hour with Jim Lehrer* transcript, PBS, March 22, 2004, http://www.pbs.org/newshour/bb/terrorism/jan-june04/clarke_3_22 .html.
35. Poll done by the Pew Charitable Research Center, "Views of a Changing World 2003," June 3, 2003, http://people-press.org/reports/display .php3?ReportID=185.
36. Kamen, *Empire,* 509.
37. Snyder, *Myths of Empire,* 4.
38. *National Security Strategy,* v, 6, 15. Of course, the president is severely stretching the traditional definition of preemptive war and implicitly acknowledges it in the document. He states: "For centuries, international law recognized that nations need not suffer an attack before they can lawfully take action to defend themselves against forces that present an imminent danger of attack. Legal scholars and international jurists often conditioned the legitimacy of preemption on the existence of an imminent threat—most often a visible mobilization of armies, navies and air forces." The president's adaptation is attacking "emerging threats before they are fully formed." Few individuals or nations would begrudge the United States, or any other country, the right to preempt an adversary's imminent attack. But the international community has traditionally frowned on attacking countries that do not pose an imminent threat but might in the future—that is, a preventative war strategy. The president's preventative war doctrine has too much room for abuse because any country can be deemed a future threat. The Bush II administration tried to make Iraq into an imminent threat to U.S. and global security but the world's almost universal opposition to the U.S. invasion indicated

that most other countries believed it was preventative war (and on shaky grounds at that, as subsequent evidence showed).

39. Alexander, *How Wars Are Won,* 47.
40. Snyder, *Myths of Empire,* 23.
41. Van Creveld, *Rise and Fall,* 344.
42. See Snyder, *Myths of Empire,* 23. Equally ironic is that a U.S. missile defense shield could theoretically give the offense a boost. It could provide a shield against enemy nuclear retaliation in the event of a U.S. conventional attack on a nation with a small nuclear arsenal. Openly acknowledging one of the hidden purposes of missile defense, neoconservative Lawrence F. Kaplan baldly admitted, "Missile defense isn't really meant to protect America. It's a tool for global dominance." Lawrence F. Kaplan, "Why the Best Offense Is a Good Missile Defense," *The New Republic,* March 12, 2001. In reality, the offensive benefits of missile defense probably would be mitigated because no missile defense is perfect, and the possibility that even one nuclear missile could get through it would probably deter any U.S. attack on a country with only a few nuclear weapons (let's hope so). Furthermore, a missile defense would be expensive to build and could still be defeated by a rapid buildup of more cheaply produced offensive nuclear weapons, giving the advantage back to the defense.
43. Chalmers Johnson, *Sorrows of Empire,* 90–91.
44. U.S. Department of Defense, "Findings of the Nuclear Posture Review" (Washington D.C.: U.S. DoD, January 9, 2002), briefing slides.
45. Evan Thomas, Richard Wolfe, and Michael Isikoff, "Selling the World on War," *Newsweek,* June 9, 2003, 27.
46. Michael Renner, "Sun Journal: Military Budgets, Warfare Waning," *Baltimore Sun,* May 13, 1998, cited in Ivan Eland, "Tilting at Windmills: Post–Cold War Military Threats to U.S. Security," *Cato Institute Policy Analysis* no. 332 (Washington, D.C.: Cato Institute, 1999).
47. Van Creveld, *Rise and Fall,* 349–53.
48. Kristof and WuDunn, *Thunder from the East,* 265.
49. Alexander, *How Wars are Won,* 29.
50. Ibid., 40.
51. Wolfowitz cited in Karen DeYoung and Walter Pincus, A18.
52. Wolfowitz's comments before the Asian security summit were first reported by the German newpapers Der Tagesspiegel and Die Welt and then quoted by George Wright, "Wolfowitz: Iraq War Was about Oil," *The Guardian,* 4 June 2003.
53. Bruce Hoffman, "The Logic of Suicide Terrorism," *Atlantic Monthly* 291, no. 5 (2003): 46.
54. Quoted in Greg Myre, "Israel's Chief of Staff Denounces Policies Against Palestinians," *New York Times,* October 30, 2003, A5.

55. *Boston Globe* editorial, "Four Wise Men in Israel," *International Herald Tribune,* November 19, 2003, http://www.iht.com/cgi-bin/generic.cgi?template=articleprint.tmplh&ArticleId=118111.
56. Chalmers Johnson, *Blowback,* 11.

CHAPTER SIX

1. Mearsheimer, *Great Power Politics,* 127.
2. Boot, *Savage Wars of Peace,* lv–xx, 329, 336–352.
3. Ibid., xvii.
4. Ibid., 345.
5. Quoted in James Chace, "In Search of Absolute Security," in *The Imperial Tense: Prospects and Problems of American Empire,* ed. Andrew Bacevich (Chicago: Ivan R. Dee, 2003), 123.
6. Burton Ira Kaufman, *Washington's Farewell Address: The View from the Twentieth Century* (Chicago: Quadrangle Books, 1969), 26–27.
7. Adrienne Koch and William Peden, eds., *The Life and Selected Writings of Thomas Jefferson* (New York: Random House, 1993), 300.
8. Bill Clinton, "Remarks at U.S. Coast Guard Academy Commencement," May 17, 2000.
9. Kupchan, *Vulnerability of Empire,* 12–13.
10. McDougal, *Promised Land,* 164.
11. Olsen, *U.S. National Defense* 9–10.
12. Mearsheimer, *Great Power Politics,* 326–27.
13. Olsen, *U.S. National Defense,* 96.
14. International Institute for Strategic Studies, *Military Balance: 2003–2004,* 247–50, 269, 276–79, 298–99.
15. Nordlinger, *Isolationism Reconfigured,* 269–70.
16. Martin, *Ancient Greece,* 150–51.
17. Olsen, *U.S. National Defense,* 11.
18. Ikenberry, "American Power," 201.
19. Carr cited in Gilpin, *War and Change,* 166.
20. U.S. Department of Defense, *Annual Report on the Military Power of the Peoples' Republic of China,* July 28, 2003, 13.
21. David Calleo, *Beyond American Hegemony: The Future of the Western Alliance* (New York: Basic Books, 1987), 142.
22. Kupchan, *Vulnerability of Empire,* 11.
23. Mearsheimer, *Great Power Politics,* 51.
24. Robert Higgs maintains that this figure should be almost doubled to get the true magnitude of U.S. spending on security. Higg's higher figure includes Department of Energy spending on nuclear weapons, homeland security, foreign assistance, veterans affairs, and interest on the national debt attributable to defense. Higgs, "The Defense Budget."

25. For more a more detailed examination of the defense budget, force structure, and equipment changes needed to create a force that would allow power projection from the United States, see Ivan Eland, *Putting "Defense" Back Into U.S. Defense Policy,* 99–227.
26. Stockholm International Peace Research Institute, *SIPRI Yearbook 2003: Armaments Disarmament and International Security* (Oxford: Oxford University Press, 2003), http://editors.sipri.org/pubs/yb03/ch10.html.
27. *Military Balance*: *2003–2004*, 269, 298.
28. John Mearsheimer usefully points out that the conventional forces of nonnuclear powers have attacked the conventional forces of nuclear powers and that the conventional forces of nuclear powers have skirmished with each other. In the former case, nonnuclear Egypt and Syria launched land attacks on nuclear-armed Israel in 1973, and a then-nonnuclear China invaded Korea and fought the forces of the nuclear United States. In the latter case, China and Russia, both nuclear powers in 1969, had border clashes on the Ussuri River that almost led to an all-out war. India and Pakistan, after they both obtained nuclear weapons, had a dangerous crisis in 1990 and fought a major border skirmish in 1999. But Mearsheimer also notes that most great power wars have been initiated by continental powers with large land armies attacking other continental countries, not offshore balancers. Mearsheimer, 132–33, 135–36. As noted earlier, the United States is naturally an offshore balancer that has abandoned that policy in favor of overseas meddling in an informal global empire. Although a substantial U.S. nuclear arsenal is not a complete guarantee from being attacked by conventional- and nuclear-armed powers, when combined with a policy of staying out of conflicts half a world away and the vast moats of ocean that any attacker would need to traverse, the United States is still extremely secure against attack. In fact, Mearsheimer notes that it may be the most secure great power in history. Also, nuclear weapons probably inhibited China and Russia and India and Pakistan from entering full-blown wars. Mearsheimer acknowledges that nuclear weapons make war between great powers less likely. Furthermore, although Egypt and Syria attacked Israel and China attacked U.S. forces in Korea, those nonnuclear countries did not threaten the Israeli or U.S. homelands, respectively, with extinction. So the attackers may have calculated that Israel and the United States would be unlikely to retaliate with nuclear weapons. In contrast, if the U.S. homeland were attacked, the United States would be likely to incinerate the perpetrating country with the most powerful nuclear arsenal on the planet.
29. For a detailed plan to reduce nuclear forces, see Eland, *Putting "Defense" Back Into U.S. Defense Policy,* 116–27, 210–11, and 217–20.

30. David R. Henderson, "The Myth of Saddam's Oil Stranglehold," in *America Entangled: The Persian Gulf Crisis and Its Consequences,* ed. Ted Galen Carpenter (Washington, D.C.: Cato Institute, 1991), 41–44.
31. Ambrose and Brinkley, *Rise to Globalism,* 386–87.
32. Both quotes are from Jonathan Marshall, "Economists Say Iraq's Threat to U.S. Oil Supply is Exaggerated," *San Francisco Chronicle,* October 29, 1990, A14.
33. William A. Niskanen, "Oil, War, and the Economy," in *The Persian Gulf Crisis,* ed. Ted Galen Carpenter, (Washington, D.C.: Cato Institute, 1991), 54.
34. Nordlinger, *Isolationism Reconfigured,* 85–86.
35. Donald Losman, "Economic Security: A National Security Folly?" *Cato Institute Policy Analysis* no. 409 (Washington, D.C.: Cato Institute, 2001), 1, 7.
36. Cited in Jerry Taylor, "Oil Not Worth the Fight," *Journal of Commerce,* September 1, 1998, 4A.
37. Losman, *Economic Security,* 6.
38. Department of Energy, *International Energy Outlook* 2003, http://www.eia.doe.gov/oiaf/ieo/tbl_d4.html. Some analysts argue that statistics on oil reserves are more important than data on oil production. The Persian Gulf accounts for 65 percent of the world's oil reserves (Department of Energy, "World Crude Oil and Natural Gas Reserves" http://www.eia.doe.gov/emeu/iea/table81.html). But when talking about energy security, production statistics would seem to be more important. The world's reserves of oil have never been larger but, in the long term, a substantial portion of those reserves may never be needed if new technologies eventually make oil obsolete or allow reduced world petroleum consumption.
39. Alan Tonelson, "NAFTA Can Play a Key Role in Energy Security," tradealert.org, February 10, 2003.
40. Losman, *Economic Security,* 8.
41. Ibid., 9.
42. Chalmers Johnson, *Blowback,* 87. Similarly, Eric Nordlinger estimates that the United States spends $40 billion per year defending $14 billion in U.S. oil imports (Nordlinger, *Isolationism Reconfigured,* 87). The varying estimates of the cost to defend Persian Gulf oil depend on assumptions about which forces in the military would be assigned the task. Cleverly, the Pentagon will not publicly estimate the cost of defending each region of the world. DoD is worried that if Congress or the president wanted to end a U.S. commitment to defend a particular region, the Pentagon's budget would be cut back by the amount the department had estimated for that sector of the globe.

43. Losman, *Economic Security,* 8.
44. Henry Clay quoted in Denson, "War and American Freedom," 8.
45. Rosecrance, "Overextension, Vulnerability, and Conflict," 162.

Index

About the Author

Ivan Eland is Senior Fellow and Director of the Center on Peace & Liberty at The Independent Institute. Dr. Eland is a graduate of Iowa State University and received an M.B.A. in applied economics and Ph.D. in national security policy from George Washington University. He has been Director of Defense Policy Studies at the Cato Institute, Principal Defense Analyst at the Congressional Budget Office, Evaluator-in-Charge (national security and intelligence) for the U.S. Government Accountability Office, and Investigator for the House Foreign Affairs Committee. He has testified on the military and financial aspects of NATO expansion before the Senate Foreign Relations Committee, CIA oversight before the House Government Reform Committee, and the Department of Homeland Security before the Senate Judiciary Committee.

Dr. Eland is the author of *Putting "Defense" Back into U.S. Defense Policy: Rethinking U.S. Security in the Post-Cold War World* and *The Efficacy of Economic Sanctions as a Foreign Policy Tool*, a contributor to numerous volumes, and the author of forty-five in-depth studies on national security issues. His articles have appeared in *Arms Control Today*, *Bulletin of the Atomic Scientists*, *Emory Law Journal*, *The Independent Review*, *Issues in Science and Technology (National Academy of Sciences)*, *Mediterranean Quarterly*, *Middle East and International Review*, *Middle East Policy*, *Nexus*, and *Northwestern Journal of International Affairs*.

Dr. Eland's material has appeared in such publications as the *Los Angeles Times*, *USA Today*, *Houston Chronicle*, *Philadelphia In-*

quirer, *Dallas Morning News*, *Insight*, *San Diego Union-Tribune*, *New York Times*, *Washington Post*, *Miami Herald*, *St. Louis Post-Dispatch*, *Newsday*, *Sacramento Bee*, *Orange County Register*, *Chicago Sun-Times*, *Washington Times*, the *Oregonian*, the *Detroit Free Press* and *Defense News*. He has appeared on ABC's "World News Tonight," NPR's "Talk of the Nation," PBS, Fox News Channel, CNBC, CNN, CNN's "Crossfire," CNN-fn, CNN International, C-SPAN, MSNBC, CBC, Radio Free Europe, Voice of America, BBC, and other local, national, and international TV and radio programs.

INDEPENDENT STUDIES IN POLITICAL ECONOMY

THE ACADEMY IN CRISIS: The Political Economy of Higher Education | *Ed. by John W. Sommer; Fwd. by Nathan Glazer*

AGAINST LEVIATHAN: Government Power and a Free Society | *Robert Higgs*

AGRICULTURE AND THE STATE: Market Processes and Bureaucracy | *E. C. Pasour, Jr.; Fwd. by Bruce L. Gardner*

ALIENATION AND THE SOVIET ECONOMY: The Collapse of the Socialist Era | *Paul Craig Roberts; Fwd. by Aaron Wildavsky*

AMERICAN HEALTH CARE: Government, Market Processes and the Public Interest | *Ed. by Roger D. Feldman; Fwd. by Mark V. Pauly*

ANTITRUST AND MONOPOLY: Anatomy of a Policy Failure | *D. T. Armentano; Fwd. by Yale Brozen*

ARMS, POLITICS, AND THE ECONOMY: Historical and Contemporary Perspectives | *Ed. by Robert Higgs; Fwd. by William A. Niskanen*

BEYOND POLITICS: Markets, Welfare and the Failure of Bureaucracy | *William C. Mitchell & Randy T. Simmons; Fwd. by Gordon Tullock*

THE CAPITALIST REVOLUTION IN LATIN AMERICA | *Paul Craig Roberts & Karen LaFollette Araujo; Fwd. by Peter T. Bauer*

CHANGING THE GUARD: Private Prisons and the Control of Crime | *Ed. by Alexander Tabarrok; Fwd. by Charles H. Logan*

CUTTING GREEN TAPE: Toxic Pollutants, Environmental Regulation and the Law | *Ed. by Richard Stroup & Roger E. Meiners; Fwd. by W. Kip Viscusi*

THE DIVERSITY MYTH: Multiculturalism and Political Intolerance on Campus | *David O. Sacks & Peter A. Thiel; Fwd. by Elizabeth Fox-Genovese*

DRUG WAR CRIMES: The Consequences of Prohibition | *Jeffrey A. Miron*

ENTREPRENEURIAL ECONOMICS: Bright Ideas from the Dismal Science | *Ed. by Alexander Tabarrok; Fwd. by Steven E. Landsburg*

FAULTY TOWERS: Tenure and the Structure of Higher Education | *Ryan C. Amacher & Roger E. Meiners*

FREEDOM, FEMINISM, AND THE STATE: An Overview of Individualist Feminism | *Ed. by Wendy McElroy; Fwd. by Lewis Perry*

HAZARDOUS TO OUR HEALTH?: FDA Regulation of Health Care Products | *Ed. by Robert Higgs; Fwd. by Joel J. Nobel*

HOT TALK, COLD SCIENCE: Global Warming's Unfinished Debate | *S. Fred Singer; Fwd. by Frederick Seitz*

LIBERTY FOR WOMEN: Freedom and Feminism in the Twenty-First Century | *Ed. by Wendy McElroy; Fwd. by Wendy Kaminer*

MARKET FAILURE OR SUCCESS: The New Debate | *Ed. by Tyler Cowen & Eric Crampton*

MONEY AND THE NATION STATE: The Financial Revolution, Government and the World Monetary System | *Ed. by Kevin Dowd & Richard H. Timberlake, Jr.; Fwd. by Merton H. Miller*

OUT OF WORK: Unemployment and Government in Twentieth-Century America | *Richard K. Vedder & Lowell E. Gallaway; Fwd. by Martin Bronfenbrenner*

A POVERTY OF REASON: Sustainable Development and Economic Growth | *Wilfred Beckerman*

PRIVATE RIGHTS & PUBLIC ILLUSIONS | *Tibor R. Machan; Fwd. by Nicholas Rescher*

RECLAIMING THE AMERICAN REVOLUTION: The Kentucky & Virginia Resolutions and Their Legacy | *William J. Watkins, Jr.; Fwd. by Richard N. Rosenfeld*

REGULATION AND THE REAGAN ERA: Politics, Bureaucracy and the Public Interest | *Ed. by Roger Meiners & Bruce Yandle; Fwd. by Robert W. Crandall*

SCHOOL CHOICES: True and False | *John D. Merrifield*

STRANGE BREW: Alcohol and Government Monopoly | *Douglas Glen Whitman*

TAXING CHOICE: The Predatory Politics of Fiscal Discrimination | *Ed. by William F. Shughart, II; Fwd. by Paul W. McCracken*

TAXING ENERGY: Oil Severance Taxation and the Economy | *Robert Deacon, Stephen DeCanio, H. E. Frech, III, & M. Bruce Johnson; Fwd. by Joseph P. Kalt*

THAT EVERY MAN BE ARMED: The Evolution of a Constitutional Right | *Stephen P. Halbrook*

TO SERVE AND PROTECT: Privatization and Community in Criminal Justice | *Bruce L. Benson; Fwd. by Marvin E. Wolfgang*

THE VOLUNTARY CITY: Choice, Community and Civil Society | *Ed. by David T. Beito, Peter Gordon & Alexander Tabarrok; Fwd. by Paul Johnson*

WINNERS, LOSERS & MICROSOFT: Competition and Antitrust in High Technology | *Stan J. Liebowitz & Stephen E. Margolis; Fwd. by Jack Hirshleifer*

WRITING OFF IDEAS: Taxation, Foundations, & Philanthropy in America | *Randall G. Holcombe*

For further information and a catalog of publications, please contact:

THE INDEPENDENT INSTITUTE
100 Swan Way, Oakland, California 94621-1428, U.S.A.
510-632-1366 • Fax 510-568-6040 • info@independent.org • www.independent.org